C++ Programming for the Absolute Beginner, Second Edition

Mark Lee

Course Technology PTR

A part of Cengage Learning

COURSE TECHNOLOGY
CENGAGE Learning™

Australia • Brazil • Japan • Korea • Mexico • Singapore • Spain • United Kingdom • United States

COURSE TECHNOLOGY
CENGAGE Learning

C++ Programming for the Absolute Beginner, Second Edition: Mark Lee

Publisher and General Manager, Course Technology PTR: Stacy L. Hiquet

Associate Director of Marketing: Sarah Panella

Manager of Editorial Services: Heather Talbot

Marketing Manager: Mark Hughes

Acquisitions Editor: Mitzi Koontz

Project Editor: Jenny Davidson

Technical Reviewer: Keith Davenport

PTR Editorial Services Coordinator: Jen Blaney

Interior Layout Tech: Value Chain International

Cover Designer: Mike Tanamachi

Indexer: Sharon Shock

Proofreader: Sara Gullion

For product information and technology assistance, contact us at
Cengage Learning Customer & Sales Support, 1-800-354-9706

For permission to use material from this text or product, submit all requests online at **cengage.com/permissions** Further permissions questions can be emailed to **permissionrequest@cengage.com**

All trademarks are the property of their respective owners.

Library of Congress Control Number: 2008939939

ISBN-13: 978-1-59863-875-2
ISBN-10: 1-59863-875-0

Course Technology, a part of Cengage Learning
20 Channel Center Street
Boston, MA 02210
USA

Cengage Learning is a leading provider of customized learning solutions with office locations around the globe, including Singapore, the United Kingdom, Australia, Mexico, Brazil, and Japan. Locate your local office at: **international. cengage.com/region**

Cengage Learning products are represented in Canada by Nelson Education, Ltd.

For your lifelong learning solutions, visit **courseptr.com**

Visit our corporate website at **cengage.com**

Printed in the United States of America
2 3 4 5 6 7 11 10

*To Dirk Henkemans,
my best friend. I am
lost without you.*

FOREWORD

The video game industry is unique in that it regularly incorporates every major discipline of computer science. From 3D graphics and artificial intelligence to operating system theory and database design, if you are designing a commercial video game, you will eventually run into problems from each of these fields. Some of these fields mean working with specialized languages, but ultimately the two languages that are as common to the game industry as crunch time, caffeinated beverages, and pizza are C and C++. Despite a few commercial games written in Java (which is very similar to C++), almost every game that you play is written in either C or C++. It doesn't matter whether the game runs on a PC, a game console, or even an arcade machine, chances are that C or C++ routines are at its heart. Even in cases when performance dictates that a routine needs to be written in assembly language to squeeze out more speed, it is common practice to first write the routine in C or C++.

During my years in the industry, I have interviewed over one hundred applicants for programming positions and have read resumes from thousands more. Through all of this, I continually look for three things in a strong candidate. The first is strong problem-solving skills. With constantly changing technologies and fierce competition, game programming is always throwing new problems at us. Consequently, excellent problem-solving skills are not only a luxury, but they are also a requirement. Second, a good candidate has been exposed to the entire spectrum of computer science disciplines. Even when programmers have specialized in one area, the solution to a problem often lies in a field outside their area of expertise. Finally, I look for strong C/C++ skills. C/C++ skills are to a game programmer what paint and brushes are to a painter. They are the tools of the trade and, as such, they need to be finely honed.

Although C++ is widely used as a teaching language, this wasn't always the case. I can still recall my first exposure to C programming. Until that time, all of my programming had been in Basic (my first video game was written in it), Pascal, and Fortran. I had heard of C; according to rumor, it was going to be the language to know. I was looking forward to my next computer science course: "Introduction to Programming Languages." I assumed that the course would teach me how to program in C. I was wrong. The only reference to C in the entire course was, "Here is your assignment. Write it in C. Hand it in on Wednesday." "Okay," I thought. "At least one of the course textbooks is about C." As it turned out, that textbook was about accessing UNIX operating system information from the C language. That was useful if I was interested in accessing process IDs or using shell commands, but not a great help if I wanted to know how to read a file or write a function.

Somehow I managed to struggle through the assignment and to actually learn something while I did it. It wasn't the best way to learn a new language, but it was better than my first exposure to C++. That was during my first job after graduation. I was working for the university's athletic department writing software for various research projects. One of the projects that I inherited from the previous programmer was only half complete and was written in C++. Once again, I had before me a sink-or-swim proposition. This time, I had access to a function reference that explained only the syntax of the language, not how to use it. I would have killed for the book that you are currently holding in your hands. Well, maybe not killed, but I certainly can't overestimate the importance of learning C++ in such an organized and straightforward manner. As you read this book, please have some sympathy for those of us who didn't have the fine learning tool you have.

Scott Greig
Director of Programming BioWare Corp.

ACKNOWLEDGMENTS

The amount of time and effort involved in the process of publishing a book is considerable, and this book is no exception. As only one cog in the vast machine of effort involved, it is difficult for me to fully appreciate all of the hands that have touched this edition. However, without the ambition and drive of my original co-author, Dirk Henkemans, this book would have remained an unrequited dream. His drive and perseverance taught me that seemingly impossible things, like writing a book, were not only possible, but readily attainable.

I thank Course Technology PTR for making this book possible and Mitzi Koontz, my acquisitions editor, for all of her efforts.

I am deeply indebted to Keith Davenport, the technical editor, whose careful eye ensured all of the code in this book works as it should.

Jenny Davidson, the project and copy editor, was an exceptional resource throughout the project and her careful editing improved this work by orders of magnitude.

I extend a special thank you to everyone else who played a role in preparing this book for publication, including Value Chain International, layout; Sara Gullion, proofreader; and Sharon Shock, indexer. All of you played a big role in making this book what it is.

We give praise to Scott Greig, the lead programmer at BioWare Corp. and the author of this book's foreword. Scott, you are our idol. Without you, who could we aspire to be?

I am deeply thankful for the scrutinizing eye of Jen Janzen whose talent for editing is unrivaled. Every line she touches is improved by orders of magnitude.

Finally, I'd like to give thanks to my parents, for putting up with and supporting me all of these years.

ABOUT THE AUTHOR

Mark Lee is a professional web developer and programmer. He has a degree in Computer Science from the University of Alberta and is proficient in the use of C, C++, Java, Ruby, PHP, AJAX, MySQL, and JavaScript.

TABLE OF CONTENTS

Chapter 3   MAKING CHOICES WITH CONTROL STATEMENTS......... 45

Chapter 4   STRUCTURING YOUR CODE WITH FUNCTIONS............. 83

Chapter 5   DESIGNING SOFTWARE: OBJECT-ORIENTED PROGRAMMING... III

Chapter 9   **USING STREAMS AND FILES**.................................. **243**

Chapter 10   **ERRORS AND EXCEPTION HANDLING**.........................**263**

INTRODUCTION

C++ is the most widely used programming language around and is an industry standard for programming applications of all kinds. In addition, C++ is a highly efficient programming language that can conserve resources more effectively than languages such as Visual Basic or Delphi.

In fact, because of its functionality and style, in many ways, C++ is the only non–Web-based programming language that you might ever need to know.

We chose to teach you C++ through game programming because initially many people experience computers through playing computer games. More important, computer games are a wonderful way to learn how to program because they teach you how to display an interface on a monitor, how to receive commands from the user, and how to manipulate information. Ultimately, games are a blend of art and science that taps into logical and creative minds, providing stimulating visual, audio, and mental experiences for programmers and users.

Over the course of this book, you will discover many innate programming techniques that apply not only to C++, but also to programming in general. These common programming techniques will make it easier for you to learn how to program in other languages and create applications other than game applications.

WHAT'S IN THIS BOOK

The book moves from simple text-based programs to more complicated games with actual graphics. If you are an absolute beginner at programming, we suggest that you go through the chapters in their natural order. On the other hand, if you already have some experience in programming, you might want to gloss over the first six chapters, which cover the basics, and jump ahead to more advanced topics.

The book is conceptually, though not physically, organized into four sections. First, Chapter 1, "Starting the Journey," through Chapter 6, "Managing Memory," give you the basic knowledge you need to program in C++. Because of the sequence of the topics in these chapters, we suggest going through them in order. For example, you will probably need to work through Chapter 4, "Structuring Your Code with Functions," before turning to Chapter 5, "Designing Software: Object-Oriented Programming."

The second section of the book (Chapter 7, "Relating Classes," through Chapter 10, "Errors and Exception Handling,") consists of the advanced C++ topics. You can cover these chapters in any order and fully comprehend them.

The third section consists of Chapter 11, "Creating the Pirate Adventure." Here you put together everything you learned in the earlier chapters and apply it to programming a rocking pirate game using industry-standard techniques.

The fourth section includes appendixes with extra information that you will find helpful, beginning with Appendix A, "Answers to Chapter Challenges," and ending with Appendix E, "Glossary."

However you read the book, remember that a big part of learning to program with C++ is hands-on experience. The more you program, the better you will become at problem-solving (an important skill in programming, as you will discover) and detecting errors in your code. Who knows, if you program enough, you might even be able to calculate pi to a million digits . . . in your head (though doing so is not guaranteed by the author of this book)!

Throughout the chapters, you will find small bits of code that illustrate concepts we present. At the end of each chapter, you will find a complete game that demonstrates the key ideas in the chapter, a summary of the chapter, and a set of challenges that tests your newfound knowledge. We hope that you will try the games and challenges because they will really help you develop the *feeling* of programming. The solutions to the challenges are in Appendix A. However, we strongly encourage you to try the challenges before looking at the solutions (even if you need help). They are all fairly short, so you can type them into your compiler (which is, again, a good way to gain experience).

What You Need to Get Started

Learning to program is an excellent way to take advantage of the power of your computer. However, before you can begin programming, you need to have the following on hand:

- A PC with a 2.0 GHz or faster processor.
- Windows XP Professional with Service Pack 2 installed, Windows Server 2003, or Windows Vista.
- At least 512MB of RAM.
- At least 8GB hard drive space.
- A compiler such as Visual Studio 2008 Express Edition.
- Knowledge, time, and patience. The information in this book will give you enough knowledge to effectively utilize both C++ and Visual Studio, or most other compilers.

In Appendix C, "Working on Mac and Linux Platforms," we discuss how to work on a non-Windows system.

Special Features in This Book

Along with the complete games and challenges at the end of the chapters, here are some other special features in this book:

 Provide a little extra information on hard topics.

 Alert you to pitfalls to avoid.

 Tips that will make programming easier and more efficient.

STARTING THE JOURNEY

The idea of programming might sound like a daunting task, but don't worry. We designed this chapter so that you can get your feet wet without having to delve into the deeper complexities of programming. The chapter begins with a discussion on computers. We'll show you how they really work. The chapter continues with the basics on creating a program. Next you'll learn how to use Visual Studio, a C++ compiler. Then you get to play with some text and numbers. With our help, and your ingenuity, you will soon be creating your own simple programs. Later, we're sure that your programs will become increasingly complex, but everyone must start the journey somewhere. Here and now, your adventure begins!

The outset of your adventure includes the following:

- How computers work
- How to write code
- How to write your first program
- How to use Visual Studio
- How the programming development cycle works
- How to use text
- How to use numbers

COMPUTER BASICS

A computer is comprised of a number of components. Some are very easy to identify: the keyboard, mouse, or the monitor. Others are internal and hidden to the novice user. These include the CPU (central processing unit) and the memory.

The CPU is the brain of the computer. It is the circuit-drenched core from which all decisions are made. If your computer one day decided to go all zombie on you and you needed to know where to stab, this would be the part to aim for. And thus, the foul beast would return to the underworld from whence it came!

Luckily, you probably won't have to worry about zombie computers for some time, so you can just file that away. The next most important component is the memory. Often called RAM (random-access memory), this is where the data and instructions are stored.

Data and instructions? Obviously you've heard these terms before, but what do they mean here? Well, data can refer to many things. Keyboard input, file contents, web server requests, any piece of information that is used by the computer. Instructions are a special kind of data. They "instruct" the CPU about what to do next. Add these two numbers, move this data here, jump to this instruction next. These are examples of CPU instructions.

The main operation of the computer is executing these instructions. Fetch the next instruction. Execute it. Fetch the next instruction. Execute it. Over and over again. Except this all happens very fast. A 1 GHz CPU can execute one billion instructions per second! Nothing to shake a stick at (though I'm not sure why one would want to shake a stick at things... the motivation seems to be lacking).

DEFINING SOURCE CODE

Computers work by executing a series of simple instructions, but, fortunately, programmers no longer need to write programs at such a low level. Special languages, called programming languages, have been developed that allow ideas to be expressed much more easily. It is up to an intermediate program, called a compiler, to translate ideas written in a programming language into a series of simple instructions that the computer can understand.

HINT   You may wonder why you cannot just tell the computer what to do. "Go to this webpage" or "Play this song" are examples of how we'd like to be able to interact with a computer. The problem is that English (and all other so-called "natural" languages, like French, German, etc.) is too complex. Programming languages like C++ are simpler and more precise. Even so, well-written code can be almost as easy to read as English.

Just like English has rules for grammar, punctuation, and spelling, so too does C++. The difference is that the rules of C++ are much stricter. If we say "The cat run slow," instead of "The cat is running slowly," the basic meaning is still conveyed. Such a lax following of the rules of C++ is a much larger problem. All sorts of errors and problems can result from not obeying the rules of C++ exactly.

And, just like English, grammar and punctuation is not all there is to it. In order to write good code, one must express his ideas succinctly and elegantly. This is an art that programmers continually refine. Professional programmers who have been working in the field for years are still working to improve their coding abilities.

But, enough talk. Let's look at some code!

Examining Hello World

Now, gentle reader, let us delve head first into the mystical world of C++. Though you may be overwhelmed at first with the odd symbols and cryptic terms, it will all become clear in time. So ready your torch and let us delve into this dark cavern!

```
//1.1 - Hello World - Mark Lee
#include <iostream>

int main( void )
{
    using std::cout;
    cout << "Hello World!\n";
    return 0;
}
```

The above is a complete C++ program. It simply displays the words, "Hello World" to the screen. Now, let's take it apart, line-by-line!

Often in research essays, there is a section at the end called the bibliography. As you likely know, this section is used to provide references for information used to write the essay. C++ is quite similar, except the bibliography goes at the beginning. A programmer can provide a "reference" to another piece of code, to indicate where that functionality comes from. The second line is such a reference:

```
#include <iostream>
```

The file being referenced is called iostream. This file provides the functionality needed to print to the screen. If you wanted to reference a different file, say, cstdio, it would look like this:

```
#include <cstdio>
```

So what is this iostream file? Where does it come from? Well, my inquisitive reader, this file is part of the C++ Standard Library. The C++ Standard Library is a collection of C++ code that provides a lot of important capabilities, like displaying text to the screen. This library is always and automatically available. Throughout the course of this book, we will introduce new parts of the library. In this program we use iostream. iostream is a component of the C++ Standard Library used to display text to the screen or read input from the keyboard.

The next line is blank. Why? Does this hold some kind of significance? Is it required to place a blank line here? The answer is no. The blank line is merely there to space things out. C++ is said to "ignore whitespace." This means that you can put spaces, tabs, and blank lines virtually anywhere without affecting the meaning. If this blank line were removed, the program would be exactly the same! So why is it there? Well, it helps make the code more readable. If all of the code was squished together without any spacing, it would be much more difficult to read and understand. It is important to make your code clear so that you don't waste time trying to figure it out.

Now we encounter some very strange words. int? void? No, void does not refer to some empty pit of despair (though C++ may feel that way at times). And int is just short for integer, but we'll cover that later in this chapter. You'll notice that this line is followed by a set of lines enclosed in curly braces ({ and }). That structure is important. The whole thing is called the main function. Every program must have a main function. In Chapter 4, we'll cover functions in more detail, but for now just place all of the code you write inside those strange braces.

The first line of the main function is another part of using the C++ Standard Library. It basically says that in this function we'll be using something from the standard library (std), and that thing is called cout. Why do we need this line? Well, everything in the C++ Standard Library is in what's called a namespace. We'll cover those in later chapters, but for now it means that everything in the library must be prefixed with std::. Putting this line at the top of the function makes this unnecessary. In the next line, we can just say cout without putting std:: in front.

So what is this cout word? And how do you even pronounce it? Well, cout is used to print things to the screen. It is pronounced "See-out." The out in cout refers to how it is used for output. Output is data that leaves your program. Input, on the other hand, is data that comes into your program. There is another word in the C++ Standard Library, cin, which is used to read input from the keyboard. We'll cover that later.

You'll notice that all of the lines in the main function end with a semicolon (;). Since whitespace is ignored, all of the statements could be on the same line. The only way to tell where one statement ends and the next one begins is to use something to separate them. C++ uses semicolons. In Chapter 3, "Making Choices with Control Statements," you'll learn about statements that do not require semicolons, but until then, every statement you encounter must terminate with a semicolon.

Now, patient reader, we have reached the crux of this program. This is where the actual displaying text to the screen happens. You probably suspected as much when you first glanced at the code. You can see "Hello World!" in quotes, and it seems to be directed towards this cout word. Well, this is how you print to the screen! The weird \n sitting there at the end symbolizes a new line. When we learn how to actually compile and run this program in the next section, you can experiment with removing this new line and see what happens.

The last line of the main function is used simply to indicate the end of the function. The word return says, "ok, this function is over," and the number 0 means that everything is okay.

Comments

The first line in the Hello World program is a comment. It has no influence on the way the program runs. Whenever you type two forward slashes (//) together, you are telling the compiler to ignore the rest of that line. The purpose of comments is to help make the code more understandable. Comments can be written in one of two ways. A single-line comment (like the preceding one) consumes only one line. Everything after the // on the line is ignored, as shown here:

```
// I am an army of one
```

Another form of the C++ comment enables you to spread a single but lengthy comment over as many lines as you want:

```
/* dragons rule the world */
```

or

```
/* dragons
rule
the
world */
```

Although it is usually confusing, you can place the multiple-line comment into code at almost any point, as illustrated here:

```
cout << /* prints out Hello World */ "Hello World\n";
```

However, just because a possibility exists does not mean that you should use it. Using comments like this can quickly make your code unreadable. A good rule of thumb is to use comments simply to make your code more understandable. If they aren't helping, take them out.

Again, nothing within a comment affects the code. Use comments only to explain, in plain English, complicated or large parts of the program. The compiler ignores the comments when it turns the program into machine code.

USING VISUAL STUDIO

In this section, you find out how to use Visual Studio to create your first program. Visual Studio is an Integrated Development Environment (IDE). A programmer requires many different tools to do his work: an editor to write code, a file browser to organize all of his files, a compiler to turn the source code into an executable program, and a debugger to examine a running program. An IDE has all of these tools packaged together into one application. Some programmers enjoy having everything all together and integrated like this, whereas others prefer to use a separate application for each tool, creating their own, customized work environment. In Appendix C, we discuss some alternatives to Visual Studio.

 We wrote this book based on the assumption that you are using Visual C++ 2008 Express Edition (which is freely available). However, it isn't a big deal if you are not. Most of the information in this chapter and the other chapters will apply regardless of the compiler that you are using. For detailed instructions on how to download and install Visual C++ 2008 Express Edition, check out http://cplus.about.com/od/learnc/ss/vc2008.htm.

It's time to start your quest into the world of programming. As we explain how to create a project with Visual Studio and present the code, try it out for yourself on your own computer. Practice makes the unfamiliar seem natural.

CREATING A NEW PROJECT

The first time you open Visual Studio, it will appear as shown in Figure 1.1. As you can see, no magic is happening (well, maybe just a little). Visual Studio is simply an application, as are Microsoft Word and Internet Explorer, except Visual Studio is an application that you use to create other applications.

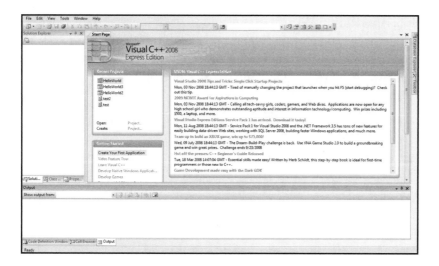

To create a new C++ project, with Visual Studio running, follow these steps (note that the names of menus, dialog boxes, and other options might be different if you have a different version of Visual Studio):

1. From the File menu, select New and then Project.
2. Select Win32 under Project Types.
3. Select Win32 Console Application under Templates.
4. Enter **Hello World** in the Name field. You will see that Solution Name also gets filled out as you type. See Figure 1.2.

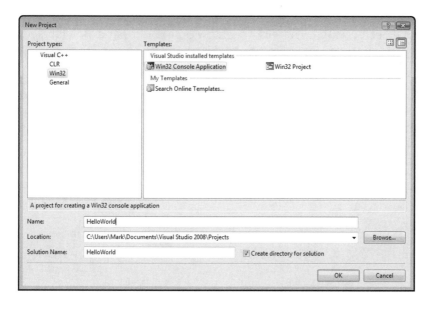

5. Click OK. The Win32 Application Wizard dialog window will appear. This is where you can further customize your project. Click Next.

6. Here you can select additional options for your project. The only option you'll need right now is Empty Project, so check that. Click Finish. See Figure 1.3.

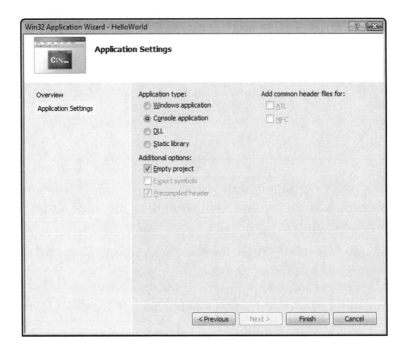

FIGURE 1.3

Setting additional
project settings.

7. The project has now been created. There is a window on the left-hand side labeled Solution Explorer. This is where you can see all of the files in your project. Right now the project is empty, so let's add a file. Right-click on the project name, Hello World, in the Solution Explorer. See Figure 1.4.

8. In the menu that appears, select Add and then New Item.

9. The Add New Item dialog window appears. Here, select C++ File (.cpp) under Templates and type **HelloWorld** in the Name field. Click Add. See Figure 1.5.

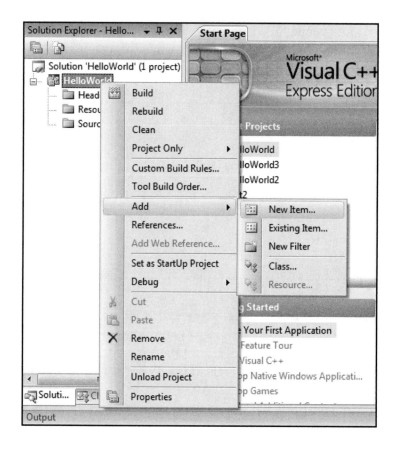

FIGURE 1.4

Interacting with
the Solution
Explorer.

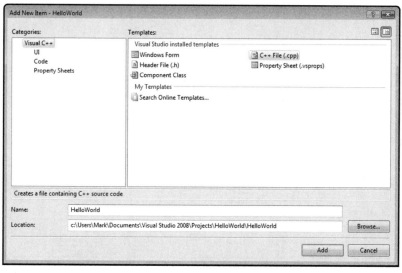

FIGURE 1.5

Adding a new file
to your project.

10. The file is now created and opened for editing. Type in the "Hello World" program from the previous section. You'll notice we skipped entering the comments for brevity. See Figure 1.6.

FIGURE 1.6

Writing your first code!

11. Once you have finished typing in the code, press Ctrl + F5, or select Start Without Debugging under the Debug menu. The results of compiling will be displayed in the bottom window, labeled Output. If there is a compilation error, you will see it here. Make sure your code matches the listing exactly. It is very easy to forget a semicolon or to make a typo.

12. You should see a new window appear as shown in Figure 1.7. Congratulations, you have just created your first program!

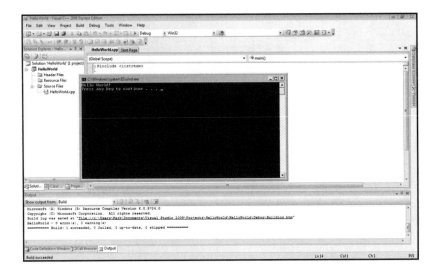

FIGURE 1.7

Executing the Hello World program.

THE SOFTWARE DEVELOPMENT CYCLE

The software development cycle is the process that all software must go through on its journey to completion. As your skills as a programmer increase, these stages will become more and more natural to you. The flowchart in Figure 1.8 illustrates this cycle.

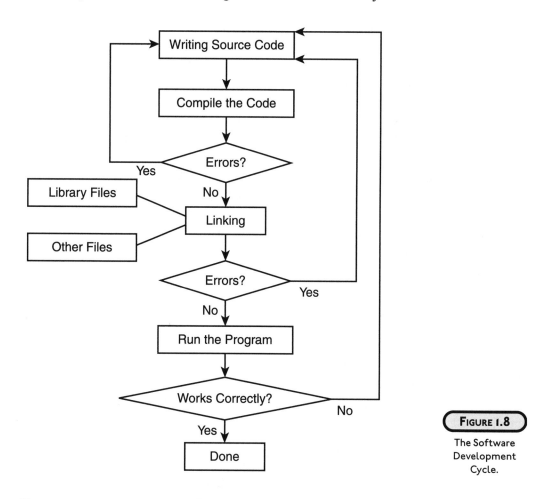

FIGURE 1.8

The Software Development Cycle.

Generally, to create a program, you follow these steps:

1. Planning! What is the program meant to do? How should the code be structured? Who is the program for and what are their needs? These are all questions that you must answer before you begin writing code!
2. Write code in the source code editor (Visual Studio or some other editor). You did a little bit of this in the earlier section, "Writing Your First Program," and you will do a lot more by the time you finish this book.

3. Compile the code. Imagine that you are an elf, and the computer is a dwarf. In order for the computer to understand your instructions, you must overcome a language barrier. You need a translator that can speak both Dwarven and Elven. In the computer world, this translator is a compiler. As we mentioned earlier, a compiler turns your language into machine code that your computer can read. However, this translation goes only one way. The compiler cannot translate machine code into source code. If there are errors, you must go back to the code to fix them. For step-by-step information on compiling code using Visual Studio, refer to the earlier section "Using Visual Studio."

4. Link the code. Linking the code is the process of bringing all of the files that make up the program together, like the joining of many brave knights in order to defeat a mighty dragon! The brave knights, in this case, include your code, but also all libraries that you use, like the C++ Standard Library. If you get an error, you must return to Step 1 to fix the error. Visual Studio does the linking step automatically when you build your project.

5. Test the program. You test the program to be sure that it functions properly. You may ask why testing is necessary if you've successfully passed the compile and linking stage. Obviously there are no errors, right? Well, some errors are more devious! Though your code may appear to work correctly, there can still be subtle problems. These are called logic errors! The bane of all programmers, much time is occupied hunting these down. It is vitally important that you thoroughly test your programs to make sure everything works as you expect it to!

6. Once your program makes it through these steps there is often still more to do! Requirements change and your program may have to adapt. Maybe errors that were missed before will be found later. Software development is a continuous process!

WORKING WITH TEXT

Before the advent of graphics, text was the basis of all programs. Text-based adventure games and text-based bulletin board systems were our first programming experiences. Text is still a very important element of programming. In this section, you find out how to assemble and store text.

Text is the simplest medium for displaying the output of programs. This book starts by using only text because text is sufficient to display the output of most programs. This approach also enables us to delay covering the complexities of graphics until the later chapters.

The technical name for a piece of text in the computer world is *string*. A string is a sequence of characters; in general, we think of a character as a symbol that you can type from the keyboard, including spaces. For example, in the "Hello World" program, `Hello World\n` is a string.

ASSEMBLING STRINGS

The computer interprets strings such as `"For Honor!!!"` as a series of characters, each occupying one letter or space (F is the first character, o is the second, and so on). Strings are always enclosed within double quotation marks. For example, `"a"`, `" "` (space), `"4"`, and `"%"` are all strings consisting of one character.

This might all seem complex, but creating strings is actually easy to do. The following are some examples of strings. As you can see, they are just a little bit of text surrounded by quotation marks.

```
"For Honor!!!"
"Pass me my sword."
"Who put my staff on the wagon?"
```

DISPLAYING STRINGS WITH COUT

Now that you know how to create a string, the first thing you are likely to want to do is display it to the screen. In this section, you learn multiple ways to do just that.

As mentioned in the dissection of the "Hello World" program, printing to the screen is not an innate part of C++. This capability is provided through the C++ Standard Library. In order to use it, you must do a few special things.

First, you must include a reference to the relevant file at the top of your program. As we saw in the Hello World program, for displaying text to the screen, this file is `iostream`. Here is the syntax (structure) for this reference:

```
#include <iostream>
```

This provides access to the relevant parts of the C++ Standard Library, but that is not the end of the story. Everything in the library is in what's called a namespace. This means that everything you use from the library must be preceded by `std::`. For example, to use `cout` now, you would have to write `std::cout`. This can get tiresome, and it is often easier to bring the relevant terms out of the std namespace. As discussed earlier, you can bring terms out of a namespace with the following code:

```
using std::cout;
```

Now you are free to use `cout` without prefixing it with `std::`.

Finally, to display a string to the screen, you use `cout` as follows:

```
cout << "Hello World";
```

You can display any string using cout, for example:

```
cout << "For Valour!";
```

Displaying Multiple Strings with cout

You can now use the basics of cout, but there's much more to learn about cout and strings. For example, you can display multiple strings at the same time. Say that you want to display two pieces of text, but they are in two different strings. According to the preceding techniques, the code will look something like this:

```
cout << "Red";
cout << " Dragon";
Output:
Red Dragon
```

However, there is an easier method. You can display as many strings as you want side-by-side and separated by <<. You can create the previous code fragment like this:

```
cout << "Red" << " Dragon";
Output:
Red Dragon
```

The output for both code fragments is identical, yet the second one is a little simpler to write. Also, because of the way C++ is written, you can split up code over more than one line. For example, the previous examples are also equivalent to the following:

```
cout << "Red"
     << " Dragon";
Output:
Red Dragon
```

This is actually a trivial example because you can use a single, larger string ("Red Dragon").

Generally, you structure your code so that it is easy to read. You should place a new cout at the beginning of each phrase. For example, to display a sentence about dragons and a sentence about elves, everything in the dragon sentence should be after one cout, and everything in the elven sentence should be after a different cout. In this way, your code is more organized and easier to read.

WORKING WITH ESCAPE CHARACTERS

You cannot express characters such as quotation marks (") and line breaks literally in a string. If you include a quotation mark as part of a string, the compiler will think that the quotation mark indicates the end of the string. For example, to create a string quoting someone, you might write:

```
"He said, "This is a quote"."
```

However, the compiler will interpret this as two separate strings, `"He said, "` and `"."` Because the words `This is a quote` are assumed to be non-strings, you wind up with a syntax error. A similar problem occurs with line breaks. All strings must be contained on a single line, so if you try to place a line break in the middle of a string, you get a syntax error. Fortunately, there is a solution to problems like these.

The solution is to use escape characters. Escape characters (or meta-characters) are used to represent characters that cannot be expressed literally. To create an escape character, you combine a backslash (\) and the particular character. For example, the escape character for a quotation mark is `\"`. Here's what it looks like in the code:

```
"He said, \"This is a quote.\"\n"
```

This code produces the desired string. If you were to output this string, `He said, "This is a quote."`, would be displayed onscreen. There are many other escape characters as well. Table 1.1 summarizes the important ones.

TABLE 1.1 ESCAPE CHARACTERS

Name	Escape Character
Newline	\n
Tab	\t
Backslash	\\
Single Quote	\'
Double Quote	\"

You will want to become familiar with most of these escape characters because they come in handy; in fact, some of them, such as the newline character (also called a line break), are essential.

STORING STRINGS

You can store strings in your program so that you don't have to write them more than once. Specifically, you store strings by putting them in memory (we cover memory in detail in Chapter 2, "Descending Deeper into Variables"). The C++ Standard Library, which provides support for displaying objects on the screen, also provides support for storing strings. The code for strings is held in a file aptly named string. As we learned with the "Hello World" program, you can use the C++ Standard Library by placing a special line of code at the top of your program:

```
#include <string>
```

Then, inside the main function, you declare what specific parts you want to bring from the standard namespace to your code, just like we did with cout:

```
using std::string;
```

When you want to store a string, you must provide a name for it so that the computer knows which string you want to access in the future. For example, we will put "A dragon is coming" into memory and name the string yell.

There is one small complication, though. C++ can store many things in memory. For example, besides strings, C++ can also store numbers. The rules for handling numbers are different from the rules for handling strings. So, you must also declare what kind of thing is being stored. We'll go into these distinctions further in Chapter 2. Here's what you must provide in order to store a string:

- The type of thing that is being stored (in this case, a string)
- The name of the string
- The characters that make up the string

Once you have all of these components assembled, you are ready to store a string in memory:

```
string yell = "A dragon is coming";
```

First comes the type of thing being stored: a string. Second comes the name of the string: yell. The equal sign tells the computer that the string, "A dragon is coming", is being stored in yell. Last comes the semicolon, which tells the computer that you have finished the statement.

DISPLAYING STORED STRINGS

Up to this point, you have displayed only literal strings. Now, you are ready to display stored strings. Using the name of the string in place of the string itself enables you to display stored strings. Here, as a quick reference, is the earlier stored string example:

```
string yell = "A dragon is coming";
```

To display the string, you use its name, which is yell, rather than the actual text:

```
cout << yell.c_str();
```

The preceding line does the same thing as the following one, which we used earlier in the section "Storing Strings":

```
cout << "A dragon is coming";
```

Don't worry about the .c_str() after the name of the string; it is just "magic" code that causes the string to display properly. We explain this magic code in Chapter 6, "Moving to Advanced Data Types."

THE TOWN CRIER PROGRAM

You've learned how to create saved strings and how to display them onscreen using cout. Now, it's time to test that knowledge by creating the Town Crier program.

Imagine that a dragon is approaching your village and you have to yell a warning to everyone. If you can yell your warning four times in a row so that everyone can hear, the village will be saved. This is obviously a job for our heroes: only the saved string and cout can save the village. Your objective, therefore, is to create a program that will display the text of your warning four times in a row.

The following is a code listing that illustrates one way to create this program, but we suggest not looking at it unless you become stuck while creating your own program:

```
//1.2 - Town Crier Program - Dirk Henkemans
#include <iostream>
#include <string>

int main(void)
{
        using std::cout;
        using std::string;
        string yell = "A dragon is coming, take cover!!!\n";
        cout << yell.c_str() << "\n"
                << yell.c_str() << "\n"
                << yell.c_str() << "\n"
                << yell.c_str() << "\n";
        return 0;
}
Output:
A dragon is coming, take cover!!!
```

```
A dragon is coming, take cover!!!
A dragon is coming, take cover!!!
A dragon is coming, take cover!!!
```

RECEIVING INPUT

Often when you are writing programs, you want to be able to receive input from the user. You want to be able to ask him questions, like what he'd like to do next or what his name is. In this section, you learn how to do just that.

The most important component of receiving input is the word `cin` (pronounced "see-in"). Just as `cout` is used to display text to the screen, `cin` is used to read input from the keyboard. `cin` is also part of the C++ Standard Library, so the proper files must be included:

```
#include <iostream>
```

Yes, that's right. It's in the same file as `cout`. `iostream` deals with both input and output capabilities. Of course, you also need a `using` declaration:

```
using std::cin;
```

And then you're finally set to begin receiving input from the user!

STORING STRINGS WITH CIN

You can store strings using `cin` much as you've stored them before, except now you declare the name and assign its value later. When you assign this value, you use the `cin` object. The `cin` object represents the keyboard or some other input device, whereas the `cout` object represents the screen or some other output device, like a file. You learn more about objects in Chapter 5, "Designing Software: Object-Oriented Programming." Here is an example of storing a user-input string:

```
string name;
cin >> name;
```

Notice that you use `cin` in much the same way that you use `cout`. Notice that the less-than signs are now greater-than signs. These signs indicate that the computer is accepting data rather than displaying it.

Here is an example of a complete program using `cin`:

```
//1.3 - Hello Program - Dirk Henkemans
#include <iostream>
#include <string>
```

```
int main(void)
{
      using std::cout;
      using std::cin;
      using std::string;
      string name = ""; // "" means empty string
      cout << "What is your name?\n";
      cin >> name;
      cout << "\nHello " << name.c_str() << "\n";
      return 0;
}
```
Output (bold text is user input):
```
What is your name?
Jackie
Hello Jackie
```

In the preceding code, `string name` tells the computer that there is space in the computer for a string called `name`. Remember that you must include the string component of the C++ Standard Library in order to use strings.

The line that reads

```
cout << "What is your name?\n";
```

displays a prompt for the user. This prompt asks the computer to write the user's name.

The next line, `cin >> name;` tells the computer to stop in order for the user to type. When the user presses Enter, the computer assigns everything that the user typed before pressing Enter to the string called `name`. Why Enter? Because reading a string by default reads to the end of the line of input.

Next, `cout << "\nHello " << name.c_str() << "\n";` begins by telling the computer to start on the next line. The computer then displays `Hello` onscreen followed by the user's name. For example, if the user types `Joe` or `Jane` for his or her name, `Hello Joe` or `Hello Jane` will be displayed. The space between `Hello` and the name is generated because a space is added at the end of the "`Hello` string (before the closing quotation mark).

Although there is much more to learn about text, you now have a basic understanding, so we can turn your attention to using numbers.

Working with Numbers

A computer is entirely number-based. Numbers are the foundation for everything that happens on the computer. Having a good grasp on numbers is essential in the computer world. In this section, you find out about basic math, the modulus operator, and how to use integers (see Chapter 2 for more on integers).

Introducing Integers

Computers can store information many ways. For now, however, we cover the basics on integers and how to use them. Integers are all the whole numbers, including zero and the positive and negative numbers. For example, 5, 0, and −100 are all integers, whereas 0.5 is not an integer. If you try to store a decimal as an integer, the computer will respond by truncating the remaining section; that is, the computer will chop off everything after the decimal.

Taking Action with Operators

In a general sense, an operator is any symbol or double symbol such as <=, and in some cases even terms such as sizeof(), that causes the compiler to take an action. The actions of adding, subtracting, multiplying, and dividing use operators. For example, when you ask a computer to add two numbers, you use the addition operator (+), which makes perfect sense, doesn't it? We all know that 2 + 2 = 4. Here's how you do the same thing in code with C++:

```
cout << 2 + 2;
```

This line displays 4 onscreen.

These four basic operators are self-explanatory; they do exactly what you probably think they do, but take a moment to review the symbol for each one:

Addition +

Subtraction -

Multiplication *

Division /

As in math, these operators do not all execute from left to right. The multiplication and division operators execute before the addition and subtraction operators, for example:

```
1 + 3 * 2
```

3 * 2 is executed first, and then 1 is added, resulting in the number 7.

Parentheses have the highest order of precedence. This means that formulas contained within parentheses are calculated first. If you take the preceding formula and add parentheses, as shown here

```
(1 + 3) * 2
```

1 + 3 executes first, producing 4, which is multiplied by 2, resulting in 8.

 TRICK Add lots of parentheses. Doing so makes debugging much easier. The rule of thumb is as follows: If you think your formula might need parentheses, put them in. This course of action will make your code easy to read and understand.

THE MODULUS OPERATOR

Remember way back to sixth grade when you did long division and your answers always worked out to be whole numbers? Then you began to work with remainders because you couldn't yet deal with decimals. Sometimes, it is especially useful to know the remainder of a number when it is divided. You get this information using the modulus operator (%). The modulus operator of x and y is the remainder of x divided by y. To find the remainder of 5 divided by 2, you write the code like this:

```
5 % 2
```

This line returns 1. Here's another easy example. Imagine that there are five pirates and 16 shiny gold coins. The pirates need to figure out whether the treasure can be divided evenly among themselves or whether they will have to get into a big, drunken brawl, which leads us to the next game. (Mind you, they will probably get into a drunken brawl anyway.)

CREATING THE PIRATE MUSKETEER GAME

It's now time to test your newfound skills. We highly suggest that you try it on your own computer. Play with the code. Try new things. This program will be your first real program and will test your knowledge on your use of numbers and text. Happy swashbuckling!

```
//1.4 - Pirate Musketeer Game - Dirk Henkemans
#include <iostream>
#include <string>

int main(void) //tells a pirate story
{
        using std::cout;
        using std::cin;
```

```cpp
using std::string;
int buddies;
int afterBattle;
string exit;
cout << "You are a pirate and are walking"
        << " along in the crime filled \n"
        << "city of Havana (in 1789). "
        << "How many of your pirate buddies \n"
        << "do you bring along? (Any number between 11 and 115)\n";

//records the amount of friends you bring along
cin >> buddies;
//calculates the amount of pirates left after the battle.
afterBattle = 1 + buddies - 10;

cout << "Suddenly 10 musketeers jump out "
        << "from the local tavern and \n"
        << "draw their swords. "
        << "10 musketeers and 10 pirates die in the \n"
        << "battle. There are only "
        << (buddies + 1 - 10)
        << " pirates left, including you.\n\n";

cout << "The fallen drop a total of 107 gold coins.\n"
        << "The bounty is split evenly, which works out to "
        << (107 / afterBattle) << " gold coins \n"
        << "for each survivor.\n";
cout << "The last " << (107 % afterBattle) << " are fought over "
        << "in a big drunken brawl.\n";
cout << "These last few coins are spent on more booze during the\n"
        << "course of the brawl. Eventually everyone retires\n"
        << "peacefully on the bar room floor.\n"
        << "Another successful day as a pirate!\n";
return 0;
}


        << (buddies + 1 - 10)
        << " pirates left, including you.\n\n";
```

```
      cout << "The fallen drop a total of 107 gold coins.\n"
           << "The loot is split evenly, which works out to "
           << (107 / afterBattle) << " gold coins \n"
           << "for each survivor, leaving ";
      cout << (107 % afterBattle) << " unclaimed coins.\n";
           << "How many of your pirate buddies \n"
           << "do you bring along? (Any number between 11 and 115)\n";
      cout << "You and the others argue over who should get the extra \n"
           << "coins, and soon a big drunken brawl breaks out!\n\n";
      cout << "In the end, you are triumphant and "
           << (107 / afterBattle) + (107 % afterBattle)
           << " coins richer!\n\n";
      return 0;
}
```

SUMMARY

The easiest way to write text or numbers to the screen and to set up things so that the user's input to the program can be read is to use the iostream library. You use cin to take and process the user's input and cout to display to the screen. In order to use cin and cout, you must include <iostream> at the beginning of your program. You can display and store strings and integers in order to use them again and again. You can use this stored data to make your programs shorter and more efficient. Also, remember that you can display many strings and integers at the same time in one cout statement, but they must be separated by <<. That's all for now; your adventure continues in Chapter 2.

CHALLENGES

1. Create a program that displays a picture of a house that looks like the ASCII house in Figure 1.9.

FIGURE 1.9

An ASCII house.

2. What is the output of the following program?

```cpp
#include <iostream>

int main( void )
{
    using std::cout;
    int x = 25;
    string str2 = "This is a test\n";
    cout << "Test" << 1 << 2 << "3";
    cout << 25 %7 << "\n" << str2.c_str();
    return 0;
}
```

3. Write a program that asks users for their names, that greets them, and that asks them for two numbers and then provides the sum.

4. What happens when you store 10.3 as an integer? What about 0.6? Can you store −101.8 as an integer?

5. Write code that will multiply some number by 2 if the number is between 1 and 100 (including 1 or 100) and if it is evenly divisible by 3; otherwise, multiply by 3 if it is between 1 and 100 but not divisible by 3; finally, if it isn't between 1 and 100, multiply the number by the number modulus 100. (Hint: Use the nested if statement.)

DESCENDING DEEPER INTO VARIABLES

The rhetoric of variables might sound intimidating to a beginning programmer; however, in this chapter, we sort through the confusion, with the hope that the information here will serve as a torch to guide you through the darkness. By the end of this chapter, you will have a good working knowledge of variables. In this chapter, you will learn the following:

- What variables are
- How to store data
- How to declare and assign values to variables
- The fundamental types
- How to determine the size of a variable
- How to use `typedef`
- How to covert hex to decimal
- How to cast from one type to another
- How to use constants

UNDERSTANDING VARIABLES

When writing code, we often want to be able to represent concepts. For example, if you were writing a fantasy role-playing game, you might want to be able to represent how many experience points the player has. You'd want to hold onto this value so that you can refer to it later. Sometimes, like when your player defeats a giant spider, you'll want to change that value, add to it, or subtract from it or some other operation.

The way you represent such a concept in your code is with a variable. So, for example, you may have a variable called exp_points that represents the player's current experience points. The name you give to a variable is important, because this is how you refer to it.

Every variable carries with it three pieces of information: its identifier, the name by which programmers refer to it; its type, which controls which operations can be performed on this variable and how to perform them; and the data itself.

Being more concrete, a variable is a certain section of memory on a computer. The data that is associated with a particular variable is stored in this section of memory. Imagine that many boxes of equal size are lined up in a row. All of them are numbered sequentially (the first is 1, the second is 2, and so on). Computer memory is very similar. Each variable is one or more boxes, and inside the boxes is the data that the variable holds. This is where variables store their data. By assigning a name to that data, you can conveniently access it from memory (as illustrated in Figure 2.1).

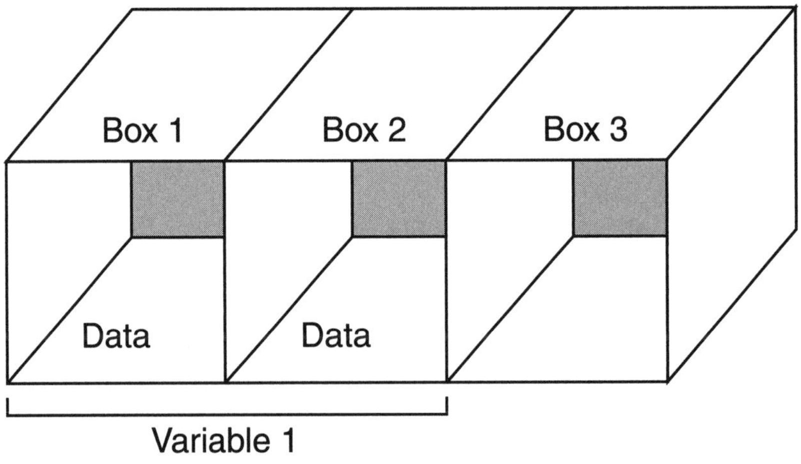

FIGURE 2.1

In this diagram, the first two boxes (bytes) are part of the memory containing variable 1. The third box is still free space because it's not used to store a variable.

SORTING OUT THE RELATIONSHIP BETWEEN VARIABLES AND MEMORY

As you advance, you will realize more and more that much of a programmer's life is spent manipulating or deciding how to manipulate data. Data is at the core of a computer's world. Know how to manipulate data, and you know how to program.

In general, you can refer to data two ways: with a variable or with a literal. Literals are, as the name implies, literal representations of data. For example, the number 2 or the word Hello are both literals. In Chapter 1, "Starting the Journey," you encountered many literals. "The dragons are coming!" is a string literal, and the number 8 is an integer literal. If you refer to data the way a non-programmer does, you are probably using a literal.

Variables, on the other hand, are quite programming-specific. The idea behind a variable is that you can refer to data without using its literal. This approach is advantageous because it provides a level of abstraction between your code and the data it manipulates, meaning that a particular line of code can manipulate different data every time it runs.

There are four basic types of variables upon which all others are built: Boolean types, character types, integer types, and floating-point types. From these four categories, you can represent any data in a program.

Before going further with variables, however, you need to learn a little bit about what memory is and how it stores data.

A computer has two primary types of memory: Random-Access Memory (RAM) and disk storage. RAM consists of special chips on a computer motherboard and some peripheral cards (video cards, sound cards, and so on). RAM stores data temporarily. This is the memory applications use as they run, and it is the kind of memory with which programmers are most concerned. Disk storage consists of hard drives, floppy disks, CD-ROM drives, or any other semi-permanent storage device. Disk storage retains its information when a computer is shut down. Our discussion is limited to RAM.

 Another kind of memory is Read-Only Memory (ROM). ROM is a non-volatile (unchanging) memory that holds the boot and self-test instructions that execute when you turn on your computer.

Computer memory is made up of millions of tiny electrical switches; each switch is called a bit. (A bit is the smallest unit of memory on a computer.) Each switch, or bit, can hold two possible voltage levels (for example, 0V and +5V). Therefore, each bit can hold two values—call them 0 and 1 or false and true, respectively. When two bits are combined, four combinations, or values, are possible (00, 01, 10, and 11). Here you have the birth of the binary numbering system, or base-two.

The most common numbering system is the decimal system. In the decimal, or base-ten, system, each digit has ten possible values (0, 1, 2, 3, 4, 5, 6, 7, 8, 9). Table 2.1 shows the numbers 0–10 in their binary and decimal forms.

TABLE 2.1	DECIMAL SYSTEM VERSUS BINARY SYSTEM
Decimal	**Binary**
0	0
1	1
2	10
3	11
4	100
5	101
6	110
7	111
8	1000
9	1001
10	1010

Don't be too intimidated by the binary system. All your old, familiar numbers are still there; the binary system just represents them differently. 0 is the same, and so is 1. The first strange one is 2. A new digit must be added to make the number 2, because binary only has two digits to work with, 0 and 1. Analogously, because decimal has only 10 digits, a new digit must be added to make the number 10. Don't worry if this is a bit confusing. The most important thing to notice is that all values can be represented by a series of 0s and 1s.

What about fractions and decimals you ask? Well there are ways to represent those too. Basically, the part before the decimal and the part after are each represented separately. It is too complex to go into the details here, but you can be assured that they can also be represented in computer memory.

As we mentioned, each electrical switch is called a bit, and a bit can hold two possible values, 0 and 1. Eight bits in a row are called a byte. A byte can hold 256 possible values, 0–255. Using the box analogy at the beginning of this chapter, where the rows of boxes represent memory, each box is one byte of memory. One byte is the smallest amount of data with which a computer can work. If more than one byte is needed, the computer uses more than one box. Remember, a kilobyte is not actually 1000 bytes per kilobyte; it's 1024 bytes. Memory doesn't follow the metric system perfectly. 1024K is a megabyte (MB). 1000MB is a gigabyte (GB). This information is summarized in Table 2.2. The number of possible values doubles with each bit added, so these numbers get large rather quickly. You always want to make sure you are not using more memory in your programs than you should.

Memory	Unit Number of Bits	Number of Possible Values
TABLE 2.2 MEMORY MEASUREMENTS		
bit	1	2
byte	8	256
kilobyte (KB)	8192	2^{8192}
megabyte (MB)	8388608	$2^{8388608}$
gigabyte (GB)	8589934592	$2^{8589934592}$
terabyte (TB)	$8.796093022 * 10^{12}$	$2^{8.796093022 * 10^{12}}$

Think of memory in a RAM chip as a sequence of bytes. Each byte has a distinct address. An address is a number, such as 10345, that tells a computer exactly which byte is being referred to. It is important to understand how each byte has its own address, but you rarely need to deal with addresses directly.

Now that you know a little more about how data is stored and represented by a computer, you are ready to dig deeper into variables.

DESCRIBING VARIABLE IDENTIFIERS

Identifiers are the names you give to your variables in order to refer to them. For example, a variable that stores user input might be called input. The rules for naming variables are as follows:

- The name must start with a letter or underscore (_).
- Every other character can be a letter, underscore, or number.
- Identifiers can be long (more than 200 characters).
- You cannot use keywords as variable names.
- C++ is case-sensitive (aVariable is different from aVARIABLE).

Some examples of valid identifiers are _file5G, String7F4, input, __my_variable, and so on. Some examples of invalid identifiers are 9variable and &variable. It is not a good idea to use identifiers beginning with two underscores because they are often reserved for special system variables. Also, keep in mind that even though an identifier is valid, it might not be useful. An identifier should be descriptive so that when you read your code three weeks later, you will fully understand your intentions.

TRAP   Don't use keywords as variable names accidentally. Using keywords in this way can cause unpredictable results and lead to many headaches. For example, `int` is already reserved to represent an integer, so if you try to use `int` as a variable name, the compiler will give you an error when the program is built.

DECLARING AND ASSIGNING VARIABLES

Before you can use a variable, you must declare it. By declaring a variable, you are telling the computer to set aside a certain amount of space to store data and to give that space a name. Different types of variables need different amounts of memory. For example, to declare an `int`, you type the following:

```
int x;
```

The syntax for the `variable` declaration is this:

```
variable_type identifier;
```

Then to assign data to that variable, you use the assignment operator (=). Operators are symbols or words that perform... well, operations. The operators can represent mathematical, relational, or other types of operators. In this chapter, we cover only the mathematical operators and the assignment operator. The assignment operator puts the values on the right side into the values on the left side. Here's an example:

```
x = 5;
```

Here, the variable, x, is now holding the value, 5. The memory that was set aside for x is filled with the value, 5. Be sure to distinguish between the equal sign in mathematics and in programming. Here, the data on the right is assigned to the variable on the left. This has nothing to do with testing whether both sides are equal. The single equal sign does not mean "is equivalent to." You might take a minute and read this information again; it is an important concept.

Variables can also be on the right side of the assignment operator, as shown here:

```
x = y;
```

This puts the value stored in y into x. This does not take the value out of y. Instead, it makes a copy of y's value and stores it in x. Remember, literal data cannot be on the left side of the assignment operator:

```
5 = x;
```

This is an illegal statement. This statement would put the value stored in x into 5, which does not make sense. If you want to assign a value to a variable right away, you can do it on the same line:

```
variable_type identifier = value;
```

This is called initializing the variable because you are giving it an initial value. For example:

```
int z = x;
```

With declaring variables and assigning them values under your belt, you are ready to learn about the different types of variables.

INTRODUCING THE FUNDAMENTAL VARIABLE TYPES

Variables come in quite a few types, but we cover only the four basic types in this chapter. The type of variable you use determines what kind of data it can store, as well as what operations can be performed with it. The four types covered in this chapter are Boolean, character, integer, and floating-point. Table 2.3 summarizes some of the different variable types.

TABLE 2.3   VARIABLE TYPES

Type	Size	Values
bool	1 byte	true (1) or false (0)
char	1 byte	a to z, A to Z, 0 to 9, space, tab, and so on
int	4 bytes	[−]2,147,483,648 to 2,147,483,647
short	2 bytes	[−]32,768 to 32,767
long	4 bytes	[−]2,147,483,648 to 2,147,483,647
float	4 bytes	$\pm(1.2 * 10^{-38}$ to $3.4 * 10^{38})$
double	8 bytes	$\pm(2.3 * 10^{-308}$ to $1.7 * 10^{308})$

THE BOOLEAN TYPE

The Boolean type is the simplest data type. It is one byte long (the smallest possible amount of data with which a computer can work). It can store two values, true and false. Use the Boolean type when you have only two possibilities. For example, you might have a variable named end, which is false until the program ends. You can use this variable to find out if you've reached the end of your program. You declare a Boolean variable using the keyword bool:

```
bool myBool = true;
cout << myBool;
```

THE CHARACTER TYPES

A character type can hold any one of 256 different characters, which can be any letter or symbol shown in the standard ASCII table.

A character literal (a literal representation of data is data that is not represented in a variable form) is surrounded by two single quotes. For example, 'a', '5', '%', and 'W' are all character literals.

You declare a character type using the keyword char:

```
char myChar = 'a';
cout<< "the character is" << myChar;
```

THE INTEGER TYPES

There are three integer types: int, short int (or short), and long int (or long).

We introduced the int type in Chapter 1. It is 4 bytes long (on most computers). It can store from −2,147,483,648 to 2,147,483,647. This type is the most commonly used data type. The integer types cannot store decimals or fractions (for example, 2.1 or 1/3). You declare it with the int keyword:

```
int myInt = -3;
cout << myInt;
```

A short type is half the size of an int—that is, 2 bytes. It can store from −32,768 to 32,767. When you have values that are relatively small, this type is very useful. It is twice as efficient because it takes only half the memory. You declare short types with the short (or short int) keyword.

```
short myShort = -56;
```

You can also display the preceding line as follows:

```
short int myShortInt = -56;
```

Next, in this exciting journey through data types is the long data type. It is the same length as an int, 4 bytes. It can store the values −2,147,483,648 to 2,147,483,647 as well. As you might have guessed, you declare the long data type with the long (or long int) keyword. It is synonymous to an int:

```
long myLong = 32056;
```

is exactly the same as:

```
long int myLong = 56789;
```

Why are there two different types that mean exactly the same thing? Well, technically, `int` and `long` can be different sizes. `short` is meant to be the smallest, `int` in the middle, and `long` the largest integer type. It has just become convention to define `int` and `long` to be the same size on standard computers.

You can put the keyword `unsigned` in front of all the integer types to assign them only positive values. An `unsigned short` has the range of 0 to 65535, and an `unsigned long` or `int` has the range of 0 to 4,294,967,295. Unsigned integers still take up the same amount of memory as normal (`signed`) integers consume. You can also use the keyword `signed` to make sure that negative values can be stored, but this is unnecessary because `signed` is the default.

```
unsigned int anUnsignedInt; // 0 to 4,294,967,295
unsigned short anUnsignedShort; // 0 to 65535
signed long aSignedLong; // -2,147,483,648 to 2,147,483,647
int anInt; // -2,147,483,648 to 2,147,483,647
```

INTEGER WRAPPING

If an integer exceeds its range, it does a peculiar thing. It starts at the beginning again. For example, if you were to store the value 4,294,967,295 in an unsigned integer (one more than its range), the unsigned integer would store its value as zero (0). An unsigned integer starts over at 0, but a signed integer starts over at its lowest negative value. An example might help clarify this point:

```
//2.1 - Integer Wrapping - Dirk Henkemans and Mark Lee
#include <iostream>

//displays an example of integer wrapping
int main()
{
    using std::cout;
    unsigned int unInt = 4294967295;
    signed short aShort = 32767;
    cout << "Unsigned int's value is: " << unInt << "\n";
    cout << "Short's value is: " << aShort << "\n";
    unInt = unInt + 1;
    aShort = aShort + 1;
```

```
        cout << "\nUnsigned int's new value is: "
        << unInt << "\n";
        cout << "Short's new value is: " << aShort << "\n";
        return 0;
}
```

Output:
Unsigned int's value is: 4294967295
Short's value is: 32767

Unsigned int's new value is: 0
Short's new value is: -32768

When unInt and aShort are declared, they are assigned their maximum values. Later, they are incremented by 1. As you can see, they have wrapped. This is a small issue, but keep it in mind—just in case.

THE INCREMENT OPERATOR

If you want to increase the value stored in an integer by exactly one, you can use the increment operator (++) to make your code much shorter. The increment operator is a kind of mathematical operator that increases the value of a variable by one. Instead of writing:

```
count = count + 1;
```

you can write:

```
count++;
```

You can also use the decrement operator (--) in the same way to decrease an integer's value by one. The decrement operator subtracts one from the value of the number. Instead of using:

```
count = count - 1;
```

you can use:

```
count--;
```

As well as being more concise and simpler to type, the increment and decrement operators compile into slightly more efficient machine code, so it is beneficial to use them whenever possible.

THE FLOATING-POINT TYPES

If you want to store decimals or fractions, you need the floating-point data types, `float` and `double`.

The `float` or single-precision floating-point data type is 4 bytes long. It can store the positive or negative decimal or non-decimal values with a maximum and minimum precision of 1.2 × 10^−38 to 3.4 × 10^38. Remember that these can be positive or negative.

Often, programmers express `float` and the other non-integers in scientific notation. Scientific notation is a way to express extremely large or small numbers in a relatively small space.

Scientific notation is just a shortcut method for writing floating-point numbers that begin to get out of hand, such as 0.0000000000000000002. Here are some numbers written in scientific notation:

```
5.6543e17  -4.02934e5  -17.204e-10  2.0e-19
```

Here's the rule to turn a scientific notational number into a regular format: Move the decimal as many places as the number to the right of the e (the number after the e is called the exponent). To convert 5.6543e17 to a regular number, you do the following:

1. Locate the number to the right of the e, the 17.
2. Move the decimal 17 places to the right. You know it's to the right because the 17 has no negative sign in front of it. Pad the new spaces with zeros. You end up with 563430000000000000.0, which is what 5.6543e17 means. This is better than typing 563430000000000000.0.

If the number has a negative exponent such as 5.6543e−17, you just move the decimal to the left 17 places and end up with 0.000000000000000056343.

Whatever number you are storing is converted into scientific notation. Then it is rounded to the nearest 10^−38 place. This is its level of precision. For example, if you store Pi (3.14159265358979323846 . . .) with a precision of two decimal places, the number will be rounded to 3.14, the standard Pi.

You declare the floating-point using the `float` keyword:

```
float aFloat = 3.156;
float negativeFloat = -678.876;
cout << aFloat << negativeFloat;
```

To store a fraction, a computer must convert it from its a/b (fractional) form to a decimal form. When you access the fraction, the `float` will give you the most accurate decimal version that it can store.

The double data type is 8 bytes long. It can store 2.2×10^{-308} to 1.7×10^{308} for positive values and -2.3×10^{-308} to -1.7×10^{308} for negative values. Thus, the double is rounded to the nearest 10^{-308} place. This is extremely high precision.

Basically, the double can handle anything you want to store. You declare a double using the double keyword.

In the following example, 2.2e-308 means the same thing as 2.2 *10^{-308}:

```
double aDouble = 2.2e-308;
double negDouble = -2.3e-308;
cout << aDouble << negDouble;
```

You're now familiar with the basic data types. In Chapter 6, "Designing Software: Object-Oriented Programming," you will learn how to create your own data types from these basic ones.

USING THE SIZEOF() OPERATOR

This relatively simple operator is built into the C++ language. Use it on any variable, and it will give the amount of memory, in bytes, that the variable consumes. You use it in the following way:

```
sizeof(identifier);
```

To display a double's size to the screen, you might use this code fragment:

```
double aDouble;
cout << "The size of a double is " << sizeof(aDouble); // is equal to 8
```

Because it represents an integer data type (the number of bytes), you can use the result of this operator anywhere that you can use an integer.

You can also use the keyword of the type rather than an identifier, as shown here:

```
cout<< "The size of 2 integers is" << 2 * sizeof(int); // is equal to 8
```

THE DATA TYPE GAME

Throughout your adventures, you happen to come across an elven village. You're in luck, intrepid adventurer, for this is the perfect chance to try your newly acquired skills. This village is under attack by a horde of dragons! To protect the village, you must summon data type warriors from the mystical forest to come to the elves' rescue.

To save the elven village, you must utilize your recently acquired skills on integers, floating-points, and doubles. Are you ready to accept the challenge? If so, read on:

```
//2.2 - Data Type Game - Dirk Henkemans and Mark Lee
#include <iostream>

//plays the data type game
int main( void )
{
     using std::cout;
     using std::cin;
     int intWarriors;
     double doubleWarriors;
     float floatWarriors;
     cout << "The village of the elves is being attacked by dragons. ";
     cout << "In order to save them, you must create each kind of "
          <<"data type warrior to defend the elven city.\n\n";
     cout << "How many int warriors do you want to send out?";
     cin >> intWarriors;
     cout << "\nLuckily, each int warrior has a strength of " <<
          sizeof(intWarriors) << ", \nwhich almost defeats the " <<
          "blue dragons.\n";
     cout << "\nQuick! How many double warriors should we send?";
     cin >> doubleWarriors;
     cout << "\n" << doubleWarriors;
     cout << " double warriors attack the last few blue dragons.\n"
          << "They kill " << sizeof(doubleWarriors) << " blue dragons."
          << " All of the blue dragons are now dead.\n\n";
     cout << "How many float warriors do you send out?";
     cin >> floatWarriors;
     cout << "\nEach of the "<< floatWarriors <<" float warriors shoots ";
     cout << sizeof(floatWarriors) << " arrows.\n";
     cout << "This is just enough to kill the green dragons.\n";
     cout << "Congratulations, you have saved the elves!\n";
}
```

MAKING LIFE EASIER WITH TYPEDEF

Sometimes, it becomes very inconvenient to keep using the keywords unsigned short int again and again. Using typedef enables you to create a new name for a type. You could rename unsigned short int to USHORT or to something even more convenient. The format for typedef is as follows:

```
typedef variable_type new_name;
```

To rename `float` to `f`, do this:

```
typedef float f;
```

Then you can declare a `float` with the newly defined keyword:

```
f radius = 4.7639;
```

 HINT Keep in mind that your new data type name should not only be convenient, but also meaningful.

Using Constants

Sometimes, when you create a variable, you want to ensure that its value cannot change. Maybe you have a variable that represents the number of cards in a player's hand, or the number of points needed to win the game. These are examples of things you want to define once and then never change again. You have entered the world of constants!

You define a constant by using the `const` keyword. The syntax is exactly the same as the syntax for declaring a regular variable, except with the `const` keyword in front:

```
const constType CONSTNAME = value;
```

 HINT You must always give your constant a value on the same line that you declare, because after this line the value cannot change. Any attempt to do so will result in a compile error. This makes it easy for you to ensure that this variable stays exactly the way you meant it to and is not changed by accident.

Using constants offers numerous advantages. Suppose that you type a number, such as 3.14, throughout the program every time you need to use the value of Pi. Then you realize that your application requires a higher precision; you'll have to change every occurrence of 3.14 to the higher prevision value such as 3.14159. If, instead, you use a constant to define Pi as 3.14 and later need to increase the precision, you will only need to change the `const` in one place and recompile the program.

If you have a really long number (such as Pi to 22 decimal places), typing it every time that you use it will also be annoying–and if you are like us, you might easily make a mistake. Using a constant simplifies this situation considerably.

Finally, it is good practice to use `const` whenever you can. This helps make your intentions clear. And it also helps the compiler to help you catch errors in your code.

THE CIRCLE GAME

For tomorrow's math assignment, you must calculate the area and circumference of a circle. Well, maybe we can help. In the following program, we do both by using constants. You use a constant to store PI (3.141592). Then the user only has to enter the radius into the program, and the program will calculate both the area and the circumference of the circle. Remember that the user's input should be stored as float so that the user can enter decimal numbers as a radius. Excellent; now it's time to build the program:

```cpp
//2.3 - The Circle Game - Dirk Henkemans and Mark Lee
#include <iostream>

//calculates the area and circumference of a circle
int main()
{
    using std::cout;
    using std::cin;
    typedef double d;
    const d PI = 3.141592;
    d radius, circumference, area;
    cout << "Welcome to the circle creator!\n";
    cout << "What would you like the radius of the circle to be? ";
    cin >> radius;

    area = PI * radius * radius;
    circumference = PI * (radius * 2);

    cout << "The area of the circle is: " << area << "\n";
    cout << "The circumference of the circle is: " << circumference << "\n";
    cout << "Thank you for playing the circle creation game!\n";
    return 0;
}
```

UNDERSTANDING THE SYNTAX

So far in this book, we have covered many different types of words—keywords, identifiers, directives, and so on—and many types of statements—assignment, include, and so on. In this section, we go through all the C++ syntax covered so far. (Syntax refers to the grammatical rules of a language.)

We start with the keywords, the basis of the C++ language. From these words, everything is built. A C++ compiler can understand only these words until it is "taught" more by the programmer.

Table 2.4 lists each of the keywords you've learned so far and gives their function and syntax.

TABLE 2.4   C++ KEYWORDS AND HOW TO USE THEM

Keyword	Function	Syntax
`const`	Used to declare a constant.	`const const_type const_name = value;`
`int`	Used to declare an integer.	`int variable_name;`
`short`	Used to declare a short.	`short variable_name;`
`long`	Used to declare a long.	`long variable_name;`
`float`	Used to declare a float.	`float variable_name;`
`double`	Used to declare a double.	`double variable_name;`
`bool`	Used to declare a Boolean.	`bool variable_name;`
`string`	Used to declare a string.	`string variable_name;`
`unsigned`	Used to declare positive-only integers.	`unsigned int_type variable_name;`
`return`	Needed at the end of the `main()` function.	`return 0;`
`sizeof()`	Returns the size of a variable or type.	`sizeof(variable_type_or_name)`
`void`	Needed to declare the `main()` function.	`int main(void)`
`main`	Needed to declare the `main()` function.	`int main(void)`
`typedef`	Used to rename types.	`typedef type new_name;`

As we indicated, keywords are the heart of the C++ language. They each have a special meaning and purpose. Know these words, and you are well on your way to being a C++ master.

Next are identifiers. You now know about two types of identifiers: literal and variable. Table 2.5 summarizes their uses and how to format them.

You have no choice about how to name literal identifiers; they are named what they are. Variable identifiers are usually all lowercase, unless they are two words combined (for example, `variableName`). Try to make your identifier names as descriptive as possible. Doing so will improve your code's readability.

We haven't covered preprocessor directives very much yet, but you know one of them. This is `#include`. As discussed earlier, directives are messages to the compiler telling it to do something when it compiles. `#include` tells the compiler to add another file to the current one. For example, in the "Hello World" program

TABLE 2.5   USE AND FORMAT OF IDENTIFIERS

Identifier	Used To Store	Format
Literal	Literal data.	No formatting rules (just use value).
Variable	Changing data.	Assign a value using the assignment operator (=).
Constant	Constant values.	Like a variable, but can only be assigned once at creation time.

```
#include <iostream>
```

tells the compiler to add the library iostream to hello.cpp when you compile. <iostream> has a lot of predefined code, such as cout.

As we mentioned earlier, operators are symbols or words that perform operations. You know about nine operators so far: the mathematical operators—addition (+), subtraction (-), multiplication (*), division (/), and modulus (%)—the increment operator (++), the assignment operator (=), and the sizeof() operator. Table 2.6 summarizes these operators and what they do.

TABLE 2.6   USE AND SYNTAX OF OPERATORS

Operator	Use	Syntax
Addition (+)	To add two numbers.	*number1 + number2*
Subtraction (-)	To subtract two numbers.	*number1 - number2*
Multiplication (*)	To multiply two numbers.	*number1 * number2*
Division (/)	To divide two numbers.	*number1 / number2*
Modulus (%)	To take the modulus of two numbers.	*number1 % number2*
Increment (++)	To increase the value of an integer by 1.	*integer1*++
Assignment (=)	To assign a value to a variable.	*variable1 = expression*
sizeof operator	To find the size of a variable or type.	sizeof(*variable_or_type*)

Feeling comfortable with variables? If not, you might want to read through parts of this chapter again and practice the sample code. Practice is the key.

CREATING THE WEAPON STORE GAME

While wandering through a dark forest, you come across a mysterious weapon store in the middle of nowhere. You are in luck, worthy traveler, for this is the perfect opportunity to test what you have learned in this chapter, including constants, casting, operators, data types, and so on. You must compile and run this program in order to visit the weapon store and purchase enough broadswords for your army's next military campaign:

```cpp
//2.4 - The Weapon Store Game - Dirk Henkemans and Mark Lee

#include <iostream>
#include <string>

//contains the code for the weapon store game.
int main (void)
{
    using std::cout;
    using std::cin;
    using std::string;
    string name;
    cout << "Welcome to the weapon store, noble knight."
        << " Come to equip the army again?\n"
        << "What is your name? ";
    cin >> name;
    cout << "Well then, Sir " << name.c_str()
        << ", let's get shopping\n";
    double gold = 50.0;
    int silver = 8;
    const double SILVERPERGOLD = 6.7;
    const double BROADSWORDCOST = 3.6;
    unsigned short broadswords;
    cout << "You have " << gold << " gold pieces and "
        << silver << " silver." << "\nThat is equal to ";
    gold += silver / SILVERPERGOLD;
    cout << gold << " gold.\n";
    cout<< "How many broadswords would you like to buy?"
        <<" (3.6 gold each) ";
    cin >> broadswords;
    gold = gold - broadswords * BROADSWORDCOST;
    cout << "\nThank you. You have " << gold << " left.\n";
    silver = (int)((gold - (int)gold) * SILVERPERGOLD);
    gold = (double)((int)(gold));
```

```
cout << "That is equal to " << gold << " gold and "
    << silver << " silver. \n"
    << "Thank you for shopping at the Weapon Store. "
    << "Have a nice day, Sir " << name.c_str() << ".\n";
return 0;
}
```

SUMMARY

You covered a lot of information in this chapter. You learned how a computer stores data in its internal memory, how you can store data temporarily for later use, and about the different types of data. You learned about constants and about typedef, sizeof(), and the assignment operator. You also reviewed the C++ syntax covered so far.

You have journeyed deep enough now to safely be called a beginning programmer. Be proud; only an elite few make it this far.

In the next chapter, we introduce you to control statements, which are the beginning of true power over your computer. Sit back for a minute and let all this information condense; then suit up, jump in, and fasten your seatbelt—you've got a great journey ahead!

CHALLENGES

1. What is the correct variable type for storing the following data?
   The number of books in a bookshelf
   The cost of this book
   The number of people in the world
   The word Hello
2. Provide meaningful variable names for the variables in the first challenge.
3. Name two reasons to use constants rather than literals.
4. Write a program that calculates and displays the sizes of all the fundamental types.
5. Test what happens if you declare a character as unsigned. Do you get the results you expected? Formulate a reason why or why not.

MAKING CHOICES WITH CONTROL STATEMENTS

In earlier chapters, you created programs that execute from start to finish. Each statement is executed only once, and every statement must be executed. However, this linearity is acceptable only for basic programming. To create advanced, dynamic programs, you must master using control statements, which enable programs to jump to a certain piece of code or to execute a section of code more than once. In this chapter, you learn about the following:

- Selection statements
- Boolean logic and operators
- Iteration statements
- Branching statements
- Random numbers

CHOOSING CODE WITH SELECTION STATEMENTS

Often, people base their decisions on certain conditions. For example, a person might go to a doctor if he feels sick. The decision, whether or not to go to the doctor, is based on a certain condition: feeling sick. The same is true when using programs. You can design your program so that it selects which code to execute based on certain conditions.

Conditions in C++ are based on Boolean values. As you have learned, Booleans have two possible values, `true` or `false`. The operators and operands that make up the condition determine a condition's value.

There are two types of selection statements: `if else` statements and `switch` statements.

Testing Conditions with if Statements

Probably the most important selection statement is the `if` statement. The idea behind the `if` statement is that a special section of code contained within the statement (called the controlled statement) will be executed only if a certain condition (called the controlling condition, or just the condition) holds true. The general syntax for the `if` statement is

```
if (condition)
    controlledStatements
```

Here, *condition* is the condition being tested, and *controlledStatements* is zero or more controlled statements. These controlled statements are executed only if *condition* evaluates to `true`. Note that there is no semicolon after *condition*. The entire two lines of this general syntax are one statement, so a semicolon is not required. Also, note that *condition* is in parentheses to separate it from the rest of the statement. These parentheses are required. If *controlledStatements* consists of only one statement, the syntax is this:

```
if (condition)
    theStatement;
```

Here *theStatement* is the single statement. Note the semicolon at the end, telling the compiler that this is the entire `if` statement. When *controlledStatements* consists of more than one statement, the syntax looks like this:

```
if (condition)
{
    statementList
}
```

Here `statementList` is zero or more C++ statements, each ending with a semicolon. Note that no semicolon is required at the end of the last curly brace (}). You might recall from Chapter 2, "Descending Deeper into Variables," that a block of code is any section of code separated by curly braces. Blocks of code can be put anywhere a single statement is allowed. This is one example. Another example, used in every program thus far, is the main function. Throughout this chapter, you will see quite a few examples of blocks of code. Keep an eye out for them.

Here is an example:

```
int swords = 9;
if(swords < 8) //the condition
{
     cout << "The number or sword is less than 8";
}
```

The `cout` statement will never be executed because the condition (the controlling condition), `swords < 8` (is the value of the integer variable `swords` less than 8?), evaluated to `false`. Nine is not less than eight. Because you want it to execute only one line of code, you can display this example in the alternate way—without the braces, as shown here:

```
int swords = 9;
if(swords < 8) //the condition
     cout << "The number of swords is less than 8";
```

In this example, because the braces are not used, the `if` statement consists of everything up to (and including) the semicolon.

As we said earlier, the `if` statement is the most common control statement. When combined with the `else if` statements and `else` statements discussed next, the `if` statement can be one of your most powerful tools.

Including else if and else Statements

Sometimes you might want to take an alternative course of action if a certain condition does not hold true. Say, for example, that you feel sick. You might go to see a doctor; otherwise, you will stay home. The statement following the word otherwise is the alternative course of action. If the condition, feeling sick, is not true, you will take the alternative action, stay home.

In C++, the word otherwise is represented with the `else` statement. An `else` statement must always follow an `if` statement. An `else` statement cannot occur by itself. The syntax for an `else` statement is this:

```
else
     controlledStatements
```

Here *controlledStatements* is one or more statements. If you have more than one statement in *controlledStatements*, you must use a block, surrounded by curly braces, as shown here:

```
else {
     statementList
}
```

In the preceding, *statementList* consists of zero or more statements, separated by semicolons. If *controlledStatements* is just one statement, a block is not needed:

```
else
     theStatement;
```

You connect an `else` statement with an `if` statement by putting the `else` statement right after the `if` statement:

```
if (condition)
     controlledStatements1
else
     controlledStatements2
```

The keyword `else` must immediately follow the `if` statement; if placed anywhere else, a compile error will occur.

Here's an example:

```
int swords = 9;
if (swords <8)
     cout << "Swords is less than 8";
else
     cout << "Swords is not less than 8.";
```

Here, the text `Swords is not less than 8` will display onscreen because the `if` statement's condition is false; the `else` statement executes automatically. If the integer variable, `swords`, were initialized to 6, for example, the text `Swords is less than 8` would display, and the entire `else` statement would be skipped.

It is possible for the statements controlled by an `else` statement to be composed of another `if` statement. This is how the infamous `else if` statement is formed:

```
if (condition1)
     controlledStatements1
else if (condition2)
     controlledStatements2
```

Here *condition1* and *condition2* are two separate conditions, and *controlledStatements1* and *controlledStatements2* are two separate sets of controlled statements. The preceding block of code executes as follows:

- If *condition1* is true, *controlledStatements1* is executed and the computer skips the rest of the if-else if structure.

- If *condition1* is false and *condition2* is true, the *controlledStatements2* is executed, and the rest of the if-else if structure is skipped.

- If *condition1* and *condition2* are both false, neither one of the controlled statements is executed.

Putting one if statement inside another if statement is called nesting. See Figure 3.1 for a diagram showing how the if-else if-else structure works.

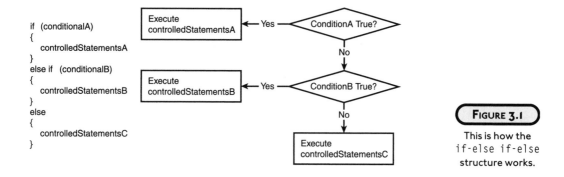

FIGURE 3.1

This is how the if-else if-else structure works.

The Three Tests of Honor Game

You are a brave knight standing in front of a labyrinth full of dark, cruel looking rooms. You must pass a number of tests that an evil wizard has set before you in order to rescue the damsel whom the evil wizard has kidnapped. If you manage to pass all these tests of honor, you and the damsel (in distress) will live happily ever after.

The first room is a room full of gold. If you take any of the gold, you fail the test; however, you get to keep the gold you take. The second room is full of diamonds. If you take these, you will prove your greed and will not be able to rescue the damsel. In the last room, you must help rescue a peasant from a dragon. If you pass all three tests, the evil wizard will release the damsel.

Here is how this example looks using if and else statements:

```
//3.1 - The Three Tests of Honour -- Mark Lee and Dirk Henkemans
#include <iostream>

int main(void)
{
    using std::cout;
```

```cpp
using std::cin;
cout << "Welcome to the Three Tests of Honour."
     << "\nAn evil wizard has kidnapped a damsel and "
     << "it is up to you to rescue her."
     << "\nHe says you must pass the three tests of "
     << "honour in his Labyrinth of Doom.";
bool goldTaken, diamondsTaken, killedByDragon;
cout << "\n\nYou enter the first room. "
     << "\nIt is full of so much gold you can hardly believe it."
     << " \nDo you take the gold (1 for yes, 0 for No)? ";
cin >> goldTaken;
if(goldTaken)
     cout << "\nYou keep the gold, "
          << "but you have failed the first test. "
          << "\nGame Over.\n\n";
else {
     cout << "Congratulations, "
          << "you have passed the first test of honour!"
          << "\n\nYou move into the second room."
          << " It is full of sparkling diamonds"
          << "\nDo you take the diamonds" " (1 for yes, 0 for No)? ";
     cin >> diamondsTaken;
     if(diamondsTaken)
          cout << "You take the diamonds, "
               << "but you have failed the second test."
               << "\nYou have proven your greed. "
               << "\nGame Over.\n\n";
     else
     {
          cout << "Congratulations, you have "
               << "passed the first and second test of honour."
               << "\n\nYou enter the third room. "
               << "\nA poor peasant is being attacked "
               << "by a dragon!" "\nDo you ignore the peasant and "
               << "move on (1 for yes, 0 for No)?";
          cin >> killedByDragon;
          if (killedByDragon)
               cout << "\nAs you sneak by, "
```

```
                        << "the dragon turns his attention to you."
                        << "\nHe burns you to a crisp "
                        << "with one breath. You are dead."
                        << "\nGame Over.\n\n";
            else
                cout << "Congratulations, you "
                        << "have passed all three tests!\n\n"
                        << "You exit the labyrinth and "
                        << "confront the evil wizard.\n\n"
                        << "He tries to turn you into a frog,"
                        << " but you manage to evade.\n"
                        << "With one swing of your "
                        << "sword it is over.\n\n"
                        << "You and the damsel live "
                        << "happily ever after.\n\n" "The End.\n\n";
        }
    }
    return 0;
}
```

As you can see in this example, the main part of the program starts with an if statement, which tests to see whether the player has chosen to take the gold or not. If the player takes the gold (by entering the number 1), the condition inside the parentheses evaluates to true (1 is equivalent to the value true), and the player can keep the gold. If the player keeps the gold, however, the player does not move on to the next test (and, therefore, the third test), the second room with the diamonds. In other words, if the first condition evaluates to true, the rest of the if-else structure is skipped.

On the other hand, if the player chooses not to take the gold, he passes the first test and moves on to the next room. If the player then chooses to take the diamonds, he can keep the diamonds, but in that case, the player will not have a chance to save the peasant or rescue the damsel. If one of the conditions holds true, the computer will execute the controlled statements that are controlled by the condition that held true. So, in this example, if the player takes the diamonds, the computer will execute the code that lets the player keep the diamonds and then it will skip to the end of the entire structure.

The third if statement is similar to the previous two. The player cannot rescue the peasant if he has taken the gold or diamonds.

The line, if (killedByDragons), is an example of one if statement. Notice that you do not need the braces around the controlled statement. However, if you choose to place braces around the cout statement, the program will not change.

Last come the else statements. The else statements are default statements, which means that if the condition of the related if statement does not hold true, the code inside the else statement will be executed. That is, if the player did not take the gold or diamonds and defeated the dragon, the player—the brave knight—may marry the damsel and live happily ever after.

The Conditional Operator

Some conditions are very trivial, making it very tedious to write a complete if statement for them. Observe the following:

```
if (x > y) // is x greater than y?
      z=y;
else
      z=x;
```

This code snippet assigns the minimum of x and y to z. Writing a complete if-else structure for something so short can be a pain. Fortunately, C++ provides an alternative: the conditional operator. The preceding example is much more concise when you use this operator:

```
z = (x>y) ? y : x;
```

The general syntax for the conditional operator is as follows:

condition ? expr1 : expr2

Here *condition* is a valid condition, and *expr1* and *expr2* are valid expressions. If *condition* is true, the conditional operator evaluates to *expr1*; otherwise, it evaluates to *expr2*. The conditional operator is an expression and can be used anywhere that other expressions can be used. You can see that this is similar to using an if statement. However, keep in mind that *expr1* and *expr2* are expressions and not statements, as opposed to if statements, whose controlled statements are full statements. You cannot, for example, do the following:

```
(x>y)? cout << "x is greater than y." : cout << "x isn't greater than y."; //error
```

Here is an example to illustrate the proper use of the conditional operator:

```
int soldiers = 5;
int tanks = 10;
int max = (b>a) ? b : a;
int min = (b<a) ? b : a;
```

```
cout << "The largest value is: " << max << "\n";
cout << "The smallest value is : " << min << "\n";
Output:
The largest value is: 10
The smallest value is: 5
```

Using the switch Statement

The second type of selection statement is the `switch` statement. Many programmers try to avoid the `switch` statement, but if used correctly, it can be a powerful tool.

Imagine that you are programming a game that displays a menu with six choices. One way to respond is to use six `if` statements in a row. Even better, use an `if-else if-else` structure. The `switch` statement is an even simpler solution. It enables you to test one variable against certain values and respond differently to each one. Here is the general syntax for the `switch` statement:

```
switch(expression)
{
    case expr1:
        controlledStatements1
        break;
    case expr2:
        controlledStatements2
        break;
    case expr3:
        controlledStatements3
        break;
    ...
}
```

Here *expression*, *expr1*, *expr2*, and *expr3* are variables or expressions whose values you want to test. We discuss the `break` statement shortly. This syntax is equivalent to an `if-else if` structure in meaning:

```
if (expression == expr1)
    controlledStatements1
else if (expression == expr2)
    controlledStatements2
else if (expression == expr3)
    controlledStatements3
...
```

You can see how much more inconvenient an if-else if structure can be. When the switch statement executes, the computer goes through each case statement and tests whether *expression* equals *exprN* (where N is any number). If they are equal, everything after the case statement will be executed until the computer encounters the break keyword. If none of the tests evaluates to true, the whole switch statement does nothing.

The break keyword is new to you. It exits (causes the program to go to the end of) the nearest enclosing switch statement or iteration statement. If the break keyword is not enclosed by a switch statement or iteration statement, a syntax error occurs when you try to compile. The break keyword is optional here. Shortly, you will learn the implications of leaving this word out, but for now, put it at the end in every case.

Now that you've made it through all the confusing definitions, it's time for an example:

```cpp
int menuChoice = 3;
switch(menuChoice) {
    case 1:
        cout << "You chose 1!\n";
        break;
    case 2:
        cout << "You chose 2!\n";
        break;
    case 3:
        cout << "You chose 3!\n";
        break;
    case 4:
        cout << "You chose 4!\n";
        break;
}
cout << "You are now out of the switch statement!\n";
Output:
You chose 3!
You are now out of the switch statement!
```

As you can see from the output, the program chose the correct case statement and executed it. All the other case statements are ignored.

Note that a break statement isn't required within every case statement (and sometimes it is useful not to have one). Observe the following example:

```
int choice;
cout << "Please enter a number: ";
cin >> choice;
cout << "\n";
switch (choice)
{
     case 1:
     case 2:
     case 3:
          cout << "You chose 1, 2, or 3.\n";
          break;
     case 4:
          cout << "You chose 4!\n";
     case 5:
          cout << "You chose 4 or 5.\n";
          break;
}
```

Output (when the user enters 1):
Please enter a number: 1
You chose 1, 2, or 3.
Output (when the user enters 4):
Please enter a number: 4
You chose 4!
You chose 4 or 5.

The default Case

You might not always be able to account for all possible values in a `switch` statement, or you might sometimes want to perform the same action for many cases. C++ provides the equivalent of an `else` statement for the `switch` statement, called the `default` statement. The `default` statement is just like the `case` statement except that there is no value to test. The syntax for the `default` statement is as follows:

```
default:
     controlledStatements
     break;
```

If the `default` statement is encountered, *controlledStatements* automatically executes. There is not a test for the `default` statement as there is for the `case` statement. You must place the `default` statement at the end of the list of `case` statements. Here is an example:

```
int choice;
cout << "Please enter a number: ";
cin >> choice;
switch (choice)
{
    default:
            cout << "\nYou chose " << choice << "\n";
}
Output:
Please enter a number: 5
You chose 5
```

USING BOOLEAN OPERATORS

In Chapter 2, we noted that the Boolean type is able to hold one of two possible values: true (1) and false (0), and all conditional statements evaluate to a Boolean value. Quite a few operands can determine the Boolean value of a condition (whether a condition is true or false); these operands are called Boolean operands. You can use these operands to form conditions (expressions that evaluate to either true or false). In this section, we discuss each of these operands in turn so that you will be able to use any one of them as needed.

The Equivalence Operator

The simplest Boolean operator is the equivalence operator. The equivalence operator (==, or two equal signs) is a binary operator, which means that it takes two operands, one on each side. The general syntax for this operator is

operand1 == *operand2*

where *operand1* and *operand2* are the two operands. This operator evaluates to true if the values of the two operands (that is, the bit patterns of the data contained within them) are the same. Here is an example to help clarify things. If you have previously declared variables as

```
long elves = 8;
int dwarves = 8;
```

you can use them in a condition like this:

```
if (elves == dwarves) //true
if (dwarves == 8) //true
if (dwarves == 0) //false
if (dwarves == elves) //true
```

Each of the preceding conditions evaluates to true, except the third one. But, wait! You might say that elves and dwarves are two different data types (integer and long integer), so their bit patterns cannot be the same, which is true, but C++ is smart enough to account for this. During execution time (run-time), when the first condition is encountered, the program converts (casts) dwarves to the type long (the largest data type involved in the statement) and then compares the values. For example, if a double (8 bytes) and an int (4 bytes) are being compared, the computer will first cast the int to a float and then compare the two. The third condition evaluates to false because the value of dwarves is not 0; it's 8.

The equivalence operator is left-associative, which means that if more than one equivalence operator is in a single statement, the operators are evaluated from left to right. For example, if you have a condition like

```
if (dwarves == elves == dragons)
```

dwarves will first be compared to elves. The value that this comparison evaluates to (true or false) will then be compared to the variable dragons. This comparison determines the result for the entire expression.

TRAP   Don't confuse the equivalence operator (==) with the assignment operator, which is one equal sign (=). The assignment operator makes the value of the variable on the left side of the assignment operator the same as the value on the right. The equivalence operator tests whether two operands are the same, but does not change them. It is common for beginners to mix them up. In other words, don't let what you already know about these symbols get in the way of what you are learning.

Introducing the Does-Not-Equal Operator

The opposite of the equivalence operator is the does-not-equal operator (!=). This operator is binary and is left-associative as well. The syntax for the does-not-equal operator is almost the same as for the equivalence operator:

```
expr1 != expr2
```

expr1 and expr2 are valid expressions. The expression formed by this operator is a condition. This operator evaluates to true if expr1 and expr2 are not equivalent. It evaluates to false if the two expressions are equivalent. For example, if you have two variables declared like so:

```
int plasmaGun = 50;
int rifle = 10;
```

you can use them with the does-not-equal operator, as shown here:

```
if (plasmaGun != rifle) //true
if (plasmaGun != 50) //false
if (rifle != 0) //true
```

The Less-Than and Greater-Than Operators

The less-than ($<$) and greater-than ($>$) signs do in computers about the same thing they do in fourth-grade math. For example, 3 $<$ 4 evaluates to `true` because 3 is less than 4. The same is the case with the greater-than sign: 4 $>$ 3 is `true` because 4 is greater than 3. Check out the following variables and what they evaluate to:

```
int elves = 4;
int dwarves = 5;
if (elves<dwarves) //true
if (dwarves < elves) //false
if (dwarves > (2 / 3)) //true
if (elves < (23 *117)) //true
```

The less-than and greater-than operators are both binary operators and are left-associative. For example, the following code might not do what you think:

```
if (0 < x < 99)
```

If you remember your math really well, you might think that this tests whether x is between 0 and 99. However, this is not what happens. First, x is compared to 0. Whatever this comparison evaluates to (`true` or `false`) is then compared to 99. Because both `true` (1) and `false` (0) are less than 99, this condition will always evaluate to `true`, regardless of the value of x.

Merging with the Equivalence Operator

You might also recall experience with the less-than-or-equal-to and the greater-than-or-equal-to signs in math. In C++, they are written slightly differently, but they still exist. Instead of a line under the less-than or greater-than sign, you put an equal sign after it. Thus, the greater-than-or-equal-to operator is $>=$, and the less-than-or-equal-to operator is $<=$.

These operators work exactly as the less-than and greater-than operators work, except that if the two things being compared are equal, the operator also returns `true`. Here are some examples:

```
if (5 <= 5) //true
if (6 >= 7) //false
if (1 <= 8) //true
```

Just like the less-than and greater-than operators, the greater-than-or-equal-to and less-than-or-equal-to operators are binary and are left associative.

The Logical or Operator

The logical or operator (||) is a binary operator. It will return `true` if one of the operands evaluates to `true`. Both sides of the or statement must first be evaluated to a Boolean form (`true` or `false`) before the or operator can be evaluated.

Table 3.1 shows the first example of a truth table (a table in which all the possible values for the operands are listed, along with the resulting value to which the operator evaluates). The first column states the value of the first operand (called A for convenience), the second column states the value of the second operand (called B), and the third column states the value of A||B.

TABLE 3.1 TRUTH TABLE FOR THE OR OPERATOR		
Value of A	**Value of B**	**Value of A||B**
True	True	True
True	False	True
False	True	True
False	False	False

Table 3.1 includes every possible combination of the operand's values. Here are examples of conditions with or statements and what they evaluate to:

```
if (true || false) //true
if ((2>3) || false) //false
if ((3*5) < 90 || (3<5)) //true
```

The or operator is left-associative as well. However, having more than one or operator in one statement is not always trivial, as it is for the less-than and greater-than operators. If any of the operands are `true`, the entire condition will be `true`.

This means that the computer executing your code can short-circuit. Short-circuiting is when a computer realizes that it doesn't have to execute the rest of a statement. For example, if the program comes across a condition with an or operand in it and the first operand is `true`, the program does not have to evaluate the second operand. It skips the second one because it knows that the whole condition will evaluate to `true`, regardless of the second operand.

The and Operator

The and operator is similar to the or operator. It is also a binary operator and left-associative. In order for the and operand to evaluate to `true`, both operands must be `true`. The and operator is represented by two ampersands (`&&`). Table 3.2 shows the truth table for the and operator.

```
if (true && true) //true
if ((3<4) && (3<5)) //true
if ((99> -32) && (-32>0.11)) //false
```

TABLE 3.2   TRUTH TABLE FOR THE AND OPERATOR

Value of A	Value of B	Value of A&&B
True	True	True
True	False	False
False	True	False
False	False	False

The not Operator

The not operator (`!`) changes a Boolean value to its reverse Boolean value—for example, `true` to `false` and `false` to `true`. It is a unary operator, which means that it takes only one operand. Table 3.3 shows the truth table for the not operator.

Here are some examples of the not operator:

```
if ( !true) // false
if ( !(2>3)) //true
if ( !( (2>3) || (3>2) ) ) //false
```

TABLE 3.3   TRUTH TABLE FOR THE NOT OPERATOR

Value of A	Value of !A
True	False
False	True

FOLLOWING THE ORDER OF OPERATION

When more than one operator is in a single expression, the computer must determine the order in which to execute them. Fortunately, operators are executed according to a standardized order called the order of operation.

You might be familiar with this standard. Does the term BEDMAS sound vaguely familiar? It is the term used in elementary school math to teach the order of operations, as shown here:

- Brackets
- Exponents
- Division/Multiplication
- Addition/Subtraction

This list is called an order of precedence list. Entries at the top of the list have the highest precedence, and entries at the bottom of the list have the lowest precedence. If two operators are at the same level in the list, they are said to have equal precedence. For example, if you have a math expression, such as

`(3+7*3)/6-2*2`

you can use the order of precedence list to determine how to evaluate the expression. First, all brackets (the operation at the top of the list; actually, they are parentheses, but PEDMAS doesn't sound quite right) are evaluated. This involves evaluating everything inside the brackets. The first thing to evaluate is the expression `3+7*3`. Two operators are in this expression: multiplication and addition. Because multiplication is higher on the list, it is evaluated first and then the addition, giving you `3+21` and then `24`.

The expression remaining is `24/6-2*2`. Next, because division and multiplication are on the same level of precedence, they are evaluated from left to right. The expression then becomes `4-4`. The expression remaining is easy to evaluate. The final answer is `0`.

C++ has a similar order of precedence list as well (see Table 3.4).

In Table 3.4, *expr* is any valid C++ expression, *lvalue* is any identifier whose value can change, and *global* is any global variable. As you can see, these rules are much more complex than the simple BEDMAS, but in a short amount of time, this list will become second nature to you. Learn to love it, but avoid code that is so complex that it depends on this list.

You can use any and all of the preceding operators together in a conditional statement. You can even make a conditional statement more than one line long. However, doing so is probably not a great idea because the conditional statement can become impossible to read. Instead, if you have a long or multiline conditional statement, try breaking it into more than

TABLE 3.4 THE ORDER OF PRECEDENCE FOR C++ OPERATORS	
Operator	**Common Name**
`::global`	Scope resolution operator
`lvalue++, lvalue--`	Postfix increment, postfix decrement
`sizeof(expr), ++lvalue, --lvalue`	`sizeof` operator, prefix increment, prefix decrement
`*, /, %`	Multiplication, division, modulus
`+, -`	Addition, subtraction
`<, <=, >, >=`	Less-than, less-than-or-equal-to, greater-than, greater-than-or-equal-to
`==, !=`	Equivalence, does not equal
`&&`	Logical and
`||`	Logical or
`expr ? expr : expr`	Conditional operator

one statement. For example, the following algorithm calculates whether the integer k is between two numbers. The first number is the summative from 1 to n (the summative from 1 to n is the sum 1 + 2 + 3 + . . . + n; the formula for this summative is n * (n + 1) / 2). The second number is the same summative but from 1 to n + 1 (the summative 1 + 2 + 3 + . . . + (n + 1); the formula is (n + 2) / 2). To get the formula, just substitute n + 1 for n in the normal formula: (n + 1) * (n + 2) / 2:

```
if (n * (n + 1) / 2 >= k && ((n + 1) * (n + 2) / 2 ) <= k)
//calculates whether or not k is between the
//summatives of n and n + 1
{
        cout << "k is between the summatives of n and n+1";
}
```

Although this example is not long, it is intensely mathematical and therefore should probably be broken into more than one line. If you look at the order of precedence list, you can see that && is evaluated last in the preceding condition. This means that the condition can be simplified to the form A&&B, where A = (n * (n + 1) /2) >= k and B = ((n + 1)*(n + 2) /2) <= k. This is a highly effective way to simplify your expression. Here is how this method looks in the code:

```
int a = (n * (n + 1) /2) >= k;
int b = ((n + 1) * (n + 2) /2) <= k;
if (a && b)
```

```
{
        cout << "k is between the summatives of n and n + 1";
}
```

CONTINUING WITH ITERATION STATEMENTS

Iteration statements are control structures that repeat continuously until a certain condition is no longer met. Perhaps we can explain this concept by comparing it to the myth of Hercules. Hercules was assigned nine tasks, and he could not continue with his life until he completed them (that is, the iteration statement would repeat continuously). Once he completed the nine tasks, however, he was free to continue with his life. In programming, these tasks can be written as a loop having to execute nine times, doing a task every time; but once the loop finishes the ninth task, the computer can continue to execute the rest of the program's code.

The while Loop

You could program the Hercules example with the while loop. The while loop will continually execute until a particular condition becomes false. The syntax for a while loop is as follows:

```
while(condition)
        controlledStatements
```

Here *condition* will be tested every time the loop executes. When *condition* is no longer true, the loop will terminate. Until then, *controlledStatements* will be executed over and over again. Remember, if the condition is not true to begin with, it is possible that the loop will never execute. Also, keep in mind that you have to make sure that your loops will terminate after a certain amount of time. Avoid infinite loops (loops that will never fail their precondition).

You are now ready to program the nine tasks of Hercules (mentioned in the preceding section). The following example shows how you can create the program using a while loop. Here you want to limit the while loop to a particular condition; you want the task number to be less than or equal to nine.

```
//3.2 - Nine Tasks of Hercules - Dirk Henkemans and Mark Lee
#include <iostream>

int main( void )
{
        using std::cout;
        //the variable that stores how many tasks you have completed.
        int taskNumber = 0;
```

```
while(taskNumber < 9) //until taskNumber >= 9
{
        taskNumber++;
        cout << "Hercules has now completed "
                << taskNumber << " tasks." << "\n";
}
return 0;
}
```

Output:
```
Hercules has now completed 1 tasks.
Hercules has now completed 2 tasks.
Hercules has now completed 3 tasks.
Hercules has now completed 4 tasks.
Hercules has now completed 5 tasks.
Hercules has now completed 6 tasks.
Hercules has now completed 7 tasks.
Hercules has now completed 8 tasks.
Hercules has now completed 9 tasks.
```

Notice that the final value for `taskNumber` is 10, not 9. This is because `taskNumber` must become 10 in order to make the condition `false`. Also, notice that `taskNumber` is incremented every time through the loop. This not only keeps track of Hercules' tasks, but also guarantees that the loop will eventually terminate. See Figure 3.2 for a diagram of how the while statement works.

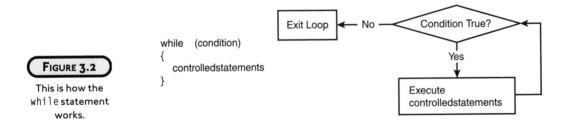

FIGURE 3.2

This is how the `while` statement works.

The Increment and Decrement Operators Revisited

You can make the preceding program more concise by incorporating the ++ operator into the condition. As we discussed before, you can incorporate multiple operators into a condition. The same is true for the condition in the "Nine Tasks of Hercules." First, you must learn about postfix and prefix operators. For both the increment and decrement operators, you put the operator before (prefix) or after (postfix) the operand as shown here:

```
operand$$ //post
$$operand //pre
```

Here $$ represents an operator, and *operand* represents an operand. However, each has a slightly different meaning. As a postfix, the operation is applied to the operand after it is retrieved, but as a prefix, the operation is applied before the value of the operand is retrieved. Here is an example:

```
int x = 5;
int y = 6;
int z = y++; // z = 6, y = 7
z = ++x; // z = 6, x = 6
```

Here is an example of how you might use these operators in the Hercules example:

```
int taskNumber = 0;
while(taskNumber++ < 9) {
    cout << "Hercules has now completed " << taskNumber << " tasks." << "\n";
}
Output:
Hercules has now completed 1 tasks.
Hercules has now completed 2 tasks.
Hercules has now completed 8 tasks.
Hercules has now completed 9 tasks.
```

The question you might ask now is whether C++ will increment taskNumber before or after it checks whether taskNumber is less than 9. The answer is simply this: If ++ comes after the variable, the variable will be incremented after the entire expression is computed. If ++ comes before the variable, the variable is incremented first, before anything else is computed.

Here is another example of using the postfix and prefix:

```
//3.3 - ++ Example Program - Dirk Henkemans and Mark Lee
#include <iostream>

int main( void )
{
    using std::cout;
    int var1 = 0, var2 = 0;
    cout << var1++ << "\n";
    cout << ++var2;
    return 0;
```

```
}
Output:
0 1
```

Although both `var1` and `var2` have a value of 1 after this program runs, you can see that `var1++` will increment `var1` after the value of `var1` is output, whereas `++var2` increments `var2` beforehand.

The `--` operator works the same way. Place this operator before the variable to make the `--` take precedence over everything else, or place it after the variable so that it is evaluated after the rest of the expression.

Looping with the do while Loop

The `do while` loop is like the `while` loop, except that the condition is tested after the iteration is finished. In this way, the loop will always execute at least once.

The syntax for the `do while` loop looks like this:

```
do {
        controlledStatements
} while(condition);
```

Remember to add the semicolon after *condition* (this is easy to forget). A `do while` loop will execute until its condition evaluates to `false`, just like a `while` loop does. However, a `do while` loop will execute once and then test the condition, so no matter what, a `do while` loop will execute once.

A good example of using the `do while` loop is when programming a game menu, as shown next. You want to display the menu in the loop, but before you ask the user for input. Then, if the user does not enter the correct information, the menu is displayed again and again until the user inputs the correct information. For example, if you number your menu items 1–4, you will want to loop until the user input is between 0 and 5 (a valid menu number). As soon as the user does enter valid input, the loop will exit.

```
//3.4 - A Simple Menu - Dirk Henkemans
#include<iostream>

int main(void)
{
        using std::cout;
        using std::cin;
        cout<<"Your party is adventuring "
```

```
            << "through hills outside of Que'll \n"
            <<"when suddenly you are "
            << "ambushed by rogues!!! \n \n";
    int response = 0;
    do
    {
            cout << "What action would you like to take? \n"
                    << " 1) Attack the evil rogues!!! \n"
                    << " 2) Run from the onslaught \n"
                    << " 3) Try to talk to the rogues \n";
            cin >> response;
    }
    while (response < 1 || response > 3);
    if (response == 1)
    {
            cout << "The battle drags into the night "
                    << "and by sunset no one knows \n"
                    << "who is still alive!\n";
    }
    else if (response == 2)
    {
            cout << "You run from the rogues into "
                    << "the trees never to see them again.\n";
    }
    else
    {
            cout << "You try talking to them "
                    << "but they seem unlikely to listen. \n"
                    << "They take all your money "
                    << "and depart happy and you poor.\n ";
    }
    return 0;
}
```

This program displays a short introduction and then allows the user to respond to the three choices given in the menu. If an invalid choice is made, the program is displayed again, and this process repeats until a valid choice is made. Each menu item selected displays a different ending.

Menus are the basis for almost everything text-based, and they provide a convenient user interface. In Chapter 4, "Writing Functions," you learn how to create a general menu for a text adventure game that can be used continuously.

Using the for Statement

The `for` statement is one of the most versatile statements that you will encounter. The `for` statement is an iteration statement that performs its own loop maintenance. The syntax for the `for` statement is shown here:

```
for (initialization; condition; expression)
    controlledStatements
```

Here *initialization* is any valid variable initialization statement or expression, *condition* is any valid condition, and *expression* is any valid expression.

A definition like this one can be overwhelming to a beginner. However, the `for` statement is really a simple device. Take a look at this example:

```
for(int count = 0; count < 10; count++)
{
    cout << count << " ";
}
Output:
0 1 2 3 4 5 6 7 8 9
```

The numbers 0 to 9 are displayed onscreen. Though this program might look complicated, it really isn't. The order in which things are executed in the `for` statement is illustrated here:

1. Execute *initialization* statement.
2. Test the *condition* (if `false`, the `for` statement is done).
3. Execute *controlledStatements*.
4. Execute *expression*.
5. Test *condition*. If `true`, go to Step 3.
6. The `for` statement is done.

The first part of the `for` statement is the *initialization* statement. It is executed as soon as the `for` statement is encountered, but is executed only once (unlike the rest of the loop). *initialization* can be any kind of variable initialization, and there are three main forms. You saw the first one in the previous example (`int count = 0`). This type includes a variable declaration and initialization. The second form occurs when a variable has been previously declared and *initialization* just sets the variable's value (for example, `count = 0`). The third form is to leave *initialization* empty. The following example illustrates these three forms:

```
for (int count = 0; count < 10; count++) //first form
     cout << count << " ";
cout << "\n";

int count;
for (count = 0; count < 10; count++) //second form
     cout << count << " ";
cout << "\n";

int index = 0;
for (; index < 10; index++) //third form
     cout << index << " ";
cout << "\n";
```
Output:
```
0 1 2 3 4 5 6 7 8 9
0 1 2 3 4 5 6 7 8 9
0 1 2 3 4 5 6 7 8 9
```

This example also illustrates another issue. Notice how count is declared twice. This is legal here because of where the declarations are located. The second declaration is in the local scope, as you've already seen, so the second count's scope lasts until the end of the function or code block (to the end of this code snippet). However, the first declaration is not local. Variables declared in initialization have a restricted scope. These variables' scopes last until the end of the for statement, which means that once the for statement ends, the variable(s) declared in initialization no longer exist. Thus, when the second declaration is encountered, there is no conflict because the first count no longer exists.

The second main part of the for statement is the condition. The condition is exactly the same as conditions in every other control statement. It is tested right after initialization is executed, and then every time through the loop. As soon as the condition evaluates to false, the for statement terminates.

You can omit the condition, as shown in the following example:

```
for (int index = 0; ; i++) cout << index;
```

This code snippet will create an infinite loop. Omitting the condition is equivalent to having a condition that is always true.

The third part of the `for` statement is the expression. The expression is executed immediately after *controlledStatements*. This means that if *controlledStatements* is never executed (the condition fails the first time), the expression is never executed.

The expression can be omitted as in the following example:

```
for (int count = 0; count < 10; )
{
    cout << count;
    count++;
}
```

Note that placing an expression (`count++`) at the end of *contolledStatements* is equivalent to placing it in the expression.

The most common way to use a `for` statement is to do some task a certain number of times. To do this, you first declare a variable and initialize it with some value in the initialization statement. In the expression, you either increment or decrement the variable declared in the initialization so that the condition will fail after a certain number of loops. Try to avoid changing the value of this "counter" variable within *controlledStatements*. The most common counter variable names are `count` or `index` (sometimes referred to as `c` and `i` for short).

NESTING

As your programs become more and more complex, you will need to nest control structures. Nesting involves placing programming structures in other programming structures. For example, you might need to put an `if` statement in a `for` statement. Any control statement can legally be placed in any other control statement. Here is an example of a `do while` loop in an `if` statement:

```
if (choice == displayMenu)
{
    do
    {
        //displayMenu
    } while(!valid Input);
}
```

You could use a multiplication table, which requires two nested `for` loops. In the following example, the inside `for` statement loops fully for each loop of the outside `for` statement. This example illustrates one way to print a multiplication table:

```
//3.5 - A Multiplication Table - Dirk Henkemans
#include<iostream>

int main(void)
{
    using std::cout;
    cout << "A multiplication table:\n"
        << " 1\t2\t3\t4\t5\t6\t7\t8\t9\n"
        << " ----------------------------------------"
        << "-------------\n";
    for(int c = 1; c < 10; c++)
    {
        cout << c << "| ";
        for(int i = 1; i < 10; i++)
        {
            cout << i * c << '\t';
        }
        cout << "\n";
    }
    return 0;
}
```

Output:

A multiplication table:

	1	2	3	4	5	6	7	8	9
1|	1	2	3	4	5	6	7	8	9
2|	2	4	6	8	10	12	14	16	18
3|	3	6	9	12	15	18	21	24	27
4|	4	8	12	16	20	24	28	32	36
5|	5	10	15	20	25	30	35	40	45
6|	6	12	18	24	30	36	42	48	54
7|	7	14	21	28	35	42	49	56	63
8|	8	16	24	32	40	48	56	64	72
9|	9	18	27	36	45	54	63	72	81

As you can see, nesting control statements is a very useful tool for many different situations.

CREATING RANDOM NUMBERS

Random numbers do not exist in computers; however, you can create pseudo random numbers using complex mathematical formulas. We do not discuss these formulas here because they are way too complex for a beginner, and you do not need to understand them in order to use them.

Random numbers are created from a random seed. A random seed is a number that is used to start the random number generator. This random seed usually comes from the current time of the computer system's clock.

This is an ideal choice for a random seed because it is so unpredictable. The chance of a program being used twice in one second is unlikely, so the random number will probably be different every time.

The process for generating random numbers consists of two parts: first, setting the seed; second, generating the random number. In order to gain access to the second hand of the computer's clock, you must include part of the standard C++ library: `<ctime>`:

```
#include <ctime>
```

The random number generator is also part of the standard library, so you must include `<cstdlib>`:

```
#include <cstdlib>
```

In order to seed the random number generator, you use the `srand()` (seed random) function (see Chapter 4 for more on functions). You put the number with which you want to seed the generator within parentheses. This can be any number, but in this case, you are using the `time()` function. The `time()` function gives the number of seconds that have passed since January 1, 1970, which seems bizarre, but it is the standard way of getting the computer's time. Once you have seeded the random number generator, you can obtain random numbers with the `rand()` function.

First, you must include these names with a `using` declaration:

```
using std::srand;
using std::rand;
using std::time;
```

Here's how you seed the random number generator:

```
srand(time(0));
```

The (0) is beyond the scope of what you are learning here, so we don't go into it. Just make sure that this line is executed only once. Don't seed the generator repeatedly; doing so can cause it to lose some randomness (a loop can sometimes take much less than a second).

Now that you have seeded the generator, you are ready to use it. To generate a random number, you use the `rand()` function. This function gives a large random number, such as 2453. Here's what the `rand()` function looks like in code:

```
cout << rand();
```

In order to generate a random number between two other numbers (for example, a random number between 1 and 10), you use this formula:

```
rand() % (max -min + 1) + min;
```

Here *max* is the higher value and *min* is the lower value. For example, to generate a number between 10 and 20, you use a formula like this one:

```
int num = rand() % 11 + 10; // (20 - 10 + 1) = 11
```

This formula works because `rand % 11` evaluates to a number from 0 to 10. Then adding 10 gives a number somewhere between 10 and 20.

The `rand()` function is very useful and is an integral part of the following game.

The Number Guessing Game

Up to this point, you have created games that do not change their behavior based on the user's input. Now is the time to learn how to use random numbers, selection statements, and iteration statements to create dynamic, responsive programs.

Throughout the rest of the book, you will create increasingly difficult games that respond to the user's input. The first of these responsive games is the "Number Guessing Game." This program works by randomly picking a number from one to 100. The user must guess the number, and the program tells the user whether the number is too high, too low, or the right one. When the user guesses the number, the program exits, telling the user how many guesses it took to get the right number.

```
//3.6 - Number Guessing Game - Dirk Henkemans

#include<iostream>
#include <ctime>
#include <cstdlib>
```

```cpp
int main(void)
{
    using std::cout;
    using std::cin;
    using std::srand;
    using std::time;
    using std::rand;

    cout << "Welcome to the number guessing game!!! \n";
    cout << "I have picked a number between 1 and 100. \n \n";
    srand((unsigned int)time(0));

    int numPicked = rand() % 100 + 1; //stores the random number
    int guess = 0; //stores the number the user guessed
    int guessNum; //stores the number of guesses

    for (guessNum = 0; guess != numPicked; guessNum++)
    {
        cout << "What would you like to guess? \n";
        cin >> guess;
        if(guess < numPicked)
            cout << "\nYou guessed too low!!! \n \n";
        else if (guess > numPicked)
            cout << "\nYou guessed too high!!! \n \n";
    }
    cout << "\nYou guessed it!!! \nIt took you " << guessNum << " guesses.";
    return 0;
}
```

Output:
Welcome to the number guessing game!!!
I have picked a number between 1 and 100.

What would you like to guess?
50
You guessed too low!!!

What would you like to guess?
75

```
You guessed too high!!!

What would you like to guess?
63
You guessed it!!!
It took you 3 guesses.
```

CREATING THE ROMAN COMMANDER GAME

While jumping around in the clouds of code city, you happen to come across the Emperor of Rome. He is desperately in need of a commander to lead an attack against the Germanian Hordes. Will you accept the challenge?

And, of course, you, seeing this as an excellent opportunity to work on your new skills, including random numbers, while loops, do while loops, if statements, switch statements, and the conditional operator, accept.

Type the following code into your compiler's source code editor and try it out. Think about each of the control statements in the code. Can you read them as though they were in English? If not, your continued practice will enable you to very soon.

```
//3.7 - The Roman Commander Game - Mark Lee and Dirk Henkemans
#include <iostream>
#include <string>
#include <ctime>
#include <cstdlib>

int main( void )
{
    using std::cout;
    using std::cin;
    using std::srand;
    using std::time;
    using std::rand;
    using std::string;

    srand((unsigned int)time(0)); //seed the random number generator
    string name; //used to store the player's name
    bool end = false; //used to test if the user chose to quit
    bool lost; //used to test if the user lost the game
```

```
int menu_choice; //stores the user's choice from the menu

//units that the player starts with
int archers = 50;
int catapults = 25;
int swordsmen = 100;

//units that the Germanians start with (random)
// random number between 70 and 20
int g_archers = rand() % (51) + 20;
int g_catapults = rand() % (41) + 10; //between 50 and 10

//between 150 and 50
int g_swordsmen = rand() % (101) + 50;

//stores which numbers correspond to which menu choices
int archers_menu, catapults_menu, swordsmen_menu;
int fight_menu;

cout << "Welcome Adventurer, what is your name?\n";
cin >> name;
cout << "Well, " << name
     << " welcome to the Roman Commander Game.\n"
     << "\nYou are the commander of the Roman Army"
     << " attacking Germania.";
while (!end) //main game loop
{
     //variables to store how many units the player sends
     int archers_sent=0, catapults_sent=0;
     int swordsmen_sent=0;
     cout << "\nYou have " << archers << " archers, " << catapults
          << " catapults, and " << swordsmen << " swordsmen.\n"
          << "\nGermania has " << g_archers << " archers, "
          << g_catapults << " catapults, and " << g_swordsmen
          << " swordsmen.\n\n";
     do //pre-battle loop
     {
          //keeps track of which menu numbers are being used
```

```cpp
int i = 1;

if (archers > 0 && ((archers - archers_sent) != 0))
{
     archers_menu = i;
     cout << "[" << i << "] Send Archers\n";
     i++;
}
else archers_menu = 0;

if (catapults > 0 && ((catapults - catapults_sent) != 0))
{
     catapults_menu = i;
     cout << "[" << i << "] Send Catapults\n";
     i++;
}
else catapults_menu = 0;

if (swordsmen > 0 && ((swordsmen - swordsmen_sent) != 0))
{
     swordsmen_menu = i;
     cout << "[" << i << "] Send Swordsmen\n";
     i++;
}
else swordsmen_menu = 0;

fight_menu = i;
cout <<"["<< i <<"] Go Fight\n";
cin >> menu_choice;

if (menu_choice == archers_menu)
{
     do {
          cout << "\nHow many archers would you "
               << "like to send?\n";
          cin >> archers_sent;
     } while (!(archers_sent > -1 &&
          archers_sent <= archers));
```

```
        } else if (menu_choice == catapults_menu)
        {
             do {
                  cout << "\nHow many catapults would you "
                       << "like to send?\n";
                  cin >> catapults_sent;
             }while (!(catapults_sent > -1 &&
                  catapults_sent <= catapults));
        } else if (menu_choice == swordsmen_menu)
        {
             do {
                  cout << "\nHow many swordsmen would you "
                       << "like to send?\n";
                  cin >> swordsmen_sent;
             } while (!(swordsmen_sent > -1 &&
                  swordsmen_sent <= swordsmen));
        }
} //end pre-battle loop
while (menu_choice != fight_menu);
cout << "\nEntering Battle...\n";
int archers_dead, catapults_dead, swordsmen_dead;
int g_archers_dead, g_catapults_dead, g_swordsmen_dead;

//each catapult kills 2 archers
archers_dead = 2 * g_catapults;
//each swordsman kills 1 catapult
catapults_dead = g_swordsmen;
//each archer kills 3 swordsmen
swordsmen_dead = 3 * g_archers;

g_archers_dead = 2 * catapults_sent;
g_catapults_dead = swordsmen_sent;
g_swordsmen_dead = 3 * archers_sent;

//makes sure that the number of units does not go below 0.
archers = (archers_dead < archers) ? archers - archers_dead : 0;
catapults = (catapults_dead < catapults) ?
catapults - catapults_dead : 0;
swordsmen = (swordsmen_dead < swordsmen) ?
```

```
            swordsmen - swordsmen_dead : 0;


        g_archers = (g_archers_dead < g_archers) ?
                        g_archers - g_archers_dead : 0;
        g_catapults = (g_catapults_dead < g_catapults) ?
                        g_catapults - g_catapults_dead : 0;
        g_swordsmen = (g_swordsmen_dead < g_swordsmen) ?
                        g_swordsmen - g_swordsmen_dead : 0;


        cout << "It was a long battle.\n"
             << archers_dead << " archers died.\n"
             << catapults_dead << " catapults died.\n"
             << swordsmen_dead << " swordsmen died.\n";


        //if player's army is dead then they have lost
        if ((archers + catapults + swordsmen) == 0)
             end = lost = true;


        //if germanium army is dead, player has won
        else if ((g_archers + g_catapults + g_swordsmen) == 0)
        {
             end = true;
             lost = false;
        }
    } //end of main game loop


    //display appropriate ending message
    if (lost)
    {
        cout << "\nYou lost. Try again next time.\n";
        return 0;
    }
    cout << "\nCongratulations, you won!\n";
    return 0;
}
```
Output:
```
Welcome Adventurer, what is your name?
Marcus
```

'

```
Well, Marcus welcome to the Roman Commander Game.

You are the commander of the Roman Army attacking Germania.
You have 50 archers, 25 catapults, and 100 swordsmen.

Germania has 61 archers, 50 catapults, and 52 swordsmen.

[1] Send Archers
[2] Send Catapults
[3] Send Swordsmen
[4] Go Fight
1
How many archers would you like to send?
50
[1] Send Catapults
[2] Send Swordsmen
[3] Go Fight
1
How many catapults would you like to send?
25
[1] Send Swordsmen
[2] Go Fight
1
How many swordsmen would you like to send?
100
[1] Go Fight
1
Entering Battle...
It was a long battle.
100 archers died.
52 catapults died.
183 swordsmen died.

You lost. Try again next time.
```

SUMMARY

In this chapter, you learned how to create a program that can make choices and adapt to user input. By learning first about conditional statements, and then about Boolean operators and iteration statements, you continued your journey into an area never before ventured into.

These lessons are an integral part of programming and will increase the functionality of your programs dramatically.

CHALLENGES

1. Write a conditional statement (an `if` statement) that will assign x/y to x if y doesn't equal 0.
2. Write a `while` loop that calculates the summative of positive integers from 1 to some number n (if you want to check this, the formula is n (n + 1) / 2).
3. Write a conditional statement that assigns x * y if x is even; otherwise, if x is odd and y doesn't equal 0, assign x to x / y; if neither of the preceding cases is `true`, output to the screen that y is equal to 0.

STRUCTURING YOUR CODE WITH FUNCTIONS

I f you have been working through this book in its natural sequence, you have progressed far on your journey. Sit for a moment and let all the information sift through your brain; then get a cup of black coffee, settle into your favorite chair, and brace yourself. You've got an exciting trip ahead.

In this chapter, you learn about the following:

- Structuring your code with functions
- Creating default arguments
- Differentiating variable scope
- The `main` function

DIVIDE AND CONQUER

Imagine that you are the commander of the Roman Empire's army, attacking the barbarian hordes in Germania. As any of your royal strategists will tell you, attacking your opponent's entire army at once is not very strategic. It is much more cunning to splinter the army into sections and attack each section separately. Doing so puts your army at a significant advantage and allows the might of the Roman Empire to grow even further.

The same is true for programming in C++. If you have a massive application to design and are working on a time limit, the easiest way to tackle the problem is to divide it into several programming tasks and then handle each task separately. As any mathematician will tell you, divide the problem into a group of problems that have already been solved, and you are done. This is the idea behind using functions.

Functions enable programmers to divide their code into many manageable pieces. Also, using functions, rather than repeating code numerous times, you can write it once and then use it again and again. With functions, instead of having to figure out a solution every time you encounter a problem, you allow a function to do that job for you. Then you can use the solution wherever it is needed.

For example, you might write a function called getWindowSize that calculates the size of a certain window. Whenever you need to know the size of a particular window, you just allow that function to calculate the size. Keep in mind that the function and the code asking the function to perform a task must communicate with each other. In the current example, the getWindowSize function needs to know which window is in question, and the function has to send the asking code the size of that window.

Before proceeding, here are some definitions we use as we continue through this chapter (you might not understand all of them now, but you will by the time you finish this chapter):

- **Block of code (or code block).** Any code enclosed within curly braces.
- **Function.** A segment of code that performs a specific task.
- **Calling procedure.** Any piece of code that tells a function to execute its code.
- **Calling a function.** Using a function's name to invoke its code.
- **Arguments/Parameters.** Pieces of information (data) that the calling procedure sends to functions.
- **Argument list/Parameter list.** A list of arguments that must be passed in order to call a certain function.
- **Return value.** Any value that a function returns to the calling procedure. Note that a given function can have only one return value, as illustrated in Figure 4.1.

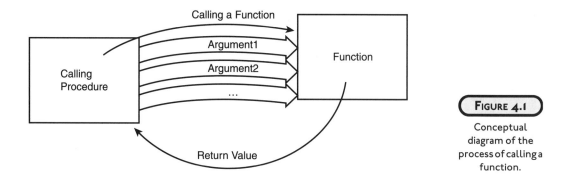

FIGURE 4.1

Conceptual diagram of the process of calling a function.

EXPLORING FUNCTION SYNTAX

In this section, we move from a theoretical to a practical level in which you learn how to write the code required for functions. To do so, you must first learn the art of function syntax. For now, however, you need to be concerned only with three parts of a function. The following three parts will be the foundation for your programs' interactions with functions and for your declaration of functions:

- The function declaration
- The function definition
- The function call

In the following sections, we discuss each of these parts.

Declaring a Function

A function declaration tells the compiler that a function exists. You tell the compiler the name of the function, what the arguments are, and what the function returns. A function declaration is also called a prototype because it is a model of the function. Here is the general syntax for a function declaration:

```
return_type function_name(argument_list);
```

Here *return_type* is the type of data that the function returns, *function_name* is the name of the function, and *argument_list* is a list of arguments that the function requires. Don't forget to add a semicolon at the end of the declaration.

If you do not want to return a value, you can use the keyword void in place of *return_type*:

```
void function_name(argument_list);
```

argument_list can be blank if there are no arguments:

return_type function_name();

Otherwise, the argument list is a list of variable declarations separated by commas:

return_type function_name(*arg1_type arg1_name, arg2_type arg2_name, …*);

Notice that each argument declaration is just a simple variable declaration (you might recognize this syntax from the material in Chapter 2, "Descending Deeper into Variables").

Example—the add Function

The idea behind the add function is relatively straightforward—take two numbers, add them, and return the result. Although we use integers for this example, any numerical data type will work.

To write the function declaration, you need three pieces of information:

- The function name
- The function return type
- The function argument list

The function name can be any valid identifier (refer to Chapter 2 for more on identifiers). However, a concise name that describes the function's purpose makes the most sense. In this case, deciding on a name is relatively easy. It is named add.

The function return type needs to be an integer. You use the integer type (int) because the function returns a number.

The last piece of information needed is the function argument list. Because the function takes two arguments, you must write two variable declarations, which we arbitrarily refer to as arguments a and b. Both a and b must be integers because they represent the two numbers that you will add. Here is the resulting argument list:

```
(int a, int b)
```

Following the general syntax, you can put the three pieces of information together to form the add() function declaration:

```
int add(int a, int b);
```

Before you continue creating this function, you need to know how to define a function.

Defining a Function

The information in this section is the heart and soul of a function. In this section, you write the code that a function contains. A function definition is like a function declaration with two curly braces ({ and }) within which you place the code. Here is the general syntax:

```
return_type function_name(argument_list)
{
    code;
}
```

Here *code* is one or more statements, each ending with a semicolon. Note that the function definition does not require a semicolon at the end. As per declaring a function, *return_type* can be void for no return value, and *argument_list* can be blank for no arguments.

One big difference between using C and C++ is your ability to declare variables wherever you need them with C++. Anywhere that you can include a statement in C++, you can also include a variable declaration.

 TRICK Even though you can include variable declarations almost anywhere, try to develop a standard way of using them. We declare them only at the beginning of code blocks. As a result, we can easily find the variable declarations.

If a function returns a value, it must have one or more return statements. Return statements begin with the keyword return followed by an expression that evaluates to be the same data type as *return_type* and a semicolon. If you were to write a function that returned a float, this would be a valid return statement:

```
return 3.141592;
```

If your function does not return a value, you can have a blank return statement:

```
return;
```

A function that does not return a value does not require a return statement at all, however. In the absence of one, it will simply terminate when the end of the function is reached.

Upon reaching a return statement, the function terminates. You can have more than one return statement in a function. Here is a common pattern in a function:

```
if (condition)
    return expression1;
return expression2;
```

This code returns only *expression1* if the *condition* evaluates to true. Otherwise, it returns *expression2*. It is often a better idea to only have one return statement at the end of the function. The return type can be stored in a variable, like this:

```
if (condition)
        ret = expression1;
else
        ret = expression2;
return ret;
```

You can use the variables created in arguments within a function. They are filled with the data that is passed when the function is called.

Example—the add Function Continued

Now you are ready to define the add function. From the description of the function, you know that the sum of the two arguments must be returned. This definition then becomes a simple task:

```
int add(int a, int b)
{
        return a + b;
}
```

As you can see, this function is relatively short and simple. In the real programming world, functions can become very long, although it is good programming practice to keep your functions as short as possible. Each function should only perform a relatively simple task. You can keep your code simple while doing very complex tasks by building simple functions on top of other simple functions.

Calling a Function

In order to use a function in a certain section of code, you must call it from within that code. When you call a function, you are telling the computer to start executing another section of code (the code within the function) before continuing with this section.

To call a function, you write the function's name followed by the arguments you are passing. Here is the general syntax:

```
function_name(data1, data2, …);
```

Here *data1* and *data2* must be of the same data types as those in the function definition. For example, if the first argument in the function definition is an integer, *data1* also must be an integer, though exceptions occur wherever the value that you pass can be converted easily into the correct value. In the preceding example, you could pass a float or double value (for example, 3.56), and the value would be truncated to make an integer (for example, 3).

If the argument list in the function declaration and function definition is empty, you can use an empty set of parentheses:

```
function_name();
```

The values that you pass to the function are assigned to each of the variables in the argument list of the function declaration. For example, if your function declaration is

```
int my_Function(int first, int second)
{
     return first;
}
```

and you call the function somewhere else:

```
my_Function(5,3)
```

the semantics of this function call are the same as the semantics of these two initializations:

```
int first = 5;
int second = 3;
```

The compiler first checks the type of data that you pass to the function against the type that the function requires. In this example, C++ checks to see whether you are passing my_Function two integers. If a conversion (cast) is required (for example, float to int), the conversion is done. If the two types of data are incompatible, the compiler returns an error. In this way, your function can access the data that you pass to it.

Return values are a little bit more confusing. When you call a function in your code, that call is replaced by the return value. Because my_Function returns an integer, you can call my_Function anywhere within code where you would normally use an integer. Here is an example:

```
my_Int = 5 + my_Function(5,3);
```

After my_Function finishes executing, the call is replaced by the value it returns (this replacement is not immediately obvious, so keep it in mind as you program):

```
my_Int = 5 + 5;
```

Example—the add Function Continued

You now have enough information to write the function call to the add function. Here is a program that asks the user for two values and uses the add function to output the sum:

```
#include <iostream>

int add(int a, int b)
{
    return a + b;
}

int main (void)
{
    using std::cout;
    using std::cin;
    int number1, number2;
    cout << "Enter the first value to be summed: ";
    cin >> number1;
    cout << "\nEnter the second: ";
    cin >> number2;
    cout << "\nThe sum is: " << add(number1, number2) << "\n";
}
```

This program first asks the user for two numbers and then gives the sum.

Putting It All Together

A complete program that contains a function has three basic components:

- An optional function declaration
- The main function
- The function definition

A function must be either declared or defined before it can be called. If you put the function definition at the beginning of your program, a declaration is not needed. However, if the function definition is at the end of the program and you call the function prior to the function definition, you need to tell your computer that the function exists. You do so by placing the function's declaration at the beginning of the program.

Here is the complete "Add Program" with the add function. This program requires a function declaration because the function definition is at the end of the program:

```
//4.1 - The Add Program - Mark Lee
#include <iostream>

//add declaration
int add(int a, int b);

//displays a sample use of the add function
int main (void)
{
    using std::cout;
    using std::cin;
    int number1, number2;
    cout << "Enter the first value to be summed: ";
    cin >> number1;
    cout << "\nEnter the second: ";
    cin >> number2;
    cout << "\nThe sum is: " << add(number1, number2) << "\n";
}

// adds two numbers and returns the sum
int add(int a, int b)
{
    return a + b;
}
```

Until now, you have placed code inside `int main (void)` and its closing brace. This section of code is called the `main` function. Function declarations and definitions must go outside this section. Don't worry if this seems confusing right now; it will become much clearer in time.

Another way to write this program is to place the `add` definition at the beginning rather than at the end of the code. In this case, you don't need a function declaration because the function definition acts as its own declaration:

```
#include <iostream>

int add(int a, int b)
{
    return a + b;
}
```

```
int main (void)
{
    int number1, number2;
    cout << "Enter the first value to be summed: ";
    cin >> number1;
    cout << "\nEnter the second: ";
    cin >> number2;
    cout << "\nThe sum is: " << add(number1, number2) << "\n";
}
```

This way, having the definition at the beginning works just as well as adding a declaration and having the definition at the end of the program. Neither way offers a particular advantage, so which one you choose is just a matter of preference.

OVERLOADING FUNCTIONS

What do you do when you are writing the add function for more than one possible data type? One approach is to write a separate function for each one, using a different name for each one. You might call one function int_add() to add two integers and another function float_add() to add two floats. This process can be quite tedious, and if you want to use the function, you must look up the proper name for the right data type.

Fortunately, C++ provides some alternatives. One approach is function overloading, discussed here, and the other is generic programming, discussed in Chapter 7, "Reusing Code: Generic Programming." For function overloading, instead of giving each function a different name, you give them all the same name. For example, every version of the add function is called add. But how does the computer tell them apart? When you call the add function, how does the computer know which version of the add function to use?

The answer is really quite simple. The computer just looks at the argument types and the number of arguments and attempts to match your function call to the correct function. Here is an example:

```
int add (int a, int b)
{
    return a + b;
}


double add (double a, double b)
{
    return a + b;
```

```
}

int main(void)
{
    cout << add(5,3);
    cout << add(5.5, 4.7);
    return 0;
}
```

The first call to `add` calls the integer version of the `add` function (the first one) because 5 and 3 are both integers and this matches the prototype for the integer version of `add`. The second call to `add` calls the floating-point version of the function.

DEFAULTING ARGUMENTS

Some functions are highly flexible, providing many different options to customize exactly how they work. This translates into many parameters needed to call the function. However, some of these parameters are likely not needed most of the time. In these cases, it is often reasonable to give these parameters a default value, so that they do not need to be specified by the caller every time.

In C++, you can specify a default value for some parameters. If the calling procedure does not pass a complete argument list, the default arguments are used.

Here is the general syntax for implementing arguments in your code:

`return_type function_name(arg_type arg_name = default_value)`

Here `default_value` is the default value for the argument. If the caller does not provide a value for this parameter, then `default_value` is used. Of course, you can still have more than one argument:

`return_type function_name(arg1 = value1, arg2 = value2)`

Here `arg1` and `arg2` are the argument types and names.

It is possible to have some arguments with default values and some without default values. The rule is that all the arguments without default values must come first in the argument list. In other words, for any particular argument with a default value, all the arguments following it in the argument list must also have default values.

To use such a function, you treat some of the arguments as nonexistent. If your function declaration is

```
int my_Function(int a, int b, int c = 0);
```

you can call this function two ways:

```
cout << my_Function(5, 3, 6);
cout << my_Function(5, 3);
```

In the first line, the value of c is 6, but in the second the line, the value of c is 0.

Defaulting arguments provides a way for you to write functions that are both highly customizable, while still very simple to call in the common case. You can get the best of both worlds. However, you should use them prudently and only when they give a real advantage and increase in clarity.

SEEING FURTHER WITH VARIABLE SCOPE

All code that you have learned to write so far can fit one of four categories, each with its own rules about which variables can access it:

- Code inside the main function
- Code in another function
- Code in a block of code, such as an if statement or a namespace
- Code outside functions

Within each of these categories are rules for how long a variable lasts (variable lifetime) and where it can be accessed (variable scope).

The general rules for variable scope and lifetime are as follows:

- If the variable is declared outside a block of code, it is called global, and its scope and lifetime are from the point of declaration until the end of the source file. As we mentioned earlier in this chapter, a block of code is any code within curly braces. This includes functions.
- If the variable is declared within a block of code, it is called local, and its scope and lifetime are until the end of the block.
- If the variable is declared within an argument list of a function, it is called a parameter, and its scope and lifetime are until the end of the function.

One implication of these rules is that functions cannot access the variables declared within the main function unless they are passed as arguments to the function.

If a variable is declared within a block that is within another block, the scope of the variable is restricted to the inner block.

Perhaps this example will help clarify the preceding rules:

```
//4.2 - Variable Scope Example - Mark Lee
#include <iostream>

int subtract (int a, int b);

int global = 5;

int main(void)
{
    using std::cout;
    int a, b;
    a = 5;
    b = 3;
    cout << "The value of main's a is: " << a
        << "\nThe value of main's b is: " << b
        << "\nThe value of global is: " << global << "\n";
    global = 2 + subtract(a,b);
    cout << "The value of main's a now is: " << a
        << "\nThe value of main's b now is: " << b
        << "\nThe value of global now is: " << global << "\n";
    return 0;
}

int subtract(int a, int b)
{
    using std::cout;
    cout << "The value of subtract's a is: " << a
        << "\nThe value of subtract's b is: " << b << "\n";
    a = a - b + global;
    return a;
}
```
Output:
```
The value of main's a is: 5
The value of main's b is: 3
The value of global is: 5
The value of subtract's a is: 5
```

```
The value of main's a now is: 5
The value of main's b now is: 3
The value of global now is: 9
```

Before any functions, the global variable, global, is declared. At the beginning of main, two local variables, a and b, are declared. When subtract is called, the values in main's a and b are copied into subtract's a and b. subtract then finds the difference and assigns it to a. When this value is returned from the subtract function, global = 2 + subtract(a,b), you have the following:

```
global = 2 + 7;
```

In other words, because subtract returns the value of subtract's a, this line is just adding 2 to the returned value, which is 7 in this case.

Remember that two separate, unrelated versions of a and b are in this code; main's a has nothing to do with subtract's a. In general, it is not a good idea to have variable names so overused like this. They should clearly indicate their purpose within their scope.

Notice that the using declaration for cout is repeated twice, once for each function. This is because it only applies to the block in which it appears. You could, if you wanted, put the using declaration at a global level, outside of every function, like so:

```cpp
//4.2 - Variable Scope Example - Mark Lee
#include <iostream>

using std::cout;

int subtract (int a, int b);

int global = 5;

int main(void)
{
    int a, b;
    a = 5;
    b = 3;
    cout << "The value of main's a is: " << a
            << "\nThe value of main's b is: " << b
            << "\nThe value of global is: " << global << "\n";
    global = 2 + subtract(a,b);
```

```
    cout << "The value of main's a now is: " << a
        << "\nThe value of main's b now is: " << b
        << "\nThe value of global now is: " << global << "\n";
    return 0;
}

int subtract(int a, int b)
{
    cout << "The value of subtract's a is: " << a
        << "\nThe value of subtract's b is: " << b << "\n";
    a = a - b + global;
    return a;
}
```

However, it is preferable to put your using declarations within the functions in which they are applicable. This helps make things clear, so you know exactly what is used where.

Specifying with the Scope Resolution Operator

Sometimes you might come across situations where a global variable and a local variable have the same name. This is legal in C++, but it can cause some confusion. Here is an example:

```
int intVar;

int main(void)
{
    int intVar; // Different from the global named intVar
    intVar = 5;
    return 0;
}
```

It is hard to tell at first glance which version of `intVar` is assigned the value 5, but a rule does exist. If a local variable has the same name as a global variable, the local variable is said to shadow the global variable. All operations performed on a variable by that name are performed on the local variable.

It is best to avoid this situation, if at all possible. If your variable names are conflicting, it is an indication of poor design. Consider reorganizing your code. However, it is good to have an understanding of how you would deal with such a situation. How then do you access the global variable in these situations?

The answer is by using the scope resolution operator. If you want to make sure that the global version of the variable is used, just put two colons (::) in front of it. For example, to make the preceding code use the global version, you change the previous code to the following:

```cpp
int intVar;

int main(void)
{
    int intVar;
    ::intVar = 5;
    return 0;
}
```

This shadowing effect can also happen with sub-blocks. For example, if you have an if statement within the main function, a variable declared within the if block can shadow a global variable or a local variable of main. However, the scope resolution operator can be used only to specify a global variable. For example, if an if statement variable shadows a main variable, you can't access the main version of that variable. Here's an illustration:

```cpp
#include <iostream>
#include <string>

using std::string;

string str = "Humans and elves can coexist. ";

//exemplifies the scope resolution operator(::)
int main(void)
{
    using std::cout;
    string str = "Elves often live in the woods. ";
    cout << str.c_str() << "---" << ::str.c_str() << "\n";
    if (true)
    {
        string str = "Humans often live in cities. ";
        cout << str.c_str() << "---" << ::str.c_str() << "\n";
    }
    return 0;
}
```

Output:
Elves often live in the woods. ---Humans and elves can coexist.
Humans often live in cities. --Humans and elves can coexist.

Using Static Variables

You will sometimes find it convenient to use the same variable within a function every time the function is called. Local variables don't work because they are re-created every time the function is called. Global variables will work fine, except you want to make sure the variable is not accessed or changed outside of the function. One solution is to use static variables.

Static variables have the same scope as normal variables, but their lifetime lasts until the end of the program. In this way, you can create a function that has a "memory."

You declare a static variable with the `static` keyword:

```
static var_type var_name;
```

The statement in which the static variable is created is executed only once for the whole program. This means that if you initialize the static variable on the same line

```
static var_type var_name = value;
```

this initialization will be executed only once.

Take a look at the following example:

```
//4.3 - Static Variables Example - Dirk Henkemans and Mark Lee
#include <iostream>

int incrementFunction1(void);
int incrementFunction2(void);

//runs the increment functions
int main(void)
{
    using std::cout;
    for(int c = 0 ; c < 4 ; c++)
    {
        cout << "Incrementing both variables.\n";
        cout << "Value of function1 is: " << incrementFunction1() << "\n";
        cout << "Value of function2 is: " << incrementFunction2() << "\n";
    }
```

```
        return 0;
}


//an increment function with a static variable
int incrementFunction1(void)
{
        static int x = 0;
        x++;
        return x;
}


//an increment function with a non-static variable
int incrementFunction2(void)
{
        int y = 0;
        y++;
        return y;
}
```
Output:
```
Incrementing both variables.
Value of function1 is: 1
Value of function2 is: 1
Incrementing both variables.
Value of function1 is: 2
Value of function2 is: 1
Incrementing both variables.
Value of function1 is: 3
Value of function2 is: 1
Incrementing both variables.
Value of function1 is: 4
Value of function2 is: 1
```

In this example, both x and y are local variables. While x is static and is initialized only once, y is initialized to 0 every time incrementFunction2 is called. For this reason, incrementFunction2 always returns 1, whereas incrementFunction1 will continue to increment x.

WELCOME TO THE SNAIL RACES

Now, it's time to try out the skills you've gained from this chapter. In the "The Snail Racing Game," be sure to watch for instances that relate to the following points:

- There is only one global variable (money). It is global because it is declared outside of functions.

- money is used as a local variable in the race() function and as a global variable; the default is the local variable; however, whenever money is used as a global variable, the scope resolution operator (::) is used.

- This example has two versions of the race() function. They take different arguments. These two race() functions are an example of overloading functions.

Now, for some mood setting: Do you ever find yourself wishing that time would go just a little slower? Go to the snail races and that wish will come true. Don't worry, eventually, one of the cute little critters will win, but you could be there a while.

```cpp
//4.4 - The Snail Racing Game -Dirk Henkemans and Mark Lee
#include <iostream>
#include <ctime>

//function declarations
int race(int, int);
void race(void);
int menu(void);
int placeBet(int);
void init(void);

//variables
int money = 200;

//the main function
int main(void)
{
    using std::cout;
    init();
    int userResponse;
    cout << "Welcome to the snail races!!!\n";
    while(userResponse = menu())
    {
```

```cpp
            switch(userResponse)
            {
            case 1:
            case 2:
            case 3:
                    ::money +=
                    race(placeBet(userResponse), userResponse);
                    break;
            case 4: //the user did not bet
                    race();
                    break;
            }
    }
    return 0;
}


//displays the main menu and returns the user's selection
int menu(void)
{
    using std::cout;
    using std::cin;
    int userResponse;
    cout << "You have " << money << " dollars.\n";
    do
    {
        cout << "Races Menu\n"
                << "1) Bet on snail 1\n"
                << "2) Bet on snail 2\n"
                << "3) Bet on snail 3\n"
                << "4) Just Watch\n"
                << "0) Leave the races\n";
        cin >> userResponse;
    } while(userResponse < 0 && userResponse > 4);
    return userResponse;
}


//decides how much a person will bet on the snail
int placeBet(int userResponse)
```

```cpp
{
     using std::cout;
     using std::cin;
     int betAmount;
     cout << "Snail " << userResponse << " is a good choice!\n";
     cout << "How much would you like to bet on your snail "
          << userResponse << "? ";
     cin >> betAmount;
     return betAmount;
}

//if they are just watching the race
void race (void)
{
     race(0, 0);
}

//if they are betting money
int race (int money, int userResponse)
{
     using std::cout;
     using std::rand;
     //stores the random number
     int winner = rand() % 3 + 1;
     cout << "And the snails are off\n"
          << "Look at them GO!!!\n"
          << "The winner is snail " << winner << "\n";
     if(winner == userResponse)
     {
          cout << "You Win!\n";
          return 2 * money;
     }
     cout << "You lose " << money << " dollars.\n";
     return -1 * money;
}

//handles program initializations
void init(void)
```

```
{
    using std::srand;
    using std::time;
    srand(time(0));
}
```

Well, what a relaxing and stress-free way to gamble! And if you lose you can make quite the gourmet appetizer. A win-win situation!

REVEALING THE MAIN FUNCTION

You've probably noticed that we keep calling main a function. There is a reason for this: main is a function. "But, it can't be!" you say, "I just learned about functions, and I've been using main since Chapter 1, 'Starting the Journey'!" Fear not, young adventurer. This is a simpler concept than you might think.

You can broadly define a function as a section of code that breaks a program into smaller, more manageable tasks. Think about your computer's operating system. If it is multitasking, it will have many programs running at once. Each of these programs has a main function. Generally, every program begins when the main function begins and ends when the main function ends.

Now, think of your operating system as a program. From it, all the other main functions are called (as illustrated in Figure 4.2).

Are you beginning to see a parallel between your operating system and a program that you create? There are also parallels between the main function and the functions that you create. This is why main is a function.

In our experience, most programmers become confused at this point about exactly how a program runs. How does the computer decide where to start? We anticipated some confusion, so we now take you through the process, step by step.

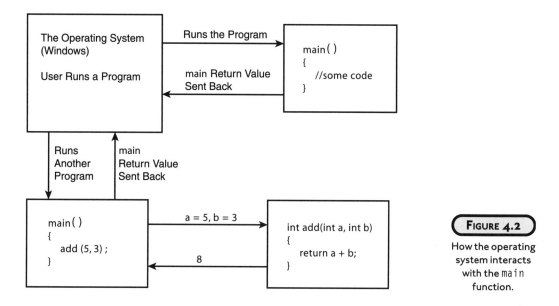

FIGURE 4.2

How the operating system interacts with the `main` function.

Examining the Sequence of Execution

Following is the order in which tasks are executed in any program:

1. All global variables are created. Globals are initialized and stored inside the runtime code at compile time.
2. The `main` function begins.
3. Each line of code in the `main` function executes sequentially.
4. All local variables are destroyed and the `main` function exits.
5. When the program unloads, all global variables are destroyed.

Global variables are initialized before the `main` function is called because they are outside the `main` function. Their scope is larger than the `main` function's scope.

From the `main` function, all other functions are called. It is the container for the entire program (except for global variables). So, even though functions are written outside the `main` function, they are, in a sense, contained within it.

Passing Arguments to main

When the operating system starts a program, the system sometimes passes information to that program. For the kind of programs that you are creating right now, only one kind of information can be passed: command-line arguments. But in other programs, such as a Windows-based program, many kinds of information can be passed.

In DOS or UNIX, you must type the program name at the command prompt in order to run a certain program. In some programs, you can provide additional information after the program name. For example, in an Internet browser, you might type a Web address after the program name, and then the browser will go immediately to that page.

If you are using Windows as your operating system, you are probably not familiar with typing command lines at a command prompt (unlike those of you who use or have used DOS or UNIX). To access the MS-DOS prompt, from the Windows taskbar, click Start and from the menu that appears, select Programs, MS-DOS Prompt (or your options might be Start, Programs, Accessories, Command Prompt). You can find command prompt tutorials on the Internet if you need more information.

In Chapter 5, "Managing Memory," you learn how to respond to these command-line arguments so that your program can use them. For now, just realize that doing so is possible.

Using the main Return Value

In all the programs presented so far, the main function has returned a value of 0. This value is the one that you will see in nearly all programs, but other possible values have different meanings.

Often, the operating system's call to your program is structured like this:

```
if (call_program)
    error_message;
```

Here *call_program* is the call to your program, and *error_message* is a piece of code that displays some sort of error message.

Because all the programs so far have returned 0, this *error_message* line has not been executed. Returning 0 means that your program executed without errors. If you return a non-zero value, the *error_message* line will be executed, which means that your program has an error.

The return value of the main function tells the compiler whether your program executed with or without errors. This information becomes important in later chapters, but for now, just keep it in mind.

CREATING THE CAVE ADVENTURE GAME

After emerging from the Dark Operating System Forest, you see some smoke in the distance. You venture closer and realize that a village is burning. Some goblins are attacking a gnome village! Noble adventurer, will you journey forth to the goblin cave and rid this world of the evil attackers? The gnomes need your help, and you will need to use everything you now know about functions in order to help them!

```cpp
//4.5 - The Cave Adventure Game - Dirk Henkemans
#include <iostream>
#include <string>

using std::string;

bool intro(void);
void room(bool enemy, bool treasure, string description);

//player stats
string name = "";

//enemy stats
string enemyName = "";

//treasure stats
string treasureName = "";
//room descriptions;
const string room1 = "You enter the mouth of the caves.";
const string room2 = "You adventure deeper into the caves.";
const string room3 = "You have reached the depths of the caves.";

int main( void )
{
    if (intro())
        return 0; //if they choose not to do it exit the program
    treasureName = "gold sword";
    enemyName = "goblin";
    room(true, true, room1);
    enemyName = "wombat";
    room(true, false, room2);
    enemyName = "hobgoblin lord.";
    treasureName = "treasure horde.";
    room(true, true, room3);
    return 0;
```

```cpp
}

bool intro(void)
{

    using std::cout;
    using std::cin;
    cout << "Brave knight!!! What is your name? \n";
    cin >> name;
    cout << "We are in need of your help, "<< name
         << ". Our village is being overrun \n"
         << "by the goblins of the Northern Caves."
         << " We need you to defeat them!\n";
         << "Will you accept the challenge?\n\n";
    cout << "1) Yes. \n"
         <<"2) No. \n\n";
    int response;
    cin >> response;
    return !(response == 1);
}


//Displays the description for the room and gives the options
void room(bool enemy, bool treasure, string description)
{
    using std::cout;
    using std::cin;
    while(true)
    {
        cout << description.c_str() << "\n\n";
        int response = 0;
        do
        {
            cout << "What would you like to do?\n";
            if(enemy)
                cout << "1) Attack the evil "
                     << enemyName.c_str() << "\n";
            else if(!enemy)
                cout << " 1) Move to the next room.";
```

Chapter 4 • Structuring Your Code with Functions

```cpp
        if(treasure)
            cout << " 2) Pick up the "
                << treasureName.c_str() << "\n";
            cin >> response;
    } while(response < 1 || response > 2);

    switch(response)
    {
    case 1:
        if(enemy)
        {
            enemy = !enemy;
            cout << "You slay the deadly "
                << enemyName.c_str() << "\n";
        }
        else if(!enemy)
            return;
        break;
    case 2:
        treasure = !treasure;
        cout << "You pick up the "
            << treasureName.c_str() << "\n";
        break;
    }
    }
}
```

Take some time. Study this code. Figure out how it works. Try compiling it. Then try making some changes to it. Make it yours. Look at how it relates to the concepts presented in this chapter.

SUMMARY

You have learned some important concepts in this chapter, and with every word, you've come one step closer to being a professional programmer. You have learned how to create and use functions and variable scope, and you've found out exactly why main is a function.

You are at a point now where you have the basic set of tools needed to create your own programs. Try programming on your own and discover what you can do. Use this book as a reference, but try to remember as much as possible on your own.

If you're feeling overwhelmed, just scan this chapter again. You want to be comfortable with the information in this chapter before moving on.

CHALLENGES

1. Write a function, called `multiply`, that multiplies two numbers and returns the result.
2. Change the function you wrote in Challenge 1 so that it remembers how many times you called it.
3. What is the difference between a global variable and a static variable? Which is better in which situation and why?
4. Try rewriting "The Cave Adventure Game" so that it does not use functions (an exercise to convince you how useful functions are).
5. If you actually made it through the last question, buy yourself a Slurpee.

DESIGNING SOFTWARE: OBJECT-ORIENTED PROGRAMMING

C++ enables you to reuse code so that you don't have to write the same code again and again. Although most programming languages allow you to reuse code, in other languages, you often have to modify the reused code quite a bit to make it work. C++'s support of object-orientated programming (OOP) makes reusing an object, such as a game's hero, almost as easy as dropping the object into your next program. You could even clone the hero multiple times into an army of fire-wielding super heroes with little additional code.

In this chapter, you learn how to do the following:

- Declare classes
- Create objects
- Create a test chassis for your objects
- Add public and private methods and members to your classes
- Utilize the fundamental principles of OOP
- Construct a multiplayer strategy game

INTRODUCTION TO OBJECT-ORIENTED PROGRAMMING

Picture a programming object just like any normal object in the real world. Each real-world object has its own properties and specific things that you can do with it. For example, a bow has specific properties—such as color, number of arrows, and weight—and specific capabilities—such as the ability to fire. If you request a bow from an armory, you do not yet know what the properties of the specific bow will be. However, once you see the bow, you can determine its color, weight, and quiver size. As you will learn in the following section, this is very similar to the way objects work in the programming world.

Before continuing with OOP, you need to understand some key terms.

A class is like a general model from which you can create objects. For example, if you create a dog class, you describe the characteristics related to the general idea of a dog.

Creating a class is the same as creating a new data type. When you create a class, you tell the computer the kind and amount of data this new type can hold. You also tell the computer what actions the new type can perform. Then you can use the class you've created to create variables from this new type (as you will see, these variables are called objects). As complicated as this might seem now, creating your own classes is an easy process, as you will learn in the following sections.

You declare all the data members and methods inside a class. Figure 5.1 shows an example of what a Bow class might look like. The Bow class describes the general properties and capabilities of a bow. A Bow class tells the computer what a bow is in terms of programming so that the computer knows what to do the next time it encounters one.

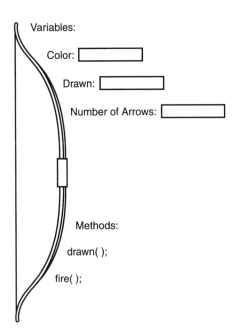

FIGURE 5.1

The Bow class with its methods and attributes.

Objects are a specific instance of a class. That is, the class declares what the properties of an object are, whereas the object stores specific values for each of these properties. For example, a Bow class describes that a bow has a certain color, but it doesn't identify the color. That way, each Bow object can have a different color. Figure 5.2 shows two Bow objects. Each is declared using the Bow class, but whereas the Bow class describes the properties of a bow, each of the two Bow objects has distinct values for these properties.

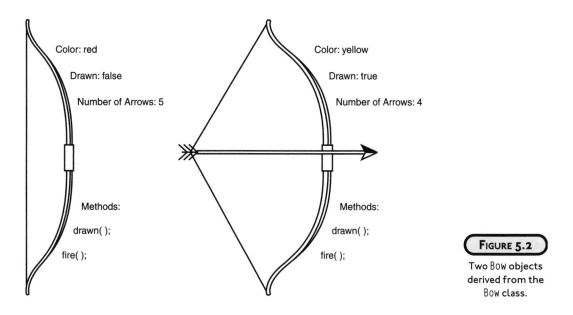

Color: red

Drawn: false

Number of Arrows: 5

Methods:

drawn( );

fire( );

Color: yellow

Drawn: true

Number of Arrows: 4

Methods:

drawn( );

fire( );

FIGURE 5.2

Two Bow objects derived from the Bow class.

Another analogy is a Knight class. You know that knights save princesses, slay dragons, are charming, and find magical items. Describing the attributes in this manner is very similar to designing a class. If you create a specific knight, for example, Sir Lancelot, you have created an object. Sure, Sir Lancelot can save princesses, slay dragons, and find magical items with King Arthur at his side just as his class specifies; however, his actual attributes, such as the name of his sword, how many princesses he saved, and exactly how charming he is, are stored by the SirLancelot object.

Methods (also known as member functions or object methods) are functions contained within a class that define how you can use objects of the class. In the example Bow class, you might want to have methods such as draw() and fire(). Methods are like the functions that we previously used, except that methods are part of the object. The methods enable you to know what the object is capable of, and they are focused primarily on manipulating the object's data (data members).

Data members of a class are the variables that define what kind of data an object of the class can store. For example, an object created from the Bow class can store the color, weight, and quiver size.

A class's members are all the methods and data members that are contained within that class. For example, the members for the Bow objects are the data members—color, weight, and quiver_size—and the methods—fire() and draw().

When you want an object to do something, you send it a message. This is how you execute the object's methods. For example, if you want bow1 to fire, you send it a fire message that will execute the fire() method. You can do this because the Bow class has a fire() method. In other words, bow1 knows how to fire because all objects in the Bow class know how to fire. It's your job, as the programmer, to send bow1 a message to fire if you want the bow to fire. You'll see how to send a message in the section "Using Objects," later in this chapter.

Discovering Classes

You can create many different forms of classes, so it's time to dive directly into the center of OOP. This may be a little frightening at first, but think about how much you have already learned. Once you start to understand the concepts, you will realize that OOP is not nearly as difficult as it seems at first. It's really not as difficult as people make it out to be. In this section, we make learning about classes easy by teaching you how to declare a class, how to create methods, how to control access to objects, and how to organize your classes into different files.

Declaring Classes

The following code is the general syntax for declaring a class. We go through it step by step following the code, but check it out carefully before moving on:

```
class ClassName
{
     memberList
};
```

Here *memberList* is the list of class members, and *ClassName* is the name of the class. Notice that *ClassName* begins with a capital letter. This is the most common convention, and we recommend it because your code will be very readable. Notice also that the class declaration ends with a semicolon. Forgetting the semicolon can cause strange errors, so be sure to include it.

memberList consists of a list of member declarations. These can be data member or method declarations. Data member declarations are normal variable declarations. For example, int x; is a data member declaration when inside a class. However, you cannot initialize data members where you declare them. They must be initialized either in a method or outside the class. For example, int x = 5; as a data member declaration causes an error. The scope of all data members is the same as the scope of the object created from the class. However, data members cannot always be accessed from outside a class. In the Bow class, these data members could store how many arrows are left, the color of the bow, and whether the bow is drawn. The data members of a class define and describe the class properties (also called attributes). Therefore, each bow object's color is a property of that object.

Method declarations are just as easy to understand, as are data member declarations. Method declarations are function declarations placed inside a class (recall that a function declaration can also include the implementation, or you can implement it separately). All methods can be accessed only through an object of the class (with the exception of static methods, which we discuss later in the chapter in "Using Static Members").

Two special kinds of methods, the constructor and the destructor, can be in a class. Both are optional, but they provide special functionality that other methods cannot provide.

A constructor is executed every time a new instance of the class is created—that is, every time you declare a new object. The constructor is normally used to set initial values for the data members. For example, in the Bow class, a constructor might set the drawn Boolean variable to be false and the number of arrows to 20. A constructor always has the same name as the class and cannot have a return value (not even void).

To understand classes and constructors, you might compare the classes you declare with the built-in data types that C++ already understands, such as float and int. All data have something like constructors, even C++'s built-in data types. For example, when you define an integer variable, you use the int keyword. C++ knows the properties of an integer. Therefore, C++ sets up a variable that can take only integer values. C++ does not, however, know what a Bow object is supposed to look like when you first define one. So your Bow class tells C++ what properties a Bow object will take on, and the constructor creates an initial Bow object with initial values.

A destructor is the opposite of a constructor and is executed when the object is destroyed. The destructor is always named the same name as the class, but with a tilde (~) at the beginning (~*ClassName*()). The destructor cannot have arguments or a return value. In the example Bow class, the destructor would be ~Bow(). A destructor is often used to perform any necessary cleanup tasks.

Here is what the Bow class looks like so far:

```
class Bow
{
        //data member declarations
        string color;
        bool drawn;
        int numOfArrows;

        Bow(string aColor); //constructor
        ~Bow(); //destructor

        //methods
        void draw();
        int fire();
};
```

The Bow class now has three data members that describe the attributes that each Bow object will take on. In addition, the Bow class contains four methods—Bow(), ~Bow(), draw(), and fire()—but you have not, as yet, added the code to those methods. The preceding code fragment will compile (because the compiler assumes that the implementation of the methods is somewhere else), but if you try to use it, the program will crash and burn because there is no implementation of the declared methods.

Creating Methods

You have, in general, walked through class declarations. Now, it is time to take a more detailed look at methods. This section provides some special rules and syntax, as well as hints on what to look out for when designing methods for classes.

First of all, you can declare a method two ways. The most common way is to declare a method inside the class declaration and then implement it outside. The second way is to declare and implement the method at the same time inside the class declaration.

You should declare most of your methods the first way. However, there is special syntax for the method implementation. Here is the general syntax for a method implementation that occurs outside a class:

```
return_type ClassName::methodName(argumentList)
{
        methodImplementation
}
```

Here *ClassName* is the name of the class, and *methodImplementation* is the code that goes inside the method. As you can see, this syntax is very similar to the function definition syntax. Notice that this is another use for the scope resolution operator (::). Here you are telling the computer to use the class's scope by putting the class's name in front.

Now, you are ready to implement the draw() and fire() methods of the Bow class. Here are the implementations:

```
//draws the bow
void Bow::draw()
{
    using std::cout;
    drawn = true;
    cout << "The " << color << " bow has been drawn.\n";
}


//fires the bow if drawn
int Bow::fire()
{
    using std::cout;
    using std::rand;
    if(!drawn)
    {
        cout << color << " has not been drawn "
            << "and therefore could not fire.\n";
        return 0;
    }
    int score;
    score = rand() % (10 - 0 + 1) + 0;
    if(score == 0)
        cout << color << " missed the target!!!\n";
    else
        cout << color << " scored " << score << " points!!!\n";
    return score;
}
```

Remember that these implementations must be outside the class declaration. Also, they must be placed after the class declaration.

The second way to declare a method is to declare and implement the method at the same time. The syntax for this is nothing new to you. Here is an example:

```
class Hello
{
    void Display() { using std::cout; cout << "Hello World.\n"; }
};
```

Declaring a method this way is pretty simple. The catch is that a method declared this way is defined as an inline method. Because there is no keyword reminding you that it is inline, be on the lookout for methods declared this way.

If you implement a method outside a class, you can still make it an inline method by putting the `inline` keyword in front of the implementation. A method or function that is inline means that when the program is compiled, the compiler replaces all calls to the method or function with the code inside the method or function. They are used to increase speed, but they also increase the size of your program files.

Designing Constructors and Destructors

Constructors and destructors are often an overwhelming concept for beginners, but in this section, we help you by cutting through the confusion.

Constructors are called automatically when an object is created, and destructors are called automatically when a function is destroyed. A constructor initializes the data members and performs all other required initialization tasks. A destructor performs all necessary cleanup tasks.

Both constructors and destructors are like methods; they can be declared and implemented at the same time or declared and implemented separately. Here is the syntax for declaring and implemenïing at the same time:

```
class ClassName
{
    //constructor
    ClassName(argumentList)
    {
        implementation
    }

    //destructor
    ~ClassName()
```

```
    {
        implementation
    }

    //other members
};
```

Here is the syntax for declaring and then implementing:

```
class ClassName
{
    ClassName(argumentList);
    ~ClassName();
    //other Members
};


ClassName::ClassName(argumentList)
{
    implementation
}


ClassName::~ClassName(argumentList)
{
    implementation
}
```

Notice that the constructor can have arguments. If you create a constructor with arguments, the user of your class must supply values for these arguments when creating an object. Having constructor arguments makes sense for many types of objects. For example, if you have a Date class, the arguments can specify which date a Date object will store.

The destructor, on the other hand, cannot have arguments. It is called automatically, so there isn't a chance for the user to provide arguments.

Because a constructor can have arguments, it might become necessary to overload the constructor. This is legal in C++ and is quite common in large classes. For example, in a Date class, you might want to enable a user to initialize a Date object with a string representation of the date or an integer version. Overloading the constructor in this way gives your class versatility and provides users of the class with many options.

The destructor cannot be overloaded. Having no return type or arguments, there is nothing with which the destructor can be overloaded.

A convenient and quick way to initialize data members in the constructor is to use an initializer list. An initializer list is a list of the data members you want to initialize, with the values to which you want to initialize them shown in parentheses. Here is the general syntax:

```
ClassName(argumentList) : dataMember1(value1), dataMember2(value2)
{
        implementation
}
```

You can have as many initializations as you want in an initializer list, though a great deal of them might make it hard to read. The syntax *dataMember1(value1)* is equivalent to *dataMember1 = value1* (that is, it does the same thing), but this syntax works only in an initializer list.

Here are the constructor and destructor for the Bow class:

```
Bow::Bow(string aColor)
{
        using std::srand;
        using std::time;
        numOfArrows = 10;
        drawn = false;
        color = aColor;
        //seeds the time
        //(we need the rand() function in the fire() method)
        srand(time(0));
}

Bow::~Bow()
{
}
```

Playing Safe with Constant Methods

Often, you will create methods that do not change the value of data members. You can make these methods constant. It is illegal (that is, impossible) to change the value of data members in a constant method. Trying to do so will cause a syntax error.

To declare a constant method, you place the keyword `const` after the argument list. Here is the syntax:

```
return_type methodName(argumentList) const;
```

Note that if you implement a constant method outside the class, the `const` keyword must be placed on both the declaration and the implementation.

The advantage of constant methods is that if a constant object is created (an object created with the `const` keyword), only constant methods can be accessed. This limited accessibility ensures that a constant object is indeed constant.

Using Access Specifiers

C++ allows you to control where the data members of your class can be accessed. This control is a powerful tool because it allows you to protect data members from accidental change (you learn more about protecting data in the section "Learning the Principles of OOP," later in this chapter). An access specifier is a word that controls where the data members in a class can be accessed. The syntax for an access specifier is as follows:

```
class ClassName
{
     classMembers
accessSpecifier:
     classMembers
};
```

An access specifier affects all members of the class (including methods) that come after it until another access specifier is encountered or until you reach the end of the class.

A class has two kinds of access specifiers: `public` and `private` (actually there are three; you learn about the third one, `protected`, in Chapter 8, "Introducing Inheritance"). The effects of these two access specifiers are outlined here:

- `public` **members.** Can be accessed anywhere that an object of the class can be accessed and from within the class (that is, in the class's methods).
- `private` **members.** Can be accessed only from within the class itself. An object of the class cannot access the `private` members, except through `public` methods. If no access specifier is provided in the class, all members default to `private`.

Here is an example of how you might use these specifiers:

```
class MyClass
{
```

```
        int x;
public:
        int y;
        int z;
private:
        int a;
};
```

In this example, x and a are private members, and y and z are public. You may have as many access specifiers as you want in your classes, but it is generally a good idea to keep things organized in one place.

Here is how the Bow class looks with access specifiers:

```
class Bow
{
        //data member declarations
        string color;
        bool drawn;
        int numOfArrows;
public:
        Bow(string aColor); //constructor
        ~Bow();             //destructor

        //methods
        void draw();
        int fire();
};
```

Separating Classes into Files

Classes often get pretty big, and having all your code in one file can quickly become unmanageable. Also, if you want to reuse your classes in other programs, you have to copy and paste them into the new program. This process can be quite a hassle.

Fortunately, there is a convention for separating classes into files. Normally, the class declaration is placed in one file, and the implementation of all the methods is put in another file. The class declaration file is normally called ClassName.h, where ClassName is the name of the class. You are familiar with using .cpp for C++ files, but .h is also a valid C++ file (however, it is used only in special situations, such as for class declarations, not for programs). The implementation is normally called ClassName.cpp.

If you use this convention, C++ allows you to do something really cool. Because you put your class into a file separate from where you are using your class, you must include it in your program with an #include directive. The syntax for the #include directive is as follows:

```
#include "filename"
```

However, instead of including two files (ClassName.h and ClassName.cpp), you have to include only ClassName.h. Visual Studio will include the .cpp file automatically as long as it is also in your project. Isn't that convenient?

Here is how the Bow class looks separated into different files:

```
//Bow.h
#include <string>
#include <iostream>

using std::string;

class Bow
{
        //data member declarations
        string color;
        bool drawn;
        int numOfArrows;
public:
        Bow(string aColor); //constructor
        ~Bow();                 //destructor

        //methods
        void draw();
        int fire();
};
//Bow.cpp
Bow::Bow(string aColor)
{
        using std::srand;
        using std::time;
        numOfArrows = 10;
        drawn = false;
        color = aColor;
```

```cpp
        //seeds the time
        //(we need the rand() function in the fire() method)
        srand((unsigned int)time(0));
}


Bow::~Bow()
{
}


//draws the bow
void Bow::draw()
{
        using std::cout;
        drawn = true;
        cout << "The " << color << " bow has been drawn.\n";
}


//fires the bow if drawn
int Bow::fire()
{
        using std::cout;
        if(!drawn)
        {
                cout << color << " has not been drawn "
                        << "and therefore could not fire.\n";
                return 0;
        }
        int score;
        score = rand() % (10 - 0 + 1) + 0;
        if(score == 0)
                cout << color << " missed the target!!!\n";
        else
                cout << color << " scored " << score << " points!!!\n";
        return score;
}
```

Class Tactics 101

This section provides some guidelines to make OOP programming a bit easier. You can use these tactics to make your code easy to debug and understand.

- Start every class name with an uppercase letter. This convention is used not only in C++, but also in almost every other object-orientated programming language.

- Add a comment at the beginning of each method and class telling the user what the following member or class does.

- Make sure that each method does only one thing. The general rule is that if a method is more than 20 lines, you are trying to do too much in that method.

- Have each class model only one concept. For example, keep the `Weapon` class separate from the `Soldier` class.

- Test each class to be sure that it works before adding it to the project. Once you know that a class works, debugging a project is simply a matter of making sure that the interaction between the classes work correctly. You will not have to worry about whether the classes themselves work, because you've already ensured that they do.

Follow these rules, and you will be much more productive—and you will save yourself time when debugging.

USING OBJECTS

After all the preceding discussion on how to create classes, you must be eager to learn about classes. Soon you will be creating your own objects from your own classes, but for now, you learn just how to create objects. In this section, you learn about object variables, default constructors, how to access members of a class, how to create a test chassis for your classes, and how to use static members.

Using Object Variables

Earlier, we wrote that creating a class is a lot like creating a data type. This relationship becomes evident when you start learning about objects. You can use the name of a class exactly like the name of a primitive data type (the data types that are built into C++). An object variable is a variable that stores the object of a certain class.

Follow these three steps to create objects:

1. Program the class that will become the template for the object. You completed this step when you created the `Bow` class.

2. Create an identifier for the object variable and determine what kind of object it will store (from what class it will be created). This process is similar to the way you declare a variable.

3. Add the arguments required by the constructor (if needed).

You can use two basic syntax forms to create objects:

Method 1:

```
className objectIdentifier(arguments);
```

Method 2:

```
className objectIdentifier = className(arguments);
```

Okay, you've waited long enough. It's time to start creating objects. Following are examples of how to create two different Bow objects:

```
Bow blue("Blue");
Bow red = Bow("Red");
```

You just created two bows, one named red and one named blue. Each of these object variables stores an object with several properties (such as a color and 20 arrows each), and each knows how to do two things: draw and fire (using the draw() and fire() methods). You can change the object stored in an object variable with the assignment operator (=), just as with normal variables. Here is an example:

```
Bow b1("blue");
Bow b2("red");
b1 = b2;
```

b1 and b2 will then each store a separate copy of a red bow.

Taking the Easy Way Out with Default Constructors

If no arguments are provided when creating an object variable, the computer will execute the default constructor. A default constructor can be one of two things. If the class has no constructor, the default constructor is a blank constructor with no arguments; if you provide a constructor that has no arguments, the default constructor is this constructor.

An empty default constructor is present in all classes until you create a constructor. If every constructor requires arguments, the class does not have a default constructor. Unless you create your own default constructor, a default constructor does nothing but create a new object variable that conforms to that object's class declaration. Here is an example of a default constructor:

```
Cpoint3d::Cpoint3d()
{
}
```

Accessing Members

When a member is public, you can access it from anywhere that an object can be accessed. You can access a public member by using the member access operator (.) between the object identifier and the member. To assign a value to a public data member, use this syntax:

```
objectIdentifier.dataMemberName = value;
```

To retrieve the value of a public data member of an object, you switch the operands like this:

```
variable = objectidentifier.variableName;
```

As you can see, objects are quite similar to normal variables. Here is an example of this syntax:

```
class S
{
public:
      int x;
};

int main(void)
{
     S s;
     s.x = 99;
}
```

Because the s object's data member x is public, all code in the program can use or change the x member (as long as the code can access the s object). As long as an s object exists, all code in the program with access to s can directly change s's data member x.

Public methods are accessed similarly. Here is the syntax to call a public method:

```
object.method(arguments)
```

Here is an example of calling a public method:

```
class S {
      int x;
public:
      int getValue() { return x; }
```

```
        void setValue (int temp) { x = temp; }
        S(int temp) : x(temp) {}
        ~S() {}
};

int main (void)
{
        S s(5);
        cout << s.getValue();
}
Output:
5
```

You cannot access private members outside a class. However, through public methods, you can usually gain limited access to private data members. Because of this limited access, the designer of the class can make sure that the data members are not misused.

Creating a Test Chassis

When you create a class, you must test it. One of the benefits of OOP is the ease with which you can test and debug classes. The idea is to test each class independently of all other classes. If the class does what it is supposed to, it should cause no more errors (in theory) when combined with the rest of the more robust program. To test a class, you create what is called a test chassis.

A test chassis is a program that tests all the capabilities of a class. The test includes all the methods, constructors, and destructors.

An example test chassis for the Bow class appears in the following code. This file is named bowTest.cpp.

```
//5.1 - The Bow Class Test Chassis - Dirk Henkemans
#include <iostream>
#include "Bow.h"

void bowTest(void);

//the main function
int main(void)
{
        bowTest();
```

```
        return 0;
}


//tests the bow class
void bowTest(void)
{
        using std::cout;
        cout << "Yellow bow created.\n";
        Bow yellow("yellow");
        cout << "Attempting to fire yellow bow\n";
        yellow.fire();
        cout << "Drawing the bow.\n";
        yellow.draw();
        cout << "Attempting to fire yellow bow.\n";
        yellow.fire();
}
```

Notice that there are lots of cout statements, so you can be sure that the class works as expected. If the program crashes for some reason, you will know exactly which line it crashed on because of the most recent cout message. Follow a similar process for each class by creating a test chassis for every class you create. Doing so will prevent many errors.

The Archery Competition

The King Nolan Bard all high and mighty has requested an archery competition to commemorate his daughter Anastasia's sixteenth birthday. The winner of the archery contest will receive the princess's hand in marriage.

To create "The Archery Competition" game, you will create the competition class. Each competition will have three contestants and an arbitrary number of rounds. The rounds will execute and then declare a winner. Study the following code and make sure that you understand what is going on.

```
//5.2 - The Archery Competition - Dirk Henkemans
#include <iostream>
#include <cstring>
#include "bow.h"

class ArcheryCompetition
{
```

```
private:
     //member variables
     int rounds;
     float redScore;
     Bow red;
     float blueScore;
     Bow blue;
public:
     //constructor
     ArcheryCompetition(int lrounds);

     //destructor
     ~ArcheryCompetition();

     //methods
     int compete(void);
};

//constructs an ArcheryCompetition object
ArcheryCompetition::ArcheryCompetition(int lrounds) :
     rounds(lrounds), red(Bow("red")),
     blue(Bow("blue")), redScore(0), blueScore(0)
{ }

//the destructor
ArcheryCompetition::~ArcheryCompetition()
{
}

//the heart of the game.
//Walks the player through an entire competition
//and figures out who won
int ArcheryCompetition::compete()
{
     using std::cout;
     //go through each round, keeping track of the score
     for(int i = 0; i < rounds; i++)
     {
```

```
            cout << "now on round " << i+1 << ".\n";
            red.draw();
            blue.draw();
            redScore = (red.fire() + redScore * i)/(i+1) ;
            blueScore = (blue.fire() + redScore * i)/(i+1);
        }
        //figure out who won
        if(redScore == blueScore)
            cout << "We have a tie!!!\n";
        else if(redScore < blueScore)
            cout << "Blue wins her hand!!\n";
        else
            cout << "red wins her hand!!\n";
        return 1;
}


int main(void)
{
        //the driver function: constructs the object and
        //calls the appropriate methods
        ArcheryCompetition plymouthSquare(2);
        plymouthSquare.compete();
        return 0;
}
```

Using Static Members

So far, each distinct object of a class has had its own copies of member variables. But what would happen if you wanted the same value for all objects of a particular class? You could use one global variable, but doing so violates the goal of data abstraction. To declare a single variable that exists across all objects in a class and to make that variable take on OOP's safety properties discussed earlier, use static members. A static member is a variable that will be the same for all instances of that class. The syntax for a static declaration member is as follows:

```
class ClassName
{
        static variableType variableIdentifier; //declaration

        //other code…..
```

```
};
```

```
//global initialization
variableType ClassName::variableIdentifier = initial_value;
```

See Figure 5.3 for a conceptual diagram of how static variables work.

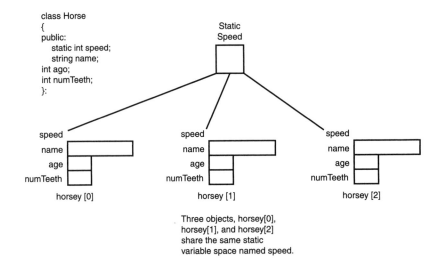

FIGURE 5.3

Static variables are the same in every object of a class.

Three objects, horsey[0], horsey[1], and horsey[2] share the same static variable space named speed.

Remember that to use a static member, you need to declare the variable in the class and also initialize the variable outside the class. That is, it must be initialized outside a class.

Imagine that you have a Horse class, and all the horses work together to pull one wagon. The speed of all the horses must be the same, but the speed might increase and decrease depending on the slope. The code for the Horse class looks something like this:

```
//5.3 - The Static Variable Demonstration program - Dirk Henkemans
#include <iostream>

class Horse
{
public:
    static int speed;

    //the remainder of the horse class
};
```

```
int Horse::speed = 3; //notice the global initialization

int main(void)
{
    using std::cout;
    Horse horse1;
    Horse horse2;
    Horse::speed = 5;
    cout << horse2.speed << "\n" << horse1.speed << "\n";
    Horse::speed = 6;
    cout << horse2.speed << "\n" << horse1.speed << "\n";

    return 0;
}
Output:
5
5
6
6
```

Notice that the speeds for both `horse1` and `horse2` are the same regardless of which horse you access the `speed` member from. This is because there is only one instance of the speed member regardless of how many horses you create to pull the carriage.

LEARNING THE PRINCIPLES OF OOP

The following three aspects of OOP make your programs easy to maintain and also make it easy to reuse objects:

- Data abstraction
- Encapsulation
- Polymorphism

You've already seen the first two OOP terms used because data abstraction and encapsulation occur when you create classes that contain private data. The following sections help further explain what these tough-sounding, but relatively simple, concepts are all about.

Understanding Data Abstraction

When you buy a certain cookie from Subway, you can identify it as a white-chocolate macadamia nut cookie. You probably can't tell what brand of flour or how much baking soda was used to make the cookie—and you probably don't care. The cookie tastes good, which is the purpose for which it was designed.

Likewise, it is often not important to know exactly how a class works, as long as it does what it is designed to do. This is the principle of data abstraction (also known as data hiding). Data abstraction is the process of hiding the data members and implementation of a class behind an interface so that the user of the class doesn't corrupt the data. The idea is that data is hidden inside the implementation for a class. You do access data members through the implementation by accessing the data members through the member function interface. That is, data is not manipulated directly, but through public functions.

The general rule is to use the smallest scope possible for all variables and members. Also, use as few global variables as possible. In doing so, only the code that should have access to data can change that data. If other code needs to use or change data inside a private object, that object's member functions can supply the routines that allow this kind of access. It is up to you, as a designer of a class, to decide exactly how much access to data the user of your class needs.

Understanding Encapsulation

Picture the manufacturing process of the nineteenth century. Individuals did everything needed to create their products. No division of labor existed. For example, a sweater maker had to do everything, from creating the wool (well... the sheep did that part, but you know what we mean) to marketing the finished product, which meant, of course, that everything took a long time to make. With the advent of specialization, people became proficient at one thing and let other people worry about the rest.

This is similar to encapsulation. Each class that you create should represent one specific thing or concept. Multiple classes then come together to represent combinations of things or concepts. Remember when you created the archery contest? The contest used multiple bows from the Bow class and a class to represent the contest itself.

Here's another example of encapsulation. Say that you want to build a car. You must build the smaller subassemblies before you can build the finished product. Each small assembly does one small thing, but they all combine to produce a car. Figure 5.4 shows the different parts of a car. Each part serves a unique purpose.

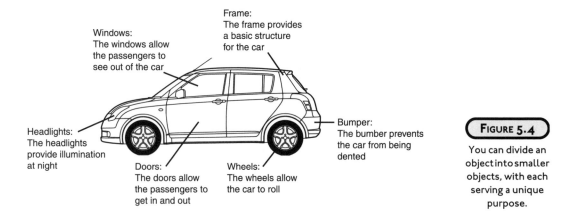

Windows:
The windows allow
the passengers to
see out of the car

Frame:
The frame provides
a basic structure
for the car

Headlights:
The headlights
provide illumination
at night

Doors:
The doors allow
the passengers to
get in and out

Wheels:
The wheels allow
the car to roll

Bumper:
The bumber prevents
the car from being
dented

FIGURE 5.4

You can divide an object into smaller objects, with each serving a unique purpose.

Understanding Polymorphism

Polymorphism is a nasty-sounding word that simply means "many forms." Polymorphism refers to a principle of OOP in which each object can be used in more than one program. The primary principle of polymorphism is that your code will analyze the conditions in which you use it and adjust to those conditions. The Bow class will always do what it is supposed to do, even if you use it on a 64-bit alpha computer or a Cray supercomputer. In Chapter 8, we cover polymorphism in greater detail. In this chapter, we continue to lay more of the C++ groundwork.

If you use these three OOP concepts (data abstraction, encapsulation, and polymorphism), your programming life will greatly improve—and so will your social life because of the time saved debugging.

DEBUGGING

Your code will not always be perfect. Things will go wrong. Sometimes, it's hard to know what is wrong with your code. Other times, you find the problem instantly. In this section, we discuss the kind of errors you can encounter while programming and how to prevent them.

There are four kinds of errors, each with different causes, and each with different ways of being fixed.

Here are the four kinds of errors and what they mean:

- **Insignificant errors.** Errors that don't affect the operation of your program. These errors generally don't cause problems. An insignificant error might occur if you do not follow a convention or forget to add comments to a section of code. These errors often go undetected until they cause obvious problems.

- **Compile-time errors.** Errors in the syntax of the programming language. For example, if you don't include the t in `int` while trying to declare an integer, you go against the syntax of the programming language and will receive the nasty error screen when you try to compile.

- **Run-time errors.** Errors that do not show up until you run the program, causing your program to crash. These errors are hard to debug—for example, errors such as declaring a constructor and forgetting to program it in. They are often hard to find and make your program crash with an unpleasant little Windows message. The compiler will not pick these up; however, the compiler might provide a warning (an error that doesn't stop the compile process). We recommend that you listen to the warnings your compiler gives and that you try to eliminate the errors from your code.

- **Logic errors.** Errors that result in your program not doing what it is supposed to do. The compiler will not pick up these errors. The program functions and will not crash but does the wrong thing. For example, imagine that the Orcs you programmed are all attacking themselves. Normally, these errors are easy to remove, although sometimes that is not the case.

Debugging is by far the most annoying part of programming, and in some cases, it can be the most time-consuming part.

The Black Box

The black box method of object-orientated programming uses the three principles listed earlier in this section on OOP principles: data abstraction, encapsulation, and polymorphism. The idea behind the black box method is that you send an object a message and the object always does the right thing, even though you don't know how it does so. This happens because the object controls all its own data. This control allows the object to protect itself from invalid parameters and data. You don't need to know and might never know what's inside the class, but by the time you finish testing with the black box, the object is well tested and functions as it should.

Black box testing makes debugging much easier. If you debug smaller sections of code and ensure that they work under all circumstances, the only errors that you might receive are those that occur when your smaller sections of code interact with the other, already debugged sections of code.

Linking Errors

Linking occurs when the computer takes all the files you have used in your program, including those from the standard libraries, and compiles them into an executable file (.exe). Linking errors are normally hard to debug, and there is no specific formula for debugging them. However, as ominous as this sounds, only two things normally cause linking errors:

- You didn't include the library files correctly, both the standard libraries and all other libraries that you use in your program.

- You tried to declare a command that doesn't exist, and the compiler didn't pick it up. For example, if you declare a constructor for an object but do not add the code, you will produce a linking error when you try to compile.

 TRICK If you can't figure out how to fix one particular error, try fixing any other existing errors. Sometimes, doing so will make the first error "go away."

CREATING THE CONQUEST GAME

You now use your skills in OOP to create the game of "Conquest," a strategic text adventure game that places you, the king, on the throne in order to conquer your enemies. You create a Nation class for each player, and each player goes through his or her turn building the nation and attacking his or her enemies.

```
//5.4 - Conquest - Dirk Henkemans - Premier Press
#include <iostream>
#include <string>

using std::string;

//handles each nation for each player
class Nation
{

public:
        int land;
        int troops;
private:
        string name;
        int food;
        int gold;
        int people;
        int farmers;
```

```cpp
        int merchants;
        int blacksmiths;
public:
        Nation(string lName);
        Nation();
        bool takeTurn(void);
private:
        void menu(void);
};

Nation nation1;
Nation nation2;

//sets the default nation values
Nation::Nation(string lName) :
        name(lName), land(20), food(50), troops(15),
        gold(100), people(100), farmers(0), merchants(0), blacksmiths(0)
{
}

//a default constructor
Nation::Nation()
{
}

//takes a turn for player
bool Nation::takeTurn()
{
        using std::cout;
        cout << "Its now " << name << "'s turn.\n";
        people += land * 0.2;
        food += farmers - people * 0.25;
        gold += merchants * 20;
        troops += blacksmiths;
        menu();
        if (nation1.land <= 0 || nation2.land <= 0)
                return false;
        return true;
```

```
}

//displays and handles the menu options
void Nation::menu()
{
    using std::cout;
    using std::cin;
    while (true)
    {
        int input = 0;
        cout << "Food " << food << "\nGold " << gold
            << "\nLand " << land << "\nMerchants " << merchants
            << "\nTroops " << troops << "\nUnemployed " << people
            << "\n";
        cout << "1) Buy land.\n"
            << "2) Hire farmers.\n"
            << "3) Hire merchants.\n"
            << "4) Hire weaponsmiths.\n"
            << "5) Attack!\n"
            << "6) Take turn.\n";
        cin >> input;
        switch (input)
        {
        case 1: //buys land
            cout << "You buy " << gold/20 << " sections of land.\n";
            land += gold/20;
            gold %= 20;
            cout << "You now have " << gold << " gold.\n";
            break;
        case 2: //hires farmers
            farmers += people;
            cout << "You hired " << people << " farmers.\n";
            people = 0;
            break;
        case 3: //hires merchants
            merchants += people;
            cout << "You hired " << people << " merchants.\n";
            people = 0;
```

```
                        break;
            case 4: //hires blacksmiths
                    blacksmiths += people;
                    cout << "You hired " << people << " blacksmiths.\n";
                    people = 0;
                    break;
            case 5: //handles the battle
                    cout << "The war wages into the night and all die!\n";
                    if (nation1.troops < nation2.troops)
                    {
                            nation2.land += 10;
                            nation1.land -= 10;
                    }
                    else if (nation1.troops > nation2.troops)
                    {
                            nation2.land -= 10;
                            nation1.land += 10;
                    }
                    nation1.troops = 0; //war is a bloody thing!!!
                    nation2.troops = 0;
                    break;
            case 6:
                    return; //ends the turn
            }
        }
}


//the main game function
int main(void)
{
        using std::string;
        using std::cout;
        using std::cin;
        string tempString;
        cout << "Welcome to the Conquest \n";
        cout << "What is your name player 1? \n";
        cin >> tempString;
        nation1 = Nation(tempString);
```

```
cout << "What is your name player 2? \n";
cin >> tempString;
nation2 = Nation(tempString);
while(nation1.takeTurn() && nation2.takeTurn())
{}
return 0;
}
```

Summary

In this chapter, you learned a lot about objects. Understanding OOP requires that you approach programming from a unique perspective. Hiding data in classes and protecting that data takes a little forethought, but it pays off later in maintainability and object reuse. Test your understanding of the OOP concepts by trying the following challenges and reviewing extra-demanding sections of this chapter before moving on to the next chapter.

CHALLENGES

1. Create a class that can be used to represent a character in a role-playing game. Store the character's name, class, and race.
2. Explain the three main principles of OOP.
3. What is the difference between a class and an object?
4. If you have a choice between declaring something public, private, global, or local without loss of functionality, which scope should you pick?
5. What attributes present in constructors and destructors are not present in other functions?

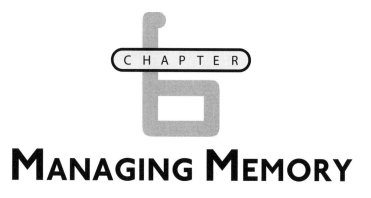

MANAGING MEMORY

Now good reader, we are moving from the basics of C++ and venturing into uncharted territory. You are ready to learn some of the more advanced aspects of the C++ language. Do not fear, however; although these concepts might be challenging, with practice, you will find them as easy as the concepts in Chapter 1, "Starting the Journey."

In this chapter, you learn how to use the following:

- Arrays
- Pointers
- C-style strings
- References
- Dynamic memory basics

EXPLAINING MEMORY

You may be curious to know how variables get stored in memory. You know of global and local variables, but how do they get *allocated* in memory? To *allocate* is to acquire memory for. All the variables you have used were allocated at some point before they could be used. In this section, we will explain more about this strange concept.

So, a computer has one chunk of memory where all of this stuff gets stored, right? Well, not quite. It turns out there are actually three main sections in memory: static memory, the stack, and the heap. Where a given variable is stored depends heavily on where and how it is declared.

Static memory is where global variables are stored. These are allocated when the program starts up, before main starts executing. They last throughout the entire course of the program, being de-allocated only when the program exits, right after main ends. So, everything in static memory must be decided upon before the program begins memory. When you declare global variables, you must know exactly which and how many you need. There is no way to decide, for instance, whether to have a global variable based on a user's input. By this point, the program is already running, so it is too late.

The stack (also called local or automatic memory) is where all of your local variables are allocated. So, an integer declared within main would go on the stack. When a function is called, its parameters would go on the stack. Every variable you've learned so far that isn't global goes on the stack.

When a program begins executing, space is allocated on the stack for all of main's local variables (see Figure 6.1(a)). As soon as another function is called, say func1, more space is allocated on top for func1's local variables and parameters (see Figure 6.1(b)). When func1 finishes executing and returns, its space on the stack is de-allocated (see Figure 6.1(c)). So, the stack grows and shrinks according to which functions are being called. This allows for a much more flexible treatment of memory. You can choose whether to call a function based on user input, and this will decide if that memory is allocated. So, your program can adapt to changing circumstances.

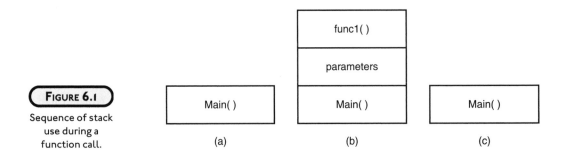

FIGURE 6.1

Sequence of stack use during a function call.

The stack is not very well suited for storing large objects. Variables that consume a lot of memory must be allocated and de-allocated every time the function is called, making your program slow. It is best to put such large variables on the heap.

The heap (or free store or dynamic memory) is the final type of memory. Sometimes you want the best of both worlds. You want memory that you can allocate whenever you need it, but you don't want it to disappear when the function ends. This is exactly how the heap works. You call a special function to allocate memory, telling it exactly how much you need, and then when you're done you call a special function to de-allocate it. This gives you total control, but also total responsibility. It is up to you to keep track of what you've allocated and to de-allocate it when you don't need it anymore.

Using Pointers

Pointers are a powerful tool if used effectively, but they can be one of the more challenging C++ tools to learn to use. However, we promise to guide you slowly through the information in this section.

The simplest definition of a pointer is this: A pointer is a variable that holds a memory address. Although this definition of a pointer is pretty straightforward, its implications are far more complex.

The memory address that the pointer stores is the address of another variable. So a pointer is said to "point to a variable."

The syntax for declaring a pointer is as follows:

pointer_type *pointer_name*;

Here, *pointer_type* is the type of the variable being pointed to, and *pointer_name* is the name of the pointer. However, declaring pointers is only a start; using them is the complicated part.

First, you must learn about a new operator, the address of operator (&). You put it directly in front of a variable, and it evaluates to the memory address of the variable. This operator is useful for assigning values to a pointer. Here is an example of how to use the address of operator:

```
int my_int;
int* my_int_pointer = &my_int;
```

This code makes my_int_pointer point to my_int. my_int_pointer stores the memory address of my_int.

Note that if a pointer has the value 0 assigned to it, the pointer does not point to a variable. This case is called a null pointer or an undeclared pointer.

If you are having trouble picturing these concepts, try this example:

```
//6.2 - Pointers - Dirk Henkemans and Mark Lee
#include <iostream>

int main(void)
{
    using std::cout;
    int an_int = 5;
    int* a_pointer = &an_int;
    cout << "The value of an_int is: " << an_int
            << "\nThe address of an_int is: " << &an_int
            << "\nThe value of a_pointer is " << a_pointer
            << "\nThe address of a_pointer is: " << &a_pointer;
}
```

ELEVATING TO THE INDIRECTION OPERATOR

You're halfway through learning about pointers. Next, you learn about the indirection operator. The indirection operator (*) is used to refer to the object pointed to by the pointer. You place the indirection operator right in front of a pointer (or an expression that evaluates to a pointer), and it evaluates to the value of the variable that the pointer points to. Although this operator is different from the *, used to declare a pointer, you'll be able to tell which is which because of the context. If it's in the pointer declaration, it's not being dereferenced.

 In the last section, you saw a pointer named a_pointer initialized using the *, but don't confuse the indirection operator with the pointer declaration. Even though there is an * symbol before the pointer when you declare it, the pointer is not actually being dereferenced.

For example, if you declare an integer and a pointer as

```
int a = 78;
int* pb = &a;
```

you can use the indirection operator to access the value of a through pb like this:

```
cout << "The value of a is: " << *pb;
```

This code displays the number 78 onscreen. You can think of the indirection operator (sometimes called the dereferencing operator) as the opposite of the address of operator.

To help clarify the relationship between the address of and indirection operators, look at this example:

```
int x = 5;
int* px = &x; // px points to x
*px = 7; // x now contains the value &x
```

In the second line, the address of &x is assigned to px. px now points to x. Note that when you change the value of *px, you are changing the value of x. After the third line, the value of x is 7.

It is also possible to have pointers to pointers. A declaration of a pointer to a pointer to an integer looks like this:

```
int** ppi;
```

It can be initialized like this:

```
int * pi;
ppi = &pi;
```

A pointer to a pointer holds the address of a pointer, which holds the address of a variable. Thus, it is possible to access the value of the variable through the pointer to a pointer. To access this value, you use the indirection operator twice:

```
cout << **ppi;
```

This code displays the value of the integer that pi points to. The concept of pointer to pointer is not always intuitive at first. It is like a road sign that points out another road sign so that you know where that road sign is located.

*ppi gives the value of the pointer pi; then using the indirection operator again, gives the value that pi points to. You could go even further, using it as many times as you want, but doing so isn't practical.

USING POINTERS AND OBJECTS

It is also possible to have pointers to objects and structures. For example, you can have a pointer to a string object like this:

```
string* ps;
```

Pointers to objects are really the same as pointers to any other type of variable. However, you need to notice some qualities. First, no object is actually being created, just a pointer to one. Because of this, you are not calling the string's constructor. (C++ calls a constructor when you declare a string because string is a class, not a built-in data type.)

To illustrate this further, let's say that we have a class to store a two-dimensional location, a point:

```
class Point
{
public:
      int X,Y;
      Point (int 1X, int 1Y) : X(1X), Y(1Y){}
      void print();
};

void Point::print()
{
      using std::cout;
      cout << "The value of X is: " << X
            << "/nThe value of Y is: " << Y << "\n";
}
```

This class is rather basic—a constructor and one method. We can create a point object like so:

```
Point p(5,3);
```

And we can create a pointer to the p object with the following line of code:

```
Point* pp = &p;
```

It is possible to access the members of this object through the pointer like this:

```
pp->X = 6;
pp->Y = 5;
```

We can access these data members only because they are public. If they were private, we could not access them directly, even through a pointer.

This code introduces a new operator, the member selection operator (->). It is just like the other member selection operator (.), except that it is for pointers to objects rather than member objects. You can also call member functions using this operator:

```
pp->print();
```

This code causes the print method to be executed, as you might suspect.

ALLOCATING FROM THE HEAP

So now, gentle reader, you are ready for a whole new world of possibility: you are ready to learn how to use the heap! This will open up many new abilities in your programming, but also a whole new set of possible bugs. In fact, the majority of bugs in C++ code have to do with the heap! It is very important to structure your code carefully so that you can keep track of everything you're allocating and de-allocate it when you are finished with it. With a few simple techniques that we will show you, most of the problems should be avoided! So, without any more introduction, let us plunge right in!

You allocate memory in the heap using the new operator. This operator returns a pointer to the newly allocated memory. The syntax for the new operator is as follows:

```
new data_type(constructor_args);
```

Here *data_type* is any valid data type or class. To use this memory, you must assign it to a pointer variable. Keeping track of memory on the heap is where pointers come in really handy. For example, to create a Point object in the heap, you can do the following:

```
Point* myPoint = new Point(2,4);
```

If you are allocating a built-in type, like an int, you do not need the brackets:

```
int* myInt = new int;
```

That's really all there is to it. The new operator is actually very easy to use. All memory that you allocate with the new operator must be de-allocated with the delete operator when you are done with it. If you do not free the memory you use, this memory will not be available to use later in the program. Forgetting to free heap memory is called a memory leak, and you should always avoid it.

The delete operator acts on a pointer to a section of memory allocated with the new operator. If the delete operator is used on anything else, it will cause an error. The syntax for the delete operator is as follows:

```
delete pointer;
```

For example, to free the memory allocated in the preceding examples, do the following:

```
delete myInt;
myInt = 0;
delete myPoint;
myPoint = 0;
```

Once you free the memory allocated with new, set the value of the pointer to 0. This ensures that you will not accidentally try to delete something that you have already deleted. A double delete can cause all sorts of problems when you try to run your program. Using the delete operator on 0 does nothing, so it is harmless.

One good way to ensure that your allocations and de-allocations match up is to have a class manage them. The allocation would take place in the constructor, and the de-allocation in the destructor. Here is an example of such a class:

```
class HeapPoint
{
public:
      HeapPoint(int x, int y);
      Point* get() { return thePoint; }
      ~HeapPoint();
private:
      Point* thePoint;
};

HeapPoint::HeapPoint(int x, int y) : thePoint(new Point(x,y))
{}

HeapPoint::~HeapPoint()
{
      delete thePoint;
      thePoint = 0;
}
```

And now you could use this HeapPoint as follows:

```
void myFunc()
{
      HeapPoint myHeapPoint(2,4);
      Point* myPoint = myHeapPoint.get();
      // do stuff with myPoint

      // no need to call delete! Called automatically!
}
```

Because myHeapPoint is a local variable, it is automatically destroyed when the function ends. This is because it is on the stack. When it is destroyed, its destructor will be called, which will de-allocate the dynamic memory. It is a good idea to build a class like this every time you use memory from the heap.

USING THE THIS POINTER

Every object of a class has a constant pointer to itself called the this pointer. With a this pointer, you can access any of the public data members or functions of the class. The syntax for using the this pointer is the same as the syntax for any other pointer to an object.

For example, in the Point class (declared in the last section), you can rewrite the print() method to use the this pointer:

```
void Point::print()
{
    using std::cout;
    cout << "The value of X is: " << this->X
        << "/nThe value of Y is: " << this->Y << "\n";
}
```

This change, however, does not change the meaning of the method. It is simply a way of explicitly stating which instance of the class you are referring to. Interestingly enough, you can also use this to get the object:

```
Point p = *this;
```

This information does not have any use to you at the moment, but it might in the future.

CONSTRUCTING CONSTANT POINTERS AND POINTERS TO CONSTANTS

You can have a constant pointer, a pointer that cannot change the memory address it stores. However, with a constant pointer, you can still change the value that the pointer points to. To create a constant pointer, place the const keyword after the * operator, as shown here:

```
char* const p; // constant pointer to char, no value
```

This code creates a constant pointer. However, because a constant pointer is a type of constant, you must initialize the pointer at the same time that you declare it:

```
char p;
char* const pc = &p;
```

The memory address that pc stores (&p) cannot be changed after this point. But you can change the value of p with pc:

```
*pc = 'd'; //this is legal, actually changes p
pc = 0; //this is illegal
```

You can also have pointers to constants. With a pointer to a constant, you can change the memory address the pointer stores, but not the constant pointed to. To declare a pointer to a constant, you add the `const` keyword before the * operator, as shown here:

```
char const* pcc; // pointer to a constant char
const int* pci; // pointer to a constant int
```

In the preceding code snippet, `pcc` can change which constant character it points to, but not the value of this constant character. Pointers to constants do not need to be initialized when declared because the pointer is still variable, but the variable pointed to isn't, as shown here:

```
char c;
pcc = &c;
*pcc = 'd'; // this is illegal
pcc = 0; // this is legal
```

You can also have constant pointers to constants, where neither the memory address nor the thing pointed to can be changed. To create such a pointer, you put the keyword `const` before and after the * operator, as shown here:

```
int x;
const int* const cpci = x;
```

The only thing you can do with `cpci` is read its value and the value of the variable it points to (x). It is important to use `const` wherever you can in your code to ensure that variables only get changed when you mean for them to!

INTRODUCING POINTERS AND FUNCTIONS

Pointers can be very useful as function parameters and return values. Having a pointer as a function parameter can make your programs much more efficient.

Normally, when you pass an argument to a function, a new copy of this argument is made and assigned to the appropriate parameter. However, if you have a pointer as a parameter, only the memory address must be copied, which can save a lot of extra copying for large data types.

Another advantage to having pointers as function parameters is that you are altering the original and not a copy that has been passed. Look at this example of what not to do:

```
#include <iostream>

class Point
{
public:
      int X = 0,Y=0;
      Point() : X(0), Y(0) {}
};

Point MoveUp(Point p)
{
      p.Y+=5;
      return point;
}

int main(void)
{
      using std::cout;
      Point point;
      point = MoveUp(point);
      cout << point.X << point.Y;
      return 0;
}
```
Output:
05

This code is not very good for two reasons. First, the entire point object must be copied twice in order to call the function MoveUp(). Second, the line point = MoveUp(point); is fairly awkward. From a design standpoint, the user of the function has to do a lot.

However, with a pointer as the parameter of MoveUp(), you can improve the function as shown here:

```
//6.3 - Passing a Pointer - Dirk Henkemans and Mark Lee
#include <iostream>

class Point
{
public:
      int X,Y;
```

```
        Point() : X(0), Y(0) {}
};

void MoveUp(Point* p)
{
        p->Y+=5;
}

int main(void)
{
        using std::cout;
        Point point;
        MoveUp(&point);
        cout << point.X << point.Y;
        return 0;
}
Output:
05
```

The efficiency of the MoveUp() function is greatly increased. Now, instead of making two copies of the Point object for each call, one copy is made of the memory address for each call. Also, the call to MoveUp() is simplified greatly. Instead of having an awkward assignment statement to call the method, you simply call the method. This is much easier for the user of the function to understand. However, you do want to make sure to document clearly that your function will change the value of its argument!

WORKING WITH ARRAYS

All the variables covered in earlier chapters can store only one particular data type. If you want to store a second piece of information, you must create another variable. These types of variables are called scalar variables. But what happens when you have to store a long list of related data? It wouldn't be convenient to create a new variable for every single piece of data. What if you have to work with thousands and thousands of employee records? The task quickly would become overwhelming.

Fortunately, most problems have a solution. In this case, arrays are the solution. Arrays are a special kind of variable that can hold a set of data, all with the same type.

An array holds a set of data. Each member of the set is called an element. Each element has a particular index associated with it. An index is a number that indicates which element of the array you are accessing.

Beginners often have difficulty with a seemingly odd thing about arrays: The numbering of the index starts at zero. So, if you have an array with five elements, the indexes will be 0, 1, 2, 3, and 4. After you work with arrays for a while, you will get used to this weird numbering, and it will start to feel natural. Figure 6.2 shows an array as boxes lined up in a row, with the array name `charArray[]` and individual array elements (such as `char_array[0]`) in each of the boxes.

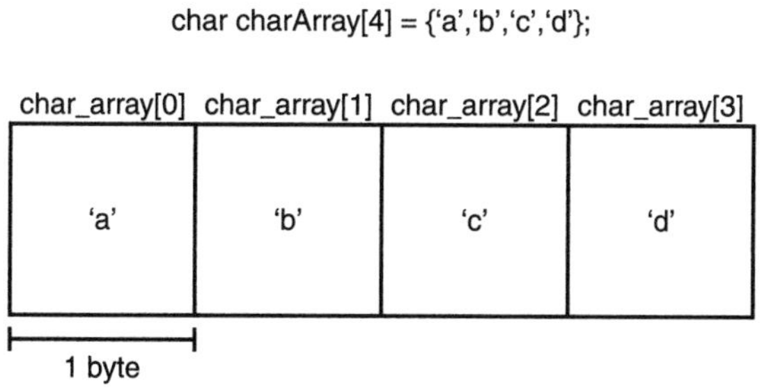

char charArray[4] = {'a','b','c','d'};

char_array[0] char_array[1] char_array[2] char_array[3]

| 'a' | 'b' | 'c' | 'd' |

|— 1 byte —|

FIGURE 6.2

You can picture arrays as a row of boxes of memory lined up side by side.

CREATING ARRAYS

Creating arrays is an easy process, especially now that you've learned about variables. To create an array, type the data type and then the variable name followed by the subscripting operator. Here is the basic syntax:

```
data_type array_name[number_of_elements];
```

This creates an array called *array_name* of type *data_type* with *number_of_elements* elements. For example, to create an array of integers called `int_array` with ten elements, you type

```
int int_array[10];
```

Remember that the indexing starts at 0, so the elements will be numbered 0 to 9. Element 10 does not actually exist in this array, even though it appears to when you are looking at the declaration.

You can create arrays of all data types, including user-defined types. If you have a class called `MyClass`, you can create an array of ten `MyClass` objects like this:

```
MyClass my_class_array[10];
```

The number between the square brackets must be a constant expression, which means that you cannot use a variable to define the number of elements in your array. As you will discover in later chapters, their inability to resize is one of the major drawbacks to using arrays—as opposed to other advanced data types.

Here are some examples of array declarations:

```
int int_array[10];
float float_array[60];
char char_array[6];
```

INITIALIZING ARRAYS

You can fill an array with data a couple of ways. First, you can initialize the array at the same time that you declare it. You do this with an initializer list, which is a list of values used to fill the array. Here is the syntax you use:

```
array_type array_name[number_of_elements] = {value1, value2, value3, ...};
```

Here *value1*, *value2*, and so on are all values of type *array_type*. Note that if you initialize in this way, you can leave *number_of_elements* blank. The computer will decide how large to make the array based on the number of elements in the initializer list. Here are some examples:

```
float float_array[3] = {0.25, .876, 3.0};
char char_array[5] = {'H','e','l','l','o'};
```

If you don't include the number of elements that an array will have but include an initializer list, the array will default to the number of elements in the initializer list. In the following line of code, char_array2 will automatically assume that the array size is 6:

```
char char_array2[] = {'d','r','a','g','o','n'};
```

If you do not have as many values in the initializer list as *number_of_elements*, the rest of the values are assumed to be 0. For example, typing

```
int my_array[5] = {1,2,3};
```

is the same as typing

```
int my_array[5] = {1,2,3,0,0};
```

Another way to initialize arrays is with a for loop. To do so, first declare the array as you normally would and then create a for loop to fill it with a value. Here is an example:

```
int int_array[10];

for (int i = 0; i < 10; i++)
{
    int_array[i] = i;
}
```

Notice that the loop executes ten times, once for each element of the array. In this example, we give each element the value of its index, but you could assign any value you like to each element.

Using Arrays

Accessing elements of an array is similar to creating an array. Each element in an array acts as a separate scalar variable. To access a particular element, you use the array's name, followed by the index number within the subscripting operator:

```
array_name[Index_number];
```

This is equivalent to using just the name of a scalar variable. For example, if you declare the array

```
char char_array[10];
```

and you want to display the value of the fourth element (index number 3), you do the following:

```
cout << char_array[3];
```

You can also access the values of an array with a pointer, as you will learn in the following section.

Relating Arrays to Pointers

Arrays and pointers are closely linked. In fact, in a strict definition, arrays are pointers. Consider this array:

```
float f[10];
```

The name of the array, f, acts as a pointer to the first element. The following displays the value of the first element:

```
cout << *f;
```

If you declare a pointer to the same type as the array's type, you can assign the pointer to the first element of the array like this:

```
float* pf = f;
```

This code snippet is synonymous to the following one:

```
float* pf = &f[0];
```

Then you can go through every element in the array by incrementing the pointer. Wait a second! You increment a pointer just like you do any other variable. Because a pointer stores a memory address, incrementing a pointer changes the memory address. Instead of going up by one, however, the value of the memory address is increased by the size of the pointer type. This effectively moves on to the next element in the array, as shown in this example:

```
float f[] = {5.5, 0.5 , 6.7};
float* pf = f;
cout << *pf;
cout << " " << *(++pf);
cout << " " <<*(++pf);
```

This code displays 5.5 0.5 6.7 onscreen. Every time you increment a pointer, it moves on to the next element of the array. If the increment operator is used on a pointer, C++ assumes that the pointer points to the array, but it doesn't actually check, so be careful that you increment pointers only to array elements.

The decrement operator (--) works the same way (see Chapter 2, "Descending Deeper into Variables"). Every time it is used on a pointer, it will move the pointer one element back in the array. Take care not to go past the beginning of the array; doing so can cause quite a few errors that might be difficult to find and debug.

You can also add to or subtract from pointers. If p is a pointer to an array, p+n moves n elements forward in the array, and p-n moves n elements back in the array.

Here is an example of how to increment through an array using a pointer:

```
int n[] = {0,1,2,3,4,5};
int* pn = n;
cout << *(pn+3) << "\n";
cout << *++pn << "\n";
*pn--;
cout <<*pn << "\n" << *(pn+4) << "\n";
Output:
```

3
1
0
4

 TRAP C++ will not prevent you from trying to access values that are no longer in the array. For example, if you increment the pointer beyond 5 in the preceding n[] array, C++ will be happy to return all the data that your computer has stored there. Worse, if you try to manipulate the data and it is required by Windows or another program, you might wind up causing the computer to crash. Accessing data that is no longer in the array is called walking off the array.

CREATING DYNAMIC ARRAYS

Normally, when creating an array, you must supply a constant expression that is the number of elements in the array. If you try to use a variable expression, the compiler will issue an error. For example, if you try to create the array

```
int x = 5;
char s[x];
```

The compiler will respond with an error saying that a constant expression was expected.

If you create an array on the free store, you can use a variable expression for the number of elements, as shown here:

```
int x = 5;
char* s = new char[x];
```

To de-allocate the memory for the preceding array, you use the delete[] operator. The delete[] operator works just like the delete operator:

```
delete[] s;
```

This frees the entire array, so you don't have to worry about each element.

MULTIDIMENSIONAL ARRAYS

Although multidimensional arrays can be a difficult concept at first, thinking of them as arrays of arrays is helpful. Looking at Figure 6.3, you see five primary elements (the big boxes) in the array, and each primary array element contains an array four elements long. This form is a 5 × 4 multidimensional array.

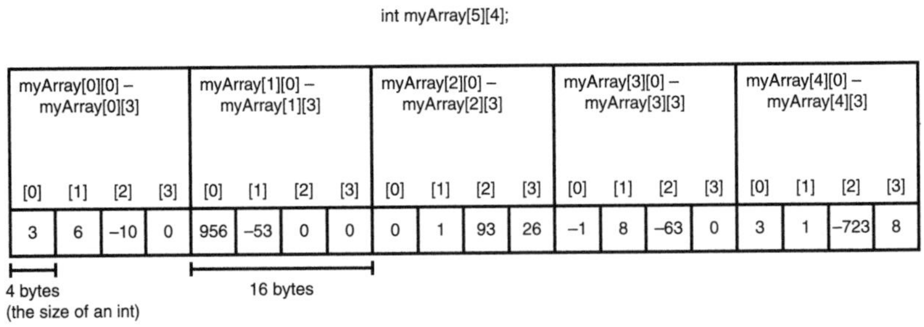

int myArray[5][4];

myArray[0][0] – myArray[0][3]				myArray[1][0] – myArray[1][3]				myArray[2][0] – myArray[2][3]				myArray[3][0] – myArray[3][3]				myArray[4][0] – myArray[4][3]			
[0]	[1]	[2]	[3]	[0]	[1]	[2]	[3]	[0]	[1]	[2]	[3]	[0]	[1]	[2]	[3]	[0]	[1]	[2]	[3]
3	6	–10	0	956	–53	0	0	0	1	93	26	–1	8	–63	0	3	1	–723	8

4 bytes
(the size of an int)

16 bytes

FIGURE 6.3

Picture a two-dimensional array as boxes of boxes. Inside each array is another array.

To create a two-dimensional array, you put a subscripting operator at the end of the declaration, as shown here:

```
array_type array_name[number_of_elements][number_of_elements2];
```

This code creates an array of *number_of_elements* arrays with *number_of_elements2* elements of type *array_type*. For example,

```
int my_Array[5][4];
```

creates an array with five elements. Each of these five elements will be an array of four integers. Picture multidimensional array elements as boxes of memory, each containing an array; again, this concept is illustrated in Figure 6.3.

You can have as many dimensions on an array as you want. However, too many arrays of arrays can quickly use up a computer's memory.

Picture a two-dimensional array as boxes of boxes. Inside each array of larger boxes is an array of smaller boxes. Arrays inside arrays are the foundation to multidimensional arrays.

Any multidimensional array can also be represented as a single dimensional array simply by multiplying all the sizes. If you have a two-dimensional array such as

```
char my_Array[10][10];
```

you can create a single-dimensional array equivalent by multiplying 10 and 10 to get 100. Thus, the array

```
char my_Array[100];
```

will have the same number of integer elements (total) as the previous two-dimensional array.

The common way to scroll through all the elements in a multidimensional array is to use a for loop within a for loop. The following example will initialize all the elements in a multidimensional array:

```
//6.1 - Multidimensional Arrays - Dirk Henkemans and Mark Lee
#include <iostream>

int main(void)
{
    using std::cout;
    int numbers[10][10];
    for (int i = 0; i < 10; i++)
        for (int c = 0; c < 10; c++)
            cout << (numbers[i][c] = (i * 10) + c) << "\n";
    return 0;
}
Output:
0 1 ... 98 99
```

Strings Revisited

We covered strings earlier in this book (refer to Chapter 1, for example). However, you have only scratched the surface of strings. Here you revisit strings for a more detailed view on how strings work and what you can do with them.

In C, strings are represented as character arrays, instead of objects like they are in C++. Because of this, you will commonly see strings represented as character arrays. As a result, we will go into some detail about how C-style strings work so that you will be able to read all C++ code.

String Literals

The official type of string literals (such as `"Hello"`) is `const char []`. The string `"Hello"` is of type `const char [6]`. But, wait! The word Hello has five letters, not six! Don't worry, we didn't make a mistake. The extra character is there because you must have a terminating null character, /0 (the value 0), that tells the computer the length of the string.

Every string literal has a hidden null character (/0) at the end so that certain algorithms will know the length of the string and when they reach the end of the string. Not all algorithms need to know the length of the string, but most do.

You can assign a string literal to a variable of type `char*`, as shown here:

```
char* x = "Hello";
```

However, the value pointed to by x cannot be manipulated. If it is not a constant, the code will produce an error, as shown in the following example.

```
*x = 'S';
```

This code causes an error because you cannot change the value of a constant. If you need to point to a string that you can modify, you must assign a string literal to a string object or to a character array. Here is an example of a way that you can change the value in a character array:

```
char s[] = "Hello";
s[0] = 'S';
```

This code is okay, and the new value of the string is "Sello".

Many of the C standard library functions for strings take char* as an argument. However, if a string is stored in a character pointer, its length is lost, which is why a string literal has a null character at the end. Without it, you will not be able to tell where the string ends.

CHARACTER ARRAYS

As you have seen, arrays of characters are another way of representing strings. You can initialize a character array with a string literal, as shown in the following example:

```
char s[] = "Hello World!";
```

Because you don't have to provide the length of the array within the subscripting operator, declaring a string this way is almost as convenient as using the string class from the standard library. C++ will allocate enough characters in the s array to hold the null zero that appears at the end of the string.

DETERMINING STRING LENGTH

To obtain the length of the string s[] (from the previous section "Character Arrays"), you could use the usual method for determining the length of an array—use the sizeof operator. For example, to obtain the length of s in the example in the preceding section, you do the following:

```
cout << sizeof(s);
```

This code displays the number 13 onscreen. We didn't divide by the size of char as you normally would to obtain array length because the size of char is always 1.

There is a slight problem with this method. The length of the string is 12, not 13. If you obtain the size through the sizeof operator, the null character is included in your length. To obtain the length of the string without the null character, you can subtract 1 from the length you obtain, or you can use the standard library.

A function called `strlen()` returns the length of any string. For example, to find the length of s in the preceding examples (`char s[] = "Hello World!";`), write this code:

```
cout << strlen(s);
```

This code displays the proper string length, 12, onscreen, rather than 13 because `strlen()` determines the length by counting the elements up to the first null character. For example, for a string such as

```
char weird_string = "Hello/0 World";
```

`strlen()` returns 5, going up to only the first null character. If you determine the length of the string with the `sizeof` operator, however, you get 14 (two null characters).

The prototype for the `strlen()` function is as follows:

```
int strlen(const char*)
```

To use this function, you must include `<string>` in your program.

USING OTHER C-STYLE STRING FUNCTIONS

You can find many other C-style string functions in the standard library. This section goes through a couple of them, just as a form of introduction to these many functions. The functions you will go through in this section are `strcopy()`, which is used for copying strings, and `strcat()`, which is used for concatenating strings.

To use these functions, you need to include `<cstring>`. To copy one string into another string, use the function `strcpy()` (string copy). The prototype for this function is as follows:

```
char* strcpy(char* p, const char* q);
```

This function puts every element in q into p. For example, calling the function as follows

```
char s[6];
strcpy(s, "Hello");
```

causes s to hold the value `"Hello"` (including the terminating null character). The `char*` that this function returns is the value of q (the value that is copied).

This function does not check to make sure that the array you pass in p is large enough to hold all the values in q. It just copies away. Because of this, you must make sure that the array you pass in for p is at least as large as q.

Here is an example of how to copy strings using the strcpy() function:

```
char s[6];
char t[] = "Hello";
cout << strcpy(s, t);
```

This code displays Hello onscreen and copies s with the string "Hello".

To concatenate two strings (to append one string to the end of another), you use the function strcat(). The prototype for the strcat() function is as follows:

```
char* strcat(char* p, const char* q);
```

This function appends the string in q to the end of p. For example, if you use the function,

```
char s[12] = "Hello";
cout << strcat(s, " World");
```

s holds the value "Hello World" (with a null character at the end). The char* that this function returns is the entire concatenated string. In the example, Hello World is displayed onscreen.

The function strncpy() will do a strcpy(), but will copy only a certain amount of q into p. The prototype for strncpy() is as follows:

```
char* strncpy(char* p. const char* q, int n);
```

This prototype copies n characters from q to the end of p. For example, writing

```
char s [7]= "Say ";
char t[]= "Hi";
cout << strncpy(s, t, 2);
```

causes the new value of s to become the character array "Say Hi". This string also displays onscreen because it is the value that strncpy() returns.

CONVERTING STRINGS TO NUMBERS

You can also use a couple of functions to convert strings that contain numeric values to the numeric value (for example, "5" to 5). These functions are declared in <cstdlib>.

To convert a string representation of an integer to an integer, use the atoi() function. The prototype for this function is as follows:

```
int atoi(const char* p);
```

To use this function, you pass in a string, and the function returns an integer. Here is an example:

```
char s[] = "567";
int x = atoi(s) + 3;
cout << x;
```

This code displays the number 570 onscreen.

You can also use functions to convert a string to a double and a string to a long; they are atof() and atol(), respectively. Their prototypes are about the same as the prototype for atoi():

```
double atof(const char* p);
long atol(const char* p);
```

These functions also work the exact same way as atoi() does.

If the string does not contain a number (for example, "HI"), 0 is returned.

These functions can be useful for receiving user input. Instead of assuming that users will enter valid numbers, you can let them enter a string. Then you can check to see whether this string can be converted to a number. This is a much safer way to receive user input.

BEGINNING WITH REFERENCES

You've come a long way. Congratulations! Now, you are ready to learn how to use references. A reference is an alias, or an alternative name, for a variable. You can think of a reference as a constant pointer that is always dereferenced. References are much like constants in that they must be initialized when declared and their value cannot be changed after that.

To create a reference, you use the reference (&) operator. Don't confuse this operator with the address of operator. You will be able to tell which is which according to the current context. Here is the syntax for declaring a reference:

```
data_type& reference_name;
```

Here *data_type* is the type of variable that the reference is a reference to and *reference_name* is the name of the reference. To initialize a reference (as you must do when you declare it), you assign a variable of type *data_type* to the reference creation:

```
data_type& reference_name = variable;
```

Here is an example of how to create and initialize a reference:

```
int x;
int& rx = x;
```

The preceding code causes rx to be a reference to the variable x. Strangely enough, operators do not act on a reference. They act only on the variable referenced by the reference. For example, if you increment rx as

```
rx++;
```

x is incremented by one. rx is just another name for x. You use references mainly as function parameters and return types.

USING REFERENCES IN FUNCTION PARAMETERS

You can legally make any function parameter a reference. This can be useful if you want to write a function that can change the argument passed to it. For example, you can write a function called decrement that has a reference parameter like this:

```
void decrement(int& x)
{
    x--;
}
```

You can then use this function as follows:

```
int a = 5;
decrement(a);
cout << a;
Output:
4
```

Because x becomes a reference to a when decrement is called, decrementing x changes the value of a. As you can see, this looks much cleaner than using references to do the same thing.

USING REFERENCES AS FUNCTION RETURN VALUES

As you might suspect, you can return a reference to a variable in a function. However, the implications of doing so are not so obvious. Consider the following example.

```
//6.4 - Reference Example - Dirk Henkemans and Mark Lee
#include <iostream>
```

```
class Point
{
     int X,Y;
public:
     Point(int lX, int lY):X(lX),Y(lY) {}
     int& GetX() {return X;}
     int& GetY() {return Y;}
};

int main(void)
{
     using std::cout;
     Point p(5,3);
     p.GetX() = 3;
     p.GetY() = 5;
     cout << p.GetX() << p.GetY() << "\n";
     return 0;
}
Output:
35
```

Because GetX() and GetY() return references to the member variables X and Y, you can use these function calls as *lvalues* (*lvalues* are values, or variables, that can be changed). Changing the value of these references changes only the values of the member variables, X and Y.

RE-CREATING THE TIC TAC TOE GAME

Now, you get to use your newfound array and pointer skills as you follow along with us to create the classic of classics: Tic Tac Toe. To make it a little easier to understand, we did not fully optimize this version of Tic Tac Toe. Later, you might want to see how you can improve on the design.

```
//6.5 - Tic Tac Toe - Dirk Henkemans and Mark Lee
#include <iostream>
#include <string>

using std::string;

enum SquareState { blank = ' ', X = 'X', O='O'};
```

```cpp
class GameBoard
{
private:
      const int WIDTH;
      const int HEIGHT;
      int* gameBoard;
public:
      GameBoard() : WIDTH(3), HEIGHT(3)
      {
            gameBoard = new int[9];
            for (int i = 0; i < 9; i++)
                  *(gameBoard + i) = blank;
      }

      ~GameBoard() {delete[] gameBoard;}
      void setX(int h, int w);
      void setO(int h, int w);
      bool isTaken(int h, int w);
      SquareState isLine();
      void draw();
};

void GameBoard::setX(int h, int w)
{
      *(gameBoard + h*HEIGHT + w) = X;
}

void GameBoard::setO(int h, int w)
{
      *(gameBoard + h*HEIGHT + w) = O;
}

bool GameBoard::isTaken (int h, int w)
{
      return *(gameBoard + h*HEIGHT + w) != ' ';
}

SquareState GameBoard::isLine()
```

```
{
    if(*gameBoard==X && *(gameBoard +1)==X && *(gameBoard +2)==X)
        return X;
    if(*gameBoard==0 && *(gameBoard +1)==0 && *(gameBoard +2)==0)
        return 0;
    if(*(gameBoard +3)==X && *(gameBoard +4)==X && *(gameBoard +5)==X)
        return X;
    if(*(gameBoard +3)==0 && *(gameBoard +4)==0 && *(gameBoard +5)==0)
        return 0;
    if(*(gameBoard +6)==X && *(gameBoard +7)==X && *(gameBoard +8)==X)
        return X;
    if(*(gameBoard +6)==0 && *(gameBoard +7)==0 && *(gameBoard +8)==0)
        return 0;
    if(*gameBoard==X && *(gameBoard +3)==X && *(gameBoard +6)==X)
        return X;
    if(*gameBoard==0 && *(gameBoard +3)==0 && *(gameBoard +6)==0)
        return 0;
    if(*(gameBoard +1)==X && *(gameBoard +4)==X && *(gameBoard +7)==X)
        return X;
    if(*(gameBoard +1)==0 && *(gameBoard +4)==0 && *(gameBoard +7)==0)
        return 0;
    if(*(gameBoard +2)==X && *(gameBoard +5)==X && *(gameBoard +8)==X)
        return X;
    if(*(gameBoard +2)==0 && *(gameBoard +5)==0 && *(gameBoard +8)==0)
        return 0;
    if(*gameBoard==X && *(gameBoard +4)==X && *(gameBoard +8)==X)
        return X;
    if(*gameBoard==0 && *(gameBoard +4)==0 && *(gameBoard +8)==0)
        return 0;
    if(*(gameBoard +2)==X && *(gameBoard +4)==X && *(gameBoard +6)==X)
        return X;
    if(*(gameBoard +2)==0 && *(gameBoard +4)==0 && *(gameBoard +6)==0)
        return 0;
    return blank;
}


void GameBoard::draw()
{
```

```cpp
    using std::cout;
    cout << "\n";
    for(int i=0; i < HEIGHT; i++)
    {
            cout << (char)*(gameBoard + i*HEIGHT);
            for(int c=1; c < WIDTH; c++)
                    cout << " | " << (char)*(gameBoard + i*WIDTH + c);
            cout << "\n" << "-------" << "/n";
    }
}


class Game
{
public:
    GameBoard* doInput(string player, gameBoard* gb);
    bool inRange(int test);
};


GameBoard* Game::doInput(string player, GameBoard* gb)
{
    using std::cout;
    using std::cin;

    gb->draw();
    string letter;
    if (player.compare("one") == 0)
        letter = "X";
    else if (player.compare("two") == 0)
        letter = "O";
    else return gb;

    int input1, input2;
    do {
        do {
            cout << "\nPlayer " << player.c_str()
                    << ", please enter a row number to put an "
                    << letter.c_str() << ": ";
            cin >> input1;
```

```
            } while(!inRange(input1));
            do {
                cout << "\nPlease enter a column number to put an "
                     << letter.c_str() << ": ";
                cin >> input2;
            } while(!inRange(input2));
        } while (gb->isTaken(input1,input2));

        if (player.compare("one") == 0)
            gb->setX(input1, input2);
        else
            gb->setO(input1, input2);
        return gb;
}

bool Game::inRange(int test)
{
        return test > -1 && test < 3;
}

int main( void )
{
        using std::cout;
        using std::cin;

        GameBoard* gb = new GameBoard;
        Game g;
        string player1, player2;
        cout << "Welcome to Tic Tac Toe!"
             << "\nPlayer one, please enter your name: ";
        cin >> player1;
        cout << "\nPlayer two, please enter your name: ";
        cin >> player2;

        while (gb->isLine() == ' ')
        {
            gb = g.doInput("one",gb);
            gb = g.doInput("two",gb);
```

```
        }
        gb->draw();
        if(gb->isLine() == X)
                cout << "\nPlayer one, you win!\nGame Over.";
        else
                cout << "\nPlayer two, you win!\nGame Over.";
        return 0;
}
```

SUMMARY

In this chapter, you learned many concepts. You started with pointers and learned how they are the basis for arrays. Then, you covered how to use references and dynamic memory. Finally, you revisited strings to learn the difference between C-style strings and the C++ strings you have used so far. Your adventure is not over though. Now, it's time to continue to Chapter 7, "Building Namespaces."

CHALLENGES

1. What is the size of the string "Hello World"? What is the length of this array named s?

```
char s[] = "Hello World";
```

2. List five reasons to use pointers.
3. What are the problems with the "Tic Tac Toe" game at the end of the chapter? How can you improve the game?
4. List three reasons to use dynamic memory.

RELATING CLASSES

A s we mentioned in Chapter 5, "Designing Software: Object-Oriented Programming," classes tend to model concepts or things. However, we haven't mentioned that these concepts or things tend to have certain relationships. As do other relationships, these relationships help clarify and provide a logical order for the world.

When you are designing classes for your programs, be sure to focus on these relationships, both for convenience and logic. In this chapter, you will learn how to express these relationships in your code:

- Composition
- Inheritance

COMBINING CLASSES WITH COMPOSITION

Let us pretend, for a moment, that you are designing a computer game. One of the classes you decide you need is a Weapon class to represent any weapons that might be encountered in the game. Perhaps the Weapon class looks something like this:

```
class Weapon
{
    int damage;
```

```
    int cost;
public:
    Weapon(int theDamage, int theCost);
    // ... other useful methods
};
```

Nothing too exciting here. Naturally, another class you would like is a `Player` class to represent the player. One thing you realize at this point is that the player needs to have a weapon. You may have already guessed it, but we have not properly discussed how you represent such a "has-a" relationship in your code. A `Player` "has-a" `Weapon`.

The people who spend their time analyzing the different relationships between classes seem to enjoy coming up with new names for them. Because of this, the technique for representing a "has-a" relationship in your code has many names: composition, aggregation, layering, containment, or embedding. We'll keep things simple and just call it composition.

Okay, we have a problem and a name for the solution. Now, my keen reader, it is time to learn what composition actually is. We'll start by simply showing you how composition looks in the `Player` class:

```
class Player
{
    Weapon myWeapon;
    // ... rest of class
};
```

As you can see, there is a `Weapon` object contained in the `Player` class. `myWeapon` is a member variable of the `Player` class. This is composition, plain and simple. The lifetime and scope of the `myWeapon` variable is restricted to that of each `Player` object. It's pretty simple and intuitive really.

Introducing Inheritance

As your game expands, it quickly becomes unrealistic and clumsy to represent all the different kinds of weapons with just one class. You might have different types of weapons, like projectile weapons, melee weapons, and magical weapons. Each of these types function a little differently and so the simple `Weapon` class we started with in the last section is no longer sufficient.

The first solution that may occur to you is to scrap the `Weapon` class entirely, in favor of three separate weapon classes:

```
class ProjectileWeapon
{
      int damage;
      int cost;
      int range;
public:
      ProjectileWeapon(int theDamage, int theCost, int theRange);
      // ... other methods
};

class MeleeWeapon
{
      int damage;
      int cost;
public:
      MeleeWeapon(int theDamage, int theCost);
      // ... other methods
};

class MagicalWeapon
{
public:
      enum MagicType { FIRE, ICE, ELECTRICAL };
private:
      int damage;
      int cost;
      MagicType magicType;
public:
      MagicalWeapon(int theDamage, int theCost, MagicType theMagicType);
      // ... other weapons
};
```

This seems to work all right at first, but there are two major problems. First, there is a lot of repetition. Member variables like damage and cost are repeated verbatim in each of the three classes. Second, how do we do composition now? There is no longer a single class to represent the concept of a weapon, so the Player class must have all three types:

```
class Player
{
        ProjectileWeapon myProjectileWeapon;
        MeleeWeapon myMeleeWeapon;
        MagicalWeapon myMagicalWeapon;
        // ... rest of class
};
```

This is clunky at best. If the player is only allowed to carry a single weapon at a time, this gets rather complicated to enforce. Especially as more weapon types are added.

Fortunately, C++ offers a way to get the best of both worlds. We can have a separate class for every weapon type while still maintaining a single weapon class to represent the general concept of a weapon and to keep all of the common code. The solution is called inheritance.

Inheritance is used to represent a "kind-of" relationship. Projectile weapons are a kind of weapon. When we implement with inheritance, there will be a general Weapon class and the ProjectileWeapon class will inherit from it. The Weapon class is said to be the parent, base, or super class, and the ProjectileWeapon class is said to be the child, derived, or sub class.

Writing Code for Inheritance

Okay, so we have three types of weapons and we need a way to represent them succinctly. We know the proper solution is inheritance, but how do we do it? Let's start with the parent class, Weapon:

```
class Weapon
{
        int damage;
        int cost;
public:
        Weapon(int theDamage, int theCost);
        // ... more methods
};

Weapon::Weapon(int theDamage, int theCost)
        : damage(theDamage), cost(theCost)
{}
```

Looks familiar, huh? Actually, if you look back at the section on composition, you'll see that it's exactly the same as the basic Weapon class we started with (except with an added constructor implementation). Now let's take a look at one of the child classes, ProjectileWeapon:

```
class ProjectileWeapon : public Weapon
{
      int range;
public:
      ProjectileWeapon(int theDamage, int theCost, int theRange);
};
```

The key thing to notice here is the very first line of code:

```
class ProjectileWeapon : public Weapon
```

You have not seen this syntax before. This is how you denote inheritance in C++. Basically, this line of code is saying that a ProjectileWeapon is a kind of Weapon. This means that everything in the Weapon class is automatically included in the ProjectileWeapon class. You'll notice that the member variables damage and cost are not declared in the ProjectileWeapon class for this reason; they are included automatically through the magic of inheritance!

Now, let's take a look at the ProjectileWeapon constructor. The naïve and incorrect way to implement it would be the following:

```
// Will not compile. ProjectileWeapon cannot access Weapon's private members
ProjectileWeapon:ProjectileWeapon(int theDamage, int theCost, int theRange)
      : damage(theDamage), cost(theCost), range(theRange)
{}
```

The problem here is a rule of C++ inheritance that seems very odd at first. A child class cannot access its parent's private members. At first that seems like a rather pointless rule that just makes things more difficult, but it does have a purpose. With this rule, you can ensure that the implementation details of the Weapon class are all kept in one place. If you change the name of the damage member, for instance, you won't need to search through every derived class for uses of this member.

Now, here is the proper way to implement a child class constructor:

```
// Right way. Call the parent's constructor
ProjectileWeapon:ProjectileWeapon(int theDamage, int theCost, int theRange)
      : Weapon(theDamage, theCost), range(theRange)
{}
```

As you can see, the proper way is to call the parent class's constructor and let it deal with initializing its own private members.

Here is the general syntax for creating a derived class:

```
class derived_class : scope_modifier base_class
```

Here *derived_class* is the name of the derived class, and *base_class* is the name of the base class. *scope_modifier* can be public, private, or protected; but for this book, you will just use public. private can be very useful in some very specialized situations, and protected should never be used.

Accessing Class Members through Inheritance

Although the rules for what the member functions of a derived class can access are straightforward, they are often difficult for a beginner, and even advanced programmers at times. In this section, we attempt to minimize the confusion and maximize your enjoyment (or at least one of the two).

First of all, recall that there are two kinds of access specifiers for members of a class: public and private. There is actually a third kind of access specifier called protected. protected only comes into play when inheritance is involved. Without inheritance, it is exactly the same as private.

The member functions of a derived class can access the following:

- All global variables.
- The class's own members.
- All public and protected members of its base class.

See, that's not so bad. If you are ever in doubt, just consult this list. A derived class has almost as much access to members as does a base class because the derived class inherits most of the base class's functionality. The only items that a derived class cannot access are the base class's private members.

As the preceding list implies, a derived class can access all the public and protected members of its base class. However, it cannot access the private members. Here is an example:

```
class Base
{
        int private_int;
protected:
        int getInt() { return private_int; }
```

```
};

class Derived : public Base
{
    // Error - cannot access private_int
    int myFunc() { return private_int; }
    // The right way
    int myFunc() { return getInt(); }
}
```

In this example, the Derived class cannot access private_int because private_int is private. It can, however, access the protected member function getInt(). Using the base class's public and protected member functions to access the private data is the proper way to access this data. Keep in mind that a Derived object still has a private_int member. It just can't access it directly. This is so that you can change the implementation of the base class without having to change each and every class that is derived from it.

In almost all other aspects, the protected access specifier is exactly the same as private. For example, if you create a Derived object, you cannot access the getInt() method that it inherits from its base class. Here is an example:

```
class Base
{
    int private_int;
protected:
    int getInt() { return private_int; }
};

class Derived : public Base
{
protected:
    int myFunc() { return 5; }
public:
    int myFunc2() { return myFunc(); }
}

int main(void)
{
    Base b;
    b.getInt(); // Error: cannot access protected member
```

```
        Derived d;
        d.getInt(); // Error: cannot access protected, inherited member
        d.myFunct(); // Error
        d.myFunc2(); // Ok! Returns 5
        return 0;
}
```

Creating Constructors and Destructors in Derived Classes

The constructors and destructors of classes involved in inheritance are a little bit more complicated than normal functions, so we're treating them as a special case.

The first rule is this: If a base class does not have a constructor or one of the base class's constructors does not require arguments, no constructor is needed in the derived class. Second, if all the base class's constructors require arguments, the derived class must have a constructor, and the constructor must explicitly invoke the base class's constructor in the initializer list. Here is an example:

```
class Base
{};

class Base2
{
public:
        Base2() { cout << "Hello"; }
};

class Base3
{
public:
        Base3(int a) { cout << a; }
};

class Derived : public Base
{
        //no constructor needed
};

class Derived2 : public Base2
{
```

```
        //no constructor needed
};

class Derived3 : public Base3
{
        //must have constructor, and must invoke Base3's constructor
public:
        // correct
        Derived3() : Base3(3) {}

        //incorrect
        Derived3() { Base3(3); }

        //incorrect
        Derived3() {};
};
```

Third, the Derived class's constructor cannot initialize the variables that it inherits from the base class in an initializer list, even if it has access to those members. It must either use the base class's constructor or initialize the relevant variables in the braces ({ and }). Here is an example:

```
class Base
{
public:
        Base() : protected_int(3) {}
protected:
        int protected_int;
};

class Derived : public Base
{
public:
        Derived();
};

//the Derived class's constructor
//the right way
Derived::Derived() : Base()
```

```
{}

//also right
Derived::Derived() : Base()
{
      protected_int = 2;
}

//error
Derived::Derived() : Base(), protected_int(2)
{}
```

In the first version of Derived class's constructor, the base class's constructor is called, and then Derived initializes its own variables. This is what you normally will see, and it is the proper way to initialize a derived class.

However, the second version is also correct. You can initialize the base class's members if the initialization is within the braces rather than in the initializer list.

The order of construction is as follows: first the base class and then the derived class. Destruction happens in the reverse order. The derived class is destroyed and then the base is destroyed. Here is an example to clarify:

```
// 7.1 - Constructors and Destructors - Mark Lee
#include <iostream>

using std::cout;

class Base
{
public:
      Base() { cout << "Base's constructor\n"; }
      ~Base() { cout << "Base's destructor\n"; }
};

class Derived : public Base
{
public:
      Derived() { cout << "Derived's constructor\n"; }
      ~Derived() { cout << "Derived's destructor\n"; }
```

```
};

int main (void)
{
    Derived d;
    return 0;
}
```

Output:

```
Base's constructor
Derived's constructor
Derived's destructor
Base's destructor
```

See, that wasn't so bad! If you're comfortable with all of these basics, the rest is easy.

Extending Inheritance

The simple inheritance that we have taught so far is not particularly useful, but it is the base from which your knowledge will grow. The following concepts are actually incredibly simple, so if you understand the past few sections, you should be on easy street.

First, a derived class can also be a base class for another derived class. Through multilevel derivation, you can get an inheritance chain. An inheritance chain is a sequence of derived classes, each of which is also a base to the class below it. The idea here is to begin with a general concept for the base class and then become more specific as you move down the chain.

The following code illustrates how this inheritance structure looks in C++:

```
class Vehicle {};
class LandVehicle : public Vehicle {};
class Car : public LandVehicle {};
class HondaInsight : public Car {};
```

As with normal inheritance, the constructors are executed from the base down, and the destructors are in reverse. For example, in the preceding inheritance chain, the order is as follows: `Vehicle` constructor, `LandVehicle` constructor, `Car` constructor, `HondaInsight` constructor; then `HondaInsight` destructor, `Car` destructor, `LandVehicle` destructor, and `Vehicle` destructor.

Figure 7.1 shows a conceptual diagram of the `Vehicle` inheritance chain. Notice how the arrows point up rather than down. This is because the arrows show the direction that classes can access other classes. A base class does not have access to a derived class, but a derived class has access to a base class.

When you call a method of a class, the computer first checks that class, then its base class, then the base's base, and so on up the chain until it finds the method.

A base class can have more than one derived class under it. In this way, you can create tree-like structures of inheritance. These structures are called class hierarchies. The MFC (Microsoft Foundation Class) is an example of a large, advanced class hierarchy. If you create advanced Windows applications, you will learn how to use it.

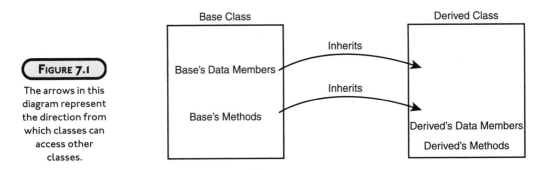

FIGURE 7.1

The arrows in this diagram represent the direction from which classes can access other classes.

A class hierarchy is not incredibly complex. The main thing is that siblings (classes with the same base class) are not affected by each other. No class has any of its siblings' members. Figure 7.2 shows a class hierarchy for vehicles.

The following code shows how this hierarchical structure looks in C++:

```cpp
class Vehicle {};
class LandVehicle : public Vehicle {};
class WaterVehicle : public Vehicle {};
class Car : public LandVehicle {};
class Bike : public LandVehicle {};
class Boat : public WaterVehicle {};
class Submarine : public WaterVehicle {};
```

You can divide this fancy class hierarchy into a bunch of inheritance chains, as illustrated in Figure 7.3.

FIGURE 7.2

You can design a class hierarchy for vehicles to look like this one.

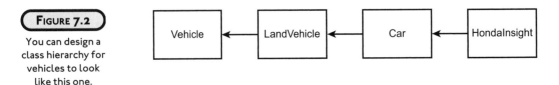

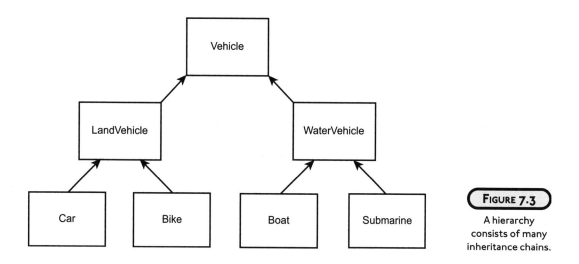

FIGURE 7.3

A hierarchy consists of many inheritance chains.

Pointers to Base Classes

A pointer to a base class can store the address of a derived object. Here is an example:

```
Base* b;
Derived d;
b = &d; //this is ok
```

This capability of storing two kinds of addresses is an important part of inheritance, and it makes C++ a very powerful language. One place where this ability might be useful is in any sort of collection. For example, you could make an array of pointers to Vehicle objects, and this array can store any subclass of Vehicle. Without this capability, you would have to create a separate array for each type of vehicle, and doing so would be annoying.

You can also write a function that takes a pointer to a base class and pass the address of any subclass to it. Here is an example:

```
class Weapon
{
    int cost;
    int damage;
public:
    Weapon(int theCost, int theDamage);
    int getCost() { return cost; }
};

Weapon::Weapon(int theCost, int theDamage)
    : cost(theCost), damage(theDamage)
```

```
{}

class ProjectileWeapon
{
      int range;
public:
      ProjectileWeapon(int theCost, int theDamage, int theRange);
};

ProjectileWeapon::ProjectileWeapon(int theCost, int theDamage, int theRange)
      : Weapon(theCost, theDamage), range(theRange)
{}

void printCost(Weapon* w)
{
      cout << "The cost is " << w->getCost() << "\n";
}

int main(void)
{
      ProjectileWeapon bow(5, 2, 10);
      printCost(&bow);
      return 0;
}
```

Output:
The cost is 5

Understanding the Three Types of Member Function Inheritance

Data members are not the only things passed down when you use inheritance. The derived class also inherits the base class's member functions. However, the story does not end there. A method is composed of two parts: an interface and an implementation. When inheriting a member function you get to choose whether to inherit the:

- Interface and implementation.
- Interface and an optional implementation.
- The interface only.

Which of these you choose depends heavily on how you intend to use the member function.

Inheriting the Interface and Implementation

The first type of member function inheritance is the easiest: inheriting both the interface and the implementation. This is what you should use for member functions that will work exactly the same way for all derived classes. The getCost() member function of the Weapon class is a good, albeit simple, example of such a function. No matter what type of weapon it is, the cost is still calculated the same way.

Here is how you inherit both the interface and implementation:

```
class Weapon
{
    int cost;
    int damage;
public:
    Weapon(int theCost, int theDamage);
    int getCost() { return cost; }
};


Weapon::Weapon(int theCost, int theDamage)
    : cost(theCost), damage(theDamage)
{}


class ProjectileWeapon
{
    int range;
public:
    ProjectileWeapon(int theCost, int theDamage, int theRange);
};
```

"But wait," you say with confusion, "there is nothing special here!" And indeed, my observant reader, you would be correct. Inheriting both the interface and implementation happens *by default*. This makes it the least complicated type of method inheritance.

The ProjectileWeapon class inherits the getCost() member function as is. You can then use it as if it were declared within that class like a normal member function:

```
int main(void)
{
    using std::cout;
    ProjectileWeapon bow(5,2,10);
```

```
        cout << "The cost is " << bow.getCost() << "\n";
        return 0;
}
```

Inheriting the Interface and an Optional Implementation

Now we get to the more interesting cases. If you want to be able to provide a different implementation of a member function for each derived class, you must make the function virtual.

To create a virtual function, use the `virtual` keyword. Here is the general syntax:

```
virtual return_type function_name(argument_list);
```

You put the `virtual` keyword in front of the function only when it is first declared. If you declare the function and then define it later, the `virtual` keyword goes only in front of the declaration. If the function is defined at the same time that it is declared, you put the `virtual` keyword in front of the function definition.

You need to put the `virtual` keyword only in front of the base class's version of the function, but you should also add it in front of every derived class's version to make it clear to everyone reading your code what is going on. Making functions virtual tells the computer to search for the correct version of the function to call. Take a look at the following example:

```
//7.2 - Virtual Functions - Mark Lee
#include <iostream>

using std::cout;

class Base
{
public:
        void Display() { cout << "Base's Display\n"; }
};

class Derived : public Base
{
public:
        void Display() { cout << "Derived's Display\n"; }
};

class Base2
{
```

```
public:
     virtual void Display() { cout << "Base2's Display\n"; }
     virtual void f(); // this is also correct
};


void Base2::f() // virtual not needed here
{}


class Derived2 : public Base2
{
public:
     void Display() { cout << "Derived2's Display\n"; }
};


int main ( void )
{
     Derived d;
     Base* b = &d;
     b->Display();
     Derived2 d2;
     Base2* b2 = &d2;
     b2->Display();
     return 0;
}
Output:
Base's Display
Derived2's Display
```

As you can see from the output, using a virtual function corrected the problem. The Base class used a non-virtual Display() function, so the incorrect function was called. Because Base2's Display() is virtual, the call to b2->Display() produces the correct output.

Inheriting the Interface Only

Some classes that you design in a hierarchy might not make sense as objects. For example, although the Vehicle class works well as a parent class to define common elements of objects derived from Vehicle, creating a Vehicle object does not have any meaning.

Another example is when you have a hierarchy of shape classes with a general Shape class at the top. Creating a Shape object does not make sense. It is a shape without shape. These classes represent abstract concepts. In contrast, a Car class can represent an actual object. Another possibility is to create a Comparable class that has the basic interface needed to make an object comparable with another object. If you derive classes from this base class, you are guaranteed to be able to compare them. However, making an object from the Comparable class wouldn't have much meaning.

C++ provides a way, called abstract classes, to represent these abstract concepts without accidentally mistaking them for normal objects. You create an abstract class by putting a pure virtual function inside the class. (You cannot create an object from an abstract class.)

A pure virtual function is a virtual function that is not implemented but is used only to create abstract classes (the base class does not provide a definition for it). To create the syntax for a pure virtual function, you simply put = 0 at the end of the virtual function declaration:

```
virtual return_type function_name(argument_list) = 0;
```

If a class has one of these pure virtual functions as one of its members (or it does not override one from its base class), the class is an abstract class. It is illegal in C++ to create an object from an abstract class. The pure virtual function just helps to ensure that you don't accidentally attempt to create an object from that base class. The base class exists, therefore, only to provide a structure for derived classes. Here is an example:

```
class Abstract
{
public:
        virtual void draw() = 0;
};

int main(void)
{
        Abstract a; //illegal - causes an error
        return 0;
}
```

If a class has an abstract base class, the class can override all the pure virtual functions so that it is not also an abstract class. Here is an example:

```
#include <iostream>

using std::cout;

class Abstract
```

```
{
public:
    virtual void draw() = 0;
};

class Derived : public Abstract
{
public:
    //overrides Abstract::draw()
    void draw() { cout << "Hello World."; }
};

int main( void )
{
    Derived d; // legal
    Abstract a; // illegal
    return 0;
}
```

However, if a derived class does not override all the pure virtual functions from its base class, it inherits them and becomes an abstract class. Here is an example:

```
class Abstract
{
    virtual int f() = 0;
    virtual float g(float) = 0;
};

class Derived : class Abstract
{
    int f(); //override pure virtual from base
    //g() is not overridden
};

int main (void)
{
    Abstract a; //illegal - abstract class
    Derived d; // illegal - also an abstract class
    return 0;
}
```

CREATING THE DRAGON LORD GAME

While wandering through a great kingdom, some noble messengers approach. "Noble Knight," they say, "You must help us!" Before you have a chance to explain that you aren't a knight, they explain their situation: "An evil dragon has kidnapped our princess! You must rescue her. We're desperate."

You can't refuse to help, so before you know it, you are riding to the dragon's lair. Can you defeat the dragon? Compile the following program and find out. Note that this program is made up of more than one file.

```cpp
//8.5 - Dragon Lord - Mark Lee
// Dragon.cpp
#include <string>
#include <ctime>
#include <cstdlib>

using std::string;

#define MAX(a,b) a>b? a:b

class Dragon
{
private:
        int speed;
        string name;
        int hitPoints;
        int armour;
        int treasure;
        int clawDamage;
        int size;
protected:
        Dragon(int theSize);
        int getArmour() { return armour; }
        int& getHitPoints() { return hitPoints; }
        int getClawDamage() { return clawDamage; }
        int getSize() { return size; }
        virtual int attack(int targetArmour, int specialDamage);
public:
        virtual int attack(int targetArmour) = 0;
```

```
        virtual void defend(int damage) = 0;
        int getTreasure() { return treasure; }
        virtual string getName() { return name; }
        int getSpeed() { return speed; }
        bool isAlive() { return hitPoints >0; }
};


Dragon::Dragon(int theSize) : size(theSize)
{
        if (size < 1 || size > 4)
                size = 3;
        clawDamage = 2 * size;
        speed = 3 * size;
        hitPoints = 4 * size;
        armour = size;
        treasure = 1000 * size;
        srand(time(0));
}


int Dragon::attack(int targetArmour, int specialDamage)
{
        int useSpecial = rand() % 2; // 0 or 1
        int damage;
        if (useSpecial)
                damage = specialDamage;
        else
                damage = getClawDamage();
        return MAX(damage - targetArmour,0);
}



//RedDragon.cpp
#include <string>

using std::string;

class RedDragon : public Dragon
{
```

```cpp
private:
      int fireDamage;
public:
      RedDragon(int theSize);
      int attack(int targetArmour);
      void defend(int damage);
      string getName() { return "Red Dragon"; }
};

RedDragon::RedDragon(int theSize) : Dragon(theSize)
{
      fireDamage = 4 * getSize();
}

int RedDragon::attack(int targetArmour)
{
      return Dragon::attack(targetArmour, fireDamage);
}

void RedDragon::defend(int damage)
{
      getHitPoints() -= (damage - getArmour())/3;
}


//BlueDragon.cpp
#include <string>

using std::string;

class BlueDragon : public Dragon
{
private:
      int iceDamage;
public:
      BlueDragon(int theSize);
      int attack(int targetArmour);
      void defend(int damage);
```

```
        string getName() { return "Blue Dragon"; }
};


BlueDragon::BlueDragon(int theSize) : Dragon(theSize)
{
        iceDamage = 3 * getSize();
}


int BlueDragon::attack(int targetArmour)
{
        return Dragon::attack(targetArmour, iceDamage);
}


void BlueDragon::defend(int damage)
{
        getHitPoints() -= (damage - getArmour())/2;
}



//BlackDragon.cpp
#include <string>

using std::string;

class BlackDragon : public Dragon
{
private:
        int poisonDamage;
public:
        BlackDragon(int theSize);
        int attack(int targetArmour);
        void defend(int damage);
        string getName() { return "Black Dragon"; }
};


BlackDragon::BlackDragon(int theSize) : Dragon(theSize)
{
        poisonDamage = getSize();
```

```cpp
}

int BlackDragon::attack(int targetArmour)
{
    return Dragon::attack(targetArmour, poisonDamage);
}

void BlackDragon::defend(int damage)
{
    getHitPoints() -= damage - getArmour();
}


//DragonLord.cpp
#include <iostream>
#include <ctime>
#include <cstdlib>
#include "Dragon.cpp"
#include "RedDragon.cpp"
#include "BlueDragon.cpp"
#include "BlackDragon.cpp"

int menuChoice();

int main (void)
{
    using std::srand;
    using std::time;
    using std::rand;
    using std::cout;
    srand((unsigned int)time(0));
    Dragon* dragons[3];
    int hp = 15;
    int armour = 2;
    int tempArmour;
    int tempAttack;
    dragons[0] = new RedDragon(rand()%4+1);
    dragons[1] = new BlackDragon(rand()%4+1);
```

```
dragons[2] = new BlueDragon(rand()%4+1);
Dragon* d = dragons[rand()%3];
cout << "Welcome noble knight.\n"
     << "You must save a princess."
     << " She has been captured by a "
     << d->getName() << ".\n"
     << "You must defeat the dragon.\n";
cout << "Your hit points are: " << hp << "\n";
while (d->isAlive() && hp>0)
{
     int choice = menuChoice();
     if (choice == 3)
          goto RUN;
     else if (choice == 1)
     {
          tempAttack = rand()%16+5;
          tempArmour = armour;
     }
     else
     {
          tempAttack = rand()%11;
          tempArmour = armour + 4;
     }

     hp -= d->attack(armour);
     d->defend(rand()%16-5);
     cout << "\nYou deliver a mighty blow and deal " << tempAttack
          << " damage.\n";
     cout << "Your hit points are: " << hp;
}
if (d->isAlive())
     cout << "\nYou have perished before"
          << " the might of the dragon.\n";
else
     cout << "\n\nYou have slain the dragon!"
          << " Congratulations.\n"
          << "The princess is saved.\n";
return 0;
```

```
RUN:
        cout << "\nYou have fled in cowardice.\n";
        return 0;
}


int menuChoice()
{
        using std::cout;
        using std::cin;
        int choice;
        do {
                cout << "\n[1]Attack\n"
                        << "[2]Defensive Mode\n"
                        << "[3]Run Away\n";
                cin >> choice;
        } while (choice < 1 && choice > 3);
        return choice;
}
```

Summary

This chapter has been a whirlwind of new concepts. You have learned about basic inheritance, the protected access modifier, multiple inheritance, virtual functions, and abstract classes. Knowing and being able to use the information in this chapter is crucial to becoming an advanced C++ programmer. If you ever move on to other programming languages, you will find that the concepts in this chapter also apply to most of those languages.

CHALLENGES

1. Create a weapon hierarchy, with at least four weapons being derived from a single parent class. What kind of data members should each contain? What about methods?

2. Design and fully implement an abstract Shape class. What should be included? What should be left to the derived classes?

Using Templates

I f you started at the beginning of this book, you are well on your way to becoming a professional programmer. You have learned the basics of C++ programming, and now you're ready for more advanced concepts. In this chapter, you learn about templates, which will serve as a springboard to the C++ standard library. You study some of the main components of the standard library. If you've ever considered designing libraries for other programmers to use, this chapter is crucial. In this chapter, you learn how to:

- Create class templates
- Create function templates
- Make template use invisible
- Use the standard library
- Use strings
- Use vectors

Creating Templates

Imagine that you are a renowned weapon maker, famous across the land for your excellent weapons. A king has come to you and asked for a bow that can shoot any kind of arrow. Foolishly, you agree to make such a bow, not realizing that the task is impossible. How can any one bow shoot every kind of arrow? Unfortunately, the bow is due tomorrow. But while studying some ancient texts on weapon making, you come across a magic spell called the "Template." "Cast this spell on a weapon," the book notes, "and the weapon will become completely versatile, able to handle any kind of ammo." You're saved! You will be able to finish the bow easily by tomorrow.

In C++, templates enable you to generalize a class or function so that it doesn't use a particular data type, and just as you might use the magic "Template" in our (newly coined) fable to create a bow that will handle all kinds of arrows, you can use templates in C++ to create a function or class that can handle all kinds of data types.

For example, each version of the add function we discussed in Chapter 4, "Writing Functions," is specific to a certain kind of data (two integers, two floating-points, and so on). With templates, however, you can create a single version that covers every C++ data type (and even user-defined data types, such as classes). Sound powerful? It is.

The theory is that when you use templates, you are performing essentially the same operation on the data no matter what data type you are working with. As a result, there's no particular reason why you can't program this operation only once. In this way, templates enable you to generalize an operation to avoid redundant programming.

Now, let us share with you the basics of programming with templates.

CREATING CLASS TEMPLATES

A class template is a class that utilizes a template in order to make the class more general. Well, that doesn't provide very much enlightenment, does it?

First, take a look at this Storage class, which stores an array of integers (without using a template):

```
class Storage
{
    int* data;
    int numElements;
public:
    Storage();
    Storage(int* array, int num) :
        data(array), numElements(num) {}
    Storage(int num) { data = new int[num]; }
    void AddElement(int newElement);
    int ElementAt(int location);
```

```
    int RemoveElementAt(int location);
    ~Storage();
};
```

This class stores an array of integers and provides methods to add, view, and remove the elements. But what would you do if you wanted to store floats or characters? You'd have to copy the preceding code and change the integers to floats or characters, which would be inefficient. Or you might somehow pass the data type that you want to store as a parameter. Then you might have a switch statement to handle each case. This would quickly become complicated and unmanageable.

The best solution to this problem is to use templates. A template version of the Storage class can store any kind of data. Templates are a simple way to pass the data type as a parameter without the methods becoming complicated and unmanageable. Here is how the Storage class looks when you use a template:

```
template<class T> class Storage
{
    T* data;
    int numElements;
public:
    Storage();
    Storage(T* array, int num) :
        data(array), numElements(num) {}
    Storage(int num) { data = new int[num]; }
    void AddElement(T newElement);
    T ElementAt(int location);
    T RemoveElementAt(int location);
    ~Storage();
};
```

As you can see, this code is fairly different. It might look a little unfamiliar to you at the moment, but soon it will become more familiar. The only thing that has changed is the replacement of int with T (but not all instances of int) and the addition of template<class T> immediately before the class.

The uses of T are easy to explain. They act as a placeholder for whichever kind of data the user of the class decides to store. So, if the user decides to store integers, all instances of T will be ints. Some uses of int remain because they aren't all part of the data. Some of them are just for the number of elements (which should always be an integer value).

The code `template<class T>` tells the computer that this class is using a template and that T is being used as a placeholder for the data type being stored. Even though you write `class T`, T doesn't have to be a class. It can be any data type.

Another way to think about a template is as an argument list. The preceding example has one argument, `class T`. When the `Storage` class is used, the user passes the type of data to store "almost" as an argument. Then T is filled with this data type. As you can see, `class T` is much like an argument declaration. Here, the keyword `class` is used in a different way to mean "data type." For this reason, you can use the keyword `typename` rather than `class` if you want (it has the exact same meaning here).

After you declare T in the first line, you can use it anywhere within the class just like any other type name (such as `int` or `float`). This means that you can declare new variables and make pointers, arrays, or anything else for which you might use a type name.

When you create an object from this class template, you must specify which type of data you are going to store. Here is an example for storing integers:

```
Storage<int> intStore;
```

As you can see, specifying the type of data for a template is much like passing an argument. When `intStore` is created, `int` takes the place of all the `T`s in the class. You can use `Storage<int>` just like you use the name of any other class. In the same way, you can store any other kind of data:

```
Storage<float> floatStore; //stores floats
Storage<string> stringStore; //stores strings
Storage<Shape*> shapeStore; //stores pointers to Shapes
```

Take a look at the syntax for creating a class template:

```
template<class TypeName> class ClassName
{
        ClassDeclaration
};
```

Here *TypeName* is an arbitrary placeholder for a data type, *ClassName* is the name of the class, and *ClassDeclaration* is the declaration of the class (just like normal classes from Chapter 5, "Fighting with OOP"). Keep in mind that *TypeName* can be any valid identifier, but it is usually a single capital letter, such as T or C.

If a method is implemented outside the class template, you must use the template syntax again for it. Here is the syntax for methods that are implemented outside of the class template:

```
template<class TypeName> returnType ClassName<TypeName>::methodName(args)
{
        methodImplementation
}
```

Here *TypeName* is the name of the parameter (such as T), and *methodImplementation* is the implementation of the method.

Because the constructor implementation uses the name of the class twice (once for the class name and once for the method name), you would normally have to put ‹*TypeName*› after each use of the class name. However, this is a bit redundant, so for the name of the method, you don't have to (but you can if you like). Here is the syntax for a constructor implemented outside of a class template:

```
template<TypeName> ClassName<TypeName>::ClassName<TypeName>(args)
{
        constructorImplementation
}
```

Or you could use this, more common, syntax:

```
template<TypeName> ClassName<TypeName>::ClassName(args)
{
        constructorImplementation
}
```

Both ways are exactly the same. It is a matter of personal preference. The first way is more formal, but the second way is more common.

 If you are making a class template, we suggest first designing the class for a specific data type. Then you can work out all the bugs and design flaws before you generalize with a template. This approach makes programming much easier.

USING TEMPLATE PARAMETERS

The declaration inside the angle brackets (for example ‹class T›) is a template parameter. As you have seen, the template parameter behaves almost the same way that a function argument does. As with function arguments, you can have more than one template parameter. In fact, you can have as many as you want.

One example of where multiple template parameters are useful is when you are creating an associative array. An associative array is like a normal array, except that two different objects are at each element. One of the two might be a string, and the other might be an integer representing the number of occurrences of the string in a section of text. Think of associative arrays as side-by-side arrays with the same number of elements. Here is how an associative array class might look:

```
template<class T, class C> class AssociativeArray;
AssociativeArray<string, int> wordFrequency;
```

In addition, a template parameter does not have to be a general type. It can be something specific, such as an integer or a floating-point. Here is an example of using a specific data type in a template parameter:

```
template<class T, int i> class Array
{
    T data[i];
    //...
};
```

You can then use this class template as follows:

```
Array<int, 10> intArray;
```

This code snippet creates an array of ten integers. Notice how the array is created with the size given from the template parameter? Doing this might be confusing. You can't create dynamic sized arrays from function arguments because an array must be declared with a constant size (except an array on the free store). A function argument does not have to be constant; however, a template parameter does. A template parameter can be a constant or a pointer. Also, a template parameter used within a class must be treated as a constant (you can't change its value).

Here is an example to illustrate these concepts:

```
int i = 10;

//error - non-constant value used for template parameter
Array<int, i> intArray;

//ok - constant value used
Array<int, 10> intArray;
```

The compiler has to know the size of all arrays created before the program actually runs. If you provide a constant expression, such as 20 - 10, the compiler will be able to evaluate the expression, so it is acceptable to use constant expressions.

However, the compiler can check only syntax errors when a template is compiled. That is, the compiler can check whether a particular type works in the template code only when you use that template with a particular data type. The point in time in which you use a template with a specific type is called the point of instantiation.

Say that you design a class template and, accidentally assuming that the type will always be a string, you use the function c_str(). In doing so, you might wind up with a problem. If an object is created with string as the type, no errors will occur. However, if the data type is not a string, problems will occur. Though assumptions of this nature do not always present a problem, they often do, so be on the lookout for them. If you design a class template that works for only certain types, make this condition very clear to the user.

CREATING FUNCTION TEMPLATES

Functions can also use templates similarly to the way classes use them. A good example is a function such as the add function covered in Chapter 4. Admittedly, add is a trivial function (because it adds only two numbers), but we can easily expand the concept of functions like this to something more complex.

As you do with class templates, you create a function template by putting the keyword template and the parameter list at the beginning of the function. Function templates are similar to overloaded functions, except that you can create one function template to handle every case rather than a different function for each case. Here is how the add function might look with a template:

```
template<class T> T add (T a, T b)
{
    return a + b;
}
```

Unfortunately, this add function is not universal. You cannot provide arguments of two different types. In the section, "Overloading Function Templates," later in this chapter, you learn ways to provide almost any argument and get the desired results.

You can use the template parameters as you do with all other data types anywhere within the function. Here is an example:

```
template<class T> void swap(T* a, T* b)
{
    T temp = *a;
    *a = *b;
    *b = temp;
}
```

This function exchanges the values of two pointers. Here is an example of how you might use this function:

```
int x = 5;
int y = 6;
swap<int>(&x, &y);
```

x now contains the value 6, and y contains the value 5. <algorithm> includes a standard library version of this function called swap, which takes two of the same type argument (regardless of which type, because the standard library swap is a function template).

UNDERSTANDING ARGUMENT RESOLUTION

Function templates are not quite the same as class templates. With function templates, you do not always have to provide a template parameter when you call the function. Sometimes, the computer can figure out what the parameters are supposed to be simply from the arguments you pass. Here is an example:

```
add(5,3);
```

Don't be fooled, brave reader; this is not the add function from Chapter 4. The version with the template is being called here. Because the arguments are both integers, the computer can deduce that the parameter (T) is supposed to be int. Now, you're venturing into the land of true programming; however, for now, you don't even have to know that the add function has a template. You simply call it like any other function.

If the arguments for the preceding function were not so clear (for example, if one were an integer and the other a floating-point), the compiler would return an error. Computers have a limited intelligence, and they can't quite decide whether the integer should be converted to a floating-point or the floating-point should be converted to an integer. If you choose not to provide parameters for function template calls, be sure that the arguments clearly designate what the parameters are supposed to be.

Also, if all the parameters are not contained in the argument list (for example, one parameter is used only for a return type), you must provide a full parameter list for the function call.

Now, as a case study, you are ready to create a function to typecast for you. (In Chapter 2, we define typecasting as the act of converting data from one type to another, retaining almost the same value.)

This function is an example of where one of the parameters is not used in the argument list, as shown here:

```
template<class C, class T> C cast(T a)
{
     return (C)a;
}
```

This function works only if a normal cast will work for the argument. Here are some examples of how you might use this function:

```
cout << cast<int, float>(3.5); //converts 3.5 to 3
cout << cast<float, int>(9); //converts 9 to 9.0

//error - cannot cast an int to a char*
cout << cast<char*, int>(35769);
```

In cases like these, you can assume from the function argument what the second template parameter is. However, as with default function arguments, you can leave out a template parameter only at the end of the parameter list. For example, if there are three parameters, you leave out the last one, the last two, or all three, provided that they can be assumed. Here is an example of how you can leave out parameters:

```
//converts 3 to 3.0 - second parameter deduced to be int
cout << cast<float>(3);

//converts 3.5 to 3 - second parameter assumed to be float
cout << cast<int>(3.5);

//error - what to cast it to?
cout << cast(35);
```

SPECIALIZING TEMPLATES

Sometimes, you might want a function template to work in a specialized way for a particular kind of data. One data type might be an exception to the rule that all other types follow. In this case, you must provide a different version of the template for that particular type. This different version is called a specialization. You use it whenever the data type in question is used.

In the section "Using Vectors," later in this chapter, you study vectors. A vector is a class template. Here is the basic declaration for the vector class template:

```
template<class T> class Vector;
```

This declaration seems pretty simple. It's just a normal class template. However, the `vector` class template has a specialization as well as this more general declaration. A vector must treat an array of void pointers differently in some way. Here is the declaration for the `Vector` class's specialization:

```
template<> class Vector<void*>;
```

The preceding code essentially denotes a specialization of `Vector` to be used whenever `void*` is used as the parameter type. That is, when you use `void*` as a parameter, the specialization is used. The specialization basically takes over. If you use any other type, the first version will be used. Here is an example of using specializations:

```
#include <iostream>
#include <string>

template<class T>class SayHi
{
     T data;
public:
     SayHi(T a) : data(a) {}
     void display() { cout << data << endl; }
};

template<> class SayHi<string>
{
     string data;
public:
     SayHi(string a) : data(a) {}
     void display() { cout << data.c_str() << endl; }
};

int main (void)
{
     SayHi<int> hi(5);
     hi.display();
     SayHi<string> hs("Hello World");
     hs.display();
     return 0;
}
Output:
5
Hello World
```

You can specialize a function template in the same way. Here is the syntax for this:

```
template<> returnType functionName<specialType>(args)
{…}
```

Here *specialType* is the type for which you are specializing.

SIMPLIFYING TEMPLATE USE

Templates can become annoying to users of your classes and functions. Fortunately, you can hide the fact that templates are used.

The first and easiest way is to use typedef. Because you can use ClassName <parameters> just as you use the name of a normal class, you can typedef the name of a class template to something shorter. For example, rather than use Vector<int>, use IntVec. Then, when users want a vector of integers, they can use IntVec. Users do not have to be aware that IntVec is part of a template. Here is how you might accomplish this renaming:

```
typedef Vector<int> IntVec;
```

An example of where typedef is used like this is in the standard library string class. The actual name of the class template for a string is basic_string. This class template takes one template parameter: the type of character being stored. Here is the typedef for this class:

```
typedef basic_string<char> string;
```

Isn't that interesting? This means that you can use basic_string<char> rather than string if you want to (if you want useless inconvenience).

A second common method of simplifying template usage is with default template parameters. As with function arguments, template parameters can have default values. The format is exactly the same:

```
template<class A, class B = int, class C = float> class ABC;
```

In this example, B and C default to int and float, respectively, if no type is passed when an object is created. Here are some ways to use this class template:

```
//A is int, B is int, C is float
ABC<int> a1;

//A is int, B is string, C is char
ABC<int, string, char> a2;

//A is double, B is double, C is float
ABC<double, double> a3;
```

You must place all default template parameters at the end of the list (as you have to with function arguments).

In the section "Understanding Argument Resolution," earlier in this chapter, we talked about the third way to make function templates less complicated.

If no parameters are provided with the function call, the computer can sometimes deduce what they should be. In this way, you can make a function template seem like a normal function.

The fourth way applies just to function templates and is discussed in the following section.

OVERLOADING FUNCTION TEMPLATES

Function templates can be overloaded, just like normal functions can. In fact, you can create many versions of a function with the same name, some being function templates and some being just normal functions.

Wait a minute! If everything we've said about templates is true (that they make a function general for every kind of data type), why would you ever need to overload a function template? Surprisingly, there are some reasons for doing so. One of the main reasons is to make a function template behave exactly like a normal function. You can write overloaded versions of a function template that handle cases where template parameters would otherwise have to be called. This ensures that the correct version is always called.

Say that you add two integers together and you want to return a floating-point (just because). Here is the new complete add function:

```
template<class T> T add (T a, T b)
{
      return a + b;
}


float add (int a, int b)
{
      return (float) a+b;
}
```

Now, if you call the add function with two integers, the overloaded version (the second one) will be called. For every other data type, the second version is ignored. But how does the computer decide which version to call? The computer follows specific rules to decide. For every function call to an overloaded function template, the computer must follow these steps:

1. Find all the versions of the function that could possibly apply to the arguments. For a call of add(5,3), this rule leaves both versions as possibilities. For a call of add(75, 'a'), this rule leaves no possibilities (because both versions take two of the same data type).
2. If one function template is a specialization of another, choose the specialization.
3. Apply the normal overload rules for functions to everything that is left.
4. If a function and a function template are left, choose the function. For a call of add(5,3), both the function and the function template were candidates until this step. The function is chosen.
5. If no possibilities remain, the call was an error. If two or more possibilities remain, the call was ambiguous and is an error.

Earlier, we said that if the parameters are not clear from the argument list, you must provide parameters when you call the function—for example, if you call the add function with an integer and a floating-point. Fortunately, there are some ways around having to provide parameters. One is to provide overloaded versions of the add function that call the function template with the parameters. This way, the user does not have to worry about the function template parameters. Here is an example of how you can overload the add function:

```
inline float add(int a, float b) { return add<float>(a,b);}
inline float add(float a, int b) { return add<float>(a.b); }
```

Now, if you call the add function with an integer and a floating-point and you don't provide a parameter, the computer will be able to figure out what to do. Notice how the preceding functions are declared inline. This is so that no extra memory is taken up for the convenience of not having to provide a parameter. You are telling the computer that when you add an integer and a floating-point, you want a floating-point to be returned. Here are some examples of using this new version of the add function:

```
cout << add(3.5, 7); //displays 10.5
cout << add(7, 3.5); //displays 10.5
```

Do not be overwhelmed by function template overloading. It really is just like normal overloading, except that you must apply a few more rules. If you are ever in doubt, just consult the list of rules.

USING THE STANDARD LIBRARY

The C++ standard library was designed to be useful for almost every C++ user. Because of this, it must be as general as possible. For example, if the standard library vector were designed for a specific data type, then its usefulness would be severely limited.

When the designers of the C++ language were creating the standard library, they set these requirements:

- It must be convenient, efficient, useful, and safe for all users.
- Users should not have to reprogram the library in order to find it useful.
- The library must provide a simple interface.
- The library must be complete in what it tries to do.
- The library must blend well with built-in data types and keywords.

Knowing these requirements, the designers then constructed the library. In our opinion, they succeeded in meeting every one of the requirements.

The standard library is organized into a set of header files, each serving a different purpose. They can be divided into ten categories: containers, general utilities, iterators, algorithms, diagnostics, strings, streams, locales, language support, and numerics.

In this section, we discuss a few of the containers and the string that has been used since Chapter 1, "Starting the Journey." Containers are types that store a set of values. Strings (as you know) store text.

Because templates are used specifically to make code more general, the standard library is a rich source for examples of how you can use templates.

Using Strings

All the C++ standard string facilities are included in `<string>`. As we mentioned previously in this chapter, `string` is a synonym for `basic_string<char>`. `basic_string` is a class template that can accept any kind of character. For example, you might create a class to store Egyptian characters called `E_char`. Then you can create a string object using Egyptian characters like this:

```
basic_string<E_char> egyptian;
```

All characters that are used as a parameter for `basic_string` must have their properties defined by another class template called `char_traits`. The basic declaration of `char_traits` is as follows:

```
template<class Ch> struct char_traits{};
```

A `struct` is exactly like a class, except that all its members are public by default rather than private. Strangely enough, this template class is never used. Every kind of character has a specialization for this template, including this example:

```
template<> struct char_traits<char>;
```

This code is the specialization for the char character type. This char_traits class template stores the properties of a particular character type. Take a look at a simplified version of the implementation of char_traits<char>:

```
template<> struct char_traits<char>
{
    typedef char char_type; //call it by a standard name

    //standard name for the integer representation
    typedef int int_type;

    //copy the second argument into the first
    static void assign(char_type& a, const char_type& b);

    //convert int to char
    static char_type to_char_type(const int_type& a);

    //convert char to int
    static int_type to_int_type(const char_type& a);

    //are the two ints the same character?
    static bool eq_int_type(const int_type& i, const int_type& j);
    //are the two chars equal?
    static bool eq(const char_type& a, const char_type& b);
    //is the first char less than the second?
    static bool lt(const char_type& a, const char_type& b);

    //move n copies of s2 into s
    static char_type* move(char_type* s, const char_type* s2, size_t n);

    //move n copies of s2 into s
    static char_type* copy(char_type* s, const char_type* s2, size_t n);

    //copy n copies of a into s
    static char_type* assign(char_type* s, size_t n, char_type a);
```

```
//compares 2 characters
static int compare(const char_type* s, const char_type* s2, size_t n);

//returns the length of the character array
static size_t length(const char_type* c);
//find c in s
static const char_type* find(const char_type* s, int n, const char_type&
c);
};
```

You've had your first glimpse at libraries. At first, they can seem unreadable, but with practice, you will become used to them. The main annoyance is that most libraries use variable names such as _E, making it hard to remember what they do. The libraries use names like this to make sure that their names don't conflict with any other names.

As you can see, `char_traits<char>` defines the basic operations when using a char or char array.

The first few lines of code you see in this definition are two `typedef`s. They give standard names to the character type and integer type so that the string class can refer to `char_traits::char_type` or `char_traits::int_type` regardless of which kind of character is used.

Because you haven't seen `size_t` before, you might be wondering what it is. You can think of it as an unsigned integer.

Implementing the methods in this class template is fairly straightforward. For example, here is the implementation for the first version of `assign`:

```
template<> void char_traits<char>::assign(char_type& a, char_type& b)
{
    a = b;
}
```

Every character type that is used as a `basic_string` must define a specialization of `char_traits` and must implement all these functions. This guarantees that the `basic_string` class will be able to perform these operations on any character.

The second most common character type is the wide character (`wchar_t`). It is similar to a normal character, except that it takes up 2 bytes (to allow more characters in the character set).

Here is the declaration for the `basic_string` class template:

```
template<class C, class T = char_traits<C>, class A = allocator<C>> class
std::basic_string;
```

As you can see, the class is part of the `std` namespace (as everything in the standard library is), and the template takes three parameters. Two of these parameters are default parameters, so you have to provide a minimum of only one. `C` is the type of character, `T` is the `char_traits` associated with that character, and `A` is a type called an allocator that deals with allocating memory for the character. By default, `T` and `A` are the specializations of their respective classes for the character type. You should leave them alone in almost all cases.

Just as the `char_traits` class defines standard names for things with `typedef`, so does the `basic_string` class. Here is the list of these `typedef`s:

```
//type of char_traits used (char_traits<char> usually)
typedef T traits_type;
//type of memory manager (allocator<char> usually)
typedef typename A allocator_type;
//kind of character being stored (char usually)
typedef typename T::char_type value_type;
//some kind of unsigned type (unsigned int maybe)
typedef typename A::size_type size_type;
//reference to individual character (char& usually)
typedef typename A::reference reference;
//pointer to individual character (char* usually)
typedef typename A::pointer pointer;
//the type used for a standard iterator
typedef compiler_dependant iterator;
//the type used for a reverse iterator
typedef std::reverse_iterator<iterator> reverse_iterator;
//used to represent every character of a string
static const size_type npos;
```

You must use `typename` at the beginning of a template parameter when you use the parameter to access things inside it. For example, to define `value_type`, you need to access `char_type` from inside the `char_traits` class. `compiler_dependant` indicates that the code placed there is based on which compiler you are using. The code is different for every compiler, but regardless of what it is, it will indicate some type of standard iterator. `npos` represents "all characters." That is, whenever you need to supply the number of characters to use for an operation, you can use `npos` to mean all of them (from whatever point to the end). Keep in mind that this doesn't necessarily mean the whole string. The most accurate meaning is "all the string."

Constructing a String

The standard library provides many ways to construct a string object. You can use another string object, a character array, a string literal, an empty constructor, and more. We cover these constructors one by one. The first is when you want to construct one string from another:

```
//construct a string from another whole or partial string
basic_string(const basic_string& s, size_type pos = 0,
            size_type n = npos, const A& a = A() );
```

The first argument is simply another string. You can use any kind of `basic_string` here. The second argument is the position (treating the string as a character array) from which to start taking values. The third argument is the number of characters to take. This argument defaults to `npos`, which loosely correlates to the largest possible value of a string. This means "go to the end of s." `pos = 0` means "start at the beginning" and `n = npos` means "take every character." The fourth argument relates to the way memory is allocated for this string. Although we don't cover the fourth argument here because it is too complicated for a beginner, here are some examples of how you might use this constructor:

```
string s = "Hello World:"; //declare a string to work with
string s1(s); //s1 and s both contain the value "Hello World"

//start at position 6, take two chars - s2 contains "Wo"
string s2(s, 6, 2);
string s3(s, 6); //error - need third argument too
```

The last call to the constructor fails because the computer mixes it up with the second constructor (explained next). The second and third constructors create a string from a character array, as shown here:

```
basic_string(const C* p, size_type n, const A& a = A());
basic_string(const C* p, const A& a = A());
```

The first argument, `p`, is the character array. `n` is the number of characters to use, and `a` has to do with the way the string is allocated (just let it have its default value, unless you feel like learning about allocators). If you don't supply `n`, the whole C-style string is used to construct the string. Here are some examples of how you might use these constructors:

```
char* p = "Hello World";
string s1(p); //s1 contains "Hello World"
string s2(p, 5); //s2 contains "Hello"
string s3(p+6, 5); //s3 contains "World"
```

The last constructor creates a string from a sequence of characters. You pass the sequence of characters with an iterator. You learn about iterators in detail in the next section, but here are the basics. For a container or a string, you can call the methods `begin()` and `end()` to get pointers to the first and last elements stored in the container or string. You can use these two values to copy the entire set of characters into the new string. Here is the constructor:

```
//uses all of the characters from first to last template<class I>
basic_string(I first, I last, const A& a = A());
```

Here are some ways that you can use this constructor:

```
string s = "Hello World";
char* c = "Hello World";
string s1(s.begin(), s.end()); //s1 contains "Hello World"
string s2(c, c+5); //s2 contains "Hello"
string s3(c+6, c+11); //s3 contains "World"
```

You can use any two pointers to characters in a sequence for this constructor. Every element between them will be used. Take care to make sure that the first argument comes before (in memory) the second and that every value between them is actually a character.

As well as constructors, the `basic_string` class has a destructor to do the cleanup that is required:

```
~basic_string();
```

ITERATING THROUGH A STRING

Iterators are common to all containers and strings. Iterators enable you to navigate through the values stored in a container or string. All iterators provide a similar interface, which is one of the main strengths of the standard library. If you learn about the interface for one container, you can easily use any container. For a `basic_string`, the individual characters in the string are the values navigated through by the iterator. All the code for these iterators is included with `<iterator>`.

Some containers (for this discussion, a string is being treated as a container of characters) can provide certain operations efficiently and some cannot. For example, a list cannot access any particular value that it stores at any given time. In other words, a list does not have random access. A vector, on the other hand, does. There are five categories of iterators, dependant on the kind of access operations that are available. They are input, output, forward, bi-directional, and random access.

Input can only read values from the elements and navigate forward through the container (input from the container to you). Output can only write values to the elements and navigate forward through the container (output from you to the container). Forward can read, write, and navigate forward through the container. Bi-directional can read, write, and navigate forward and backward. Random access can read, write, and navigate to any element at random.

The operations available to each type of iterator are summarized in Table 8.1.

TABLE 8.1 ITERATOR OPERATIONS					
Operation Type	**Out**	**In**	**Forward**	**Bi**	**Rand**
Forward Iteration (++)	Yes	Yes	Yes	Yes	Yes
Backward Iteration (--)	No	No	No	Yes	Yes
Random Access ([ ], +=, -=, +, -)	No	No	No	No	Yes
Read (*Iterator)	No	Yes	Yes	Yes	Yes
Write (*Iterator =)	Yes	No	Yes	Yes	Yes
Member Access (->)	No	Yes	Yes	Yes	Yes
Comparison (==, !=)	No	Yes	Yes	Yes	Yes
More Comparison (<, >, <=, >=)	No	No	No	No	Yes

As you can see from the operations in Table 8.1, iterators are similar to pointers to arrays. In fact, a pointer to an array is an iterator for the array. All iterators provide operators that match those of pointers. To the untrained eye, an iterator can appear to be a pointer because it is used exactly like one.

The categories of iterators form a hierarchy:

```
struct input_iterator_tag {};
struct output_iterator_tag {};
struct forward_iterator_tag : public input_iterator_tag {};
struct bidirectional_iterator_tag : public forward_iterator_tag {};
struct random_access_iterator_tag : public bidirectional_iterator_tag {};
```

This hierarchy matches the capabilities of each type. For example, a random access iterator can function as an input iterator, but not vice versa. Output iterators are left out of the hierarchy because they don't quite fit with the rest. If one were included, it would become a second base class to forward_iterator_tag, but that does not create any significant advantages, so it's not.

Now, you are ready for the basic iterator class. After a few minutes of study, it will seem fairly simple, so here it is:

```
template <class C, class T, class Dist = ptrdiff_t,
     class Ptr = T*, class Ref = T&> struct iterator
{
     //a class from the hierarchy above
     typedef C iterator_category;
     //the type of element being iterated upon
     typedef T value_type;
     //type of distance between two elements
     typedef Dist difference_type;
     typedef Ptr pointer; //pointer to element type
     tyepdef Ref reference; //reference to element type
};
```

Here C is the kind of iterator (indicated by a type from the preceding hierarchy), T is the type of element, Dist is the type used to measure the distance between elements, Ptr is the type used as a pointer to an element, and Ref is the type used as a reference to an element. ptrdiff_t is defined to be the standard distance between two pointers. As you can see, all that this class does is define names, because it is just a base class from which each container can derive its own version. You use this class to define all these types to meet your requirements, whatever they are.

Just as each character class has a char_traits associated with it, each iterator has an iterator_traits associated with it. Here is the iterator_traits template class:

```
template<class Iter> struct iterator_traits
{
     typedef typename Iter::iterator_category iterator_category;
     typedef typename Iter::value_type value_type;
     typedef typename Iter::difference_type difference_type;
     typedef typename Iter::pointer pointer;
     typedef typename Iter::reference reference;
};
```

When a programmer designs an algorithm that uses iterators, she can use iterator_traits<Iter>::iterator_category to design different behavior for each different iterator type. That way, the user of the code does not have to be aware of iterators. The most appropriate version of the code is automatically used. It is one more powerful way to make the implementation invisible to the user.

All strings and containers provide standard methods to generate an iterator of their elements. Here are the iterator methods for the `basic_string` class:

```
//generates an iterator that points at the first element
iterator begin();
//iterator that points at one past the last element
iterator end();
```

Often, both these methods are required if you are using the iterator as a sequence of characters. For example, the string constructor that takes an input sequence can use the results of these two methods to produce a string:

```
string s = "Hello World";
string s1(s.begin(), s.end()); //s1 now contains "Hello World"
```

Sometimes, you might want to iterate through a container in reverse order. A class template, called `reverse_iterator`, accomplishes this feat. This class template is derived from the iterator class. Here is the `reverse_iterator` class template:

```
template<class Iter> class reverse_iterator : public
        iterator<iterator_traits<Iter>::iterator_category,
            iterator_traits<Iter>::value_type,
            iterator_traits<Iter>::difference_type,
            iterator_traits<Iter>::pointer,
            iterator_traits<Iter>::reference>
{
protected:

        //used to internally iterate backwards with a normal iterator
        Iter current;

public:
        //give the iterator type a standard name
        typedef Iter iterator_type;

        //default constructor
        reverse_iterator() : current() {}

        //constructor from a normal iterator
        reverse_iterator(Iter x) : current(x) {}
```

```
//construct from another reverse_iterator
template<class U> reverse_iterator(const reverse_iterator<U>& x) :
       current(x.base()) {}



//return the normal iterator that this class uses
Iter base() const { return current; }

//dereferencing
reference operator* () const
{
       Iter tmp = current;
       return *--tmp;
}

pointer operator-> () const;

//access member operator
reference operator[] (difference_type n) const;

//go backwards (reverse)
reverse_iterator& operator++ ()
{
       --current;
       return *this;
}

reverse_iterator operator++ (int)
{
       reverse_iterator t = current;
       --current;
       return t;
}

//go forwards (reverse)
reverse_iterator& operator-- ()
{
       ++current;
```

```
        return *this;
}


reverse_iterator operator-- (int)
{
        reverse_iterator t = current;
        ++current;
        return t;
}


reverse_iterator operator+ (difference_type n) const;
reverse_iterator operator+= (difference_type n);
reverse_iterator operator- (difference_type n) const;
reverse_iterator operator -= (difference_type n);
};
```

The reverse_iterator contains an iterator, called current, that reverse_iterator uses to iterate. reverse_iterator increments and decrements this iterator internally and uses its value whenever the user requests a value. The meaning of the ++ operator for an iterator is "go to the next element." However, a reverse_iterator goes through the elements backward, so a ++ on a reverse_iterator is equivalent to a -- on a normal iterator (both move the same direction in the container). This is why current is decremented in the implementation of the ++ operator function.

Normally, when an iterator reaches the end of a container, the iterator is pointing to one past the last element of the container. However, because a reverse_iterator moves backward, the end will be when the iterator points to 1 before the first value. This is an illegal value to access and might cause problems. To avoid this complication, current points to one element after whatever the iterator points to. In other words, when the iterator is at the end, current will point to the first element of the container. This design is much safer than pointing to 1 before the first element.

A reverse_iterator, like all iterators, supports operators that make it behave exactly like a pointer.

To create a reverse iterator from a container or string, you use the rbegin() and rend() methods. Here they are for the basic_string class:

```
//reverse iterator starting at end of string and moving backwards
reverse_iterator rbegin();
```

```
//reverse iterator starting at the beginning of the string
reverse_iterator rend();
```

Here are some examples of how you might use a `reverse_iterator`:

```
string s = "Hello World";
cout << *s.rbegin(); //"d" is displayed
cout << *++s.rbegin(); //"l" is displayed
cout << s.rbegin()[4]; //"W" is displayed
```

ACCESSING STRINGS

The standard library provides numerous ways to access the data contained in a string. In this section, we go through each of them to give you a thorough understanding of the `basic_string` class.

Because a `basic_string` is really just an advanced character array, it stands to reason that you should be able to access a `basic_string` like an array, and, fortunately, you can. You can access individual elements of an array two ways: with the subscripting operator (`[]`) or with the `at()` method. Here are the declarations for both:

```
reference operator[] (size_type n);
reference at(size_type n);
```

`n` is the index indicating the position in the string for both these methods (starting at 0, just like an array). The difference between the two is that the `at()` method checks to make sure that the index is within the string (an error occurs if it's not). The subscripting operator does not. It assumes that a character is stored there and accesses the position in memory. Here are some examples of how you might use these methods:

```
string s = "Asus Motherboards Rule!!";
cout << s[3]; //the fourth character - 's'
cout << s.at(2); //the 3rd character - 'u'
```

As you can see, these methods are straightforward and easy to use.

Another common way to access a string is to convert it to a C-style string. In Chapter 1, you learned about one of the methods, `c_str()`, for doing this. There are also two others, `data()` and `copy()`. Here are the declarations for all three:

```
const C* c_str() const;
const C* data() const;
size_type copy(C* p, size_type n, size_type pos = 0) const;
```

The `data()` method returns a pointer to a constant array of characters. The string maintains ownership of the array, so you cannot change it in any way. It is just for viewing purposes. The `c_str()` method does the same thing, except that it adds a null character at the end of the array (making the array a proper C-style string). You use the `copy()` method to copy the elements into an array so that you can then manipulate them. This method copies n elements into array p, starting with element pos. The number of elements copied is returned. Here are some examples of how you might use these methods:

```
string s = "SyncMaster 3";
char array[15];
s.copy(array, 4, 7); //array now contains "ster"
array[4] = 0; //now it is a proper c-style string
cout << s.c_str(); //an old favorite
const char* p = s.data();
p[4] = 'a'; //error, can't manipulate the array
```

These functions have limited use, unless you are using the functions for C-style strings.

One way to obtain information about a string is to compare it to another string. A `basic_string` can be compared to another `basic_string` and to character arrays (of the same character type). You use the method `compare()` to compare two strings. It is overloaded to provide many possibilities:

```
int compare(const basic_string& s) const;
int compare(const C* p) const;
int compare(size_type pos, size_type n, const basic_string& s) const;
int compare(size_type pos, size_type n, const basic_string& s, size_type pos2,
size_type n2 = npos) const;
```

Every version of the `compare()` method returns an integer. This integer is 0 if the things being compared are equal (as defined by `char_trait<C>::compare()`), negative if the first is less than the second, and positive if the first is greater than the second. The idea of one string being greater than another might seem strange, but it is the integer values of the characters that are actually compared (so a is less than b).

The first two versions are pretty clear-cut. Simply provide a string or a character array, and the `compare()` method will compare them. However, sometimes you want to compare only parts of a string. This is where the last two versions come in. pos is the position from which you start comparing, and n is the number of characters to compare. In the third version, part of a string is being compared to all of s. In the fourth, only parts of both strings are being compared. Here are some examples:

```
string s1 = "Get the Fish";
string s2 = "Getting Started";
char array[] = "5-Port Starter Kit";
cout << s1.compare(s2); //-1 is displayed
cout << s2.compare(array); //1 is displayed
cout << s1.compare(0,3,s2); //-1 is displayed
cout << s1.compare(0.3.s2.0,3); //0 is displayed
```

These methods are very important if you ever want to sort a set of strings (for example, to put a list of names in alphabetical order).

The standard library also provides functions for the standard comparison operators (==, !=, <, >, <=, and >=). These are declared outside the basic_string class. Here are a few of the declarations:

```
template<class C, class T, class A>
bool operator==(const basic_string<C,T,A>&, const basic_string<C,T,A>&);

template<class C, class T, class A>
bool operator==(const C*, const basic_string<C,T,A>&);

template<class C, class T, class A>
bool operator==(const basic_string<C,T,A>&, const C*);
```

From these functions, you can test the equality of two strings or of a string and a character array. Here is an example of testing a string and a character array:

```
string continent = "Europe";
if (continent == "Europe") //true
     cout << "The continent is Europe!";
```

Don't worry too much about how the computer decides whether two strings are equal. Basically, if they hold an equal set of characters, they are equal.

At times, you will need to search for a particular sequence of characters (a substring) within a string. The basic_string class provides 24 different ways to do this. The first is the find() method. It searches from a particular point in a string and returns the position (the index) if it finds the sequence. If it does not, it returns npos (which represents an illegal index). The sequence that you are looking for can be a string, a character array, or a single character. Here are the declarations for all the versions of the find() method:

```
size_type find(const basic_string& s, size_type i = 0) const;
size_type find(const C* p, size_type i, size_type n) const;
size_type find(const C* p, size_type i = 0) const;
size_type find(C c, size_type i = 0) const;
```

Here i is the position to start searching from, and n is the number of characters from the character array to search for. Here are some examples:

```
string s = "The basic_string class is extremely versatile.";
string s1 = "basic_string";

//displays 4
cout << s.find(s1);

//displays 4294967295 - indicating that the string wasn't found
cout << s.find(s1, 5);

//displays 17 - match found for "class"
cout << s.find("classes", 17, 5);

//displays 4294967295 - couldn't find "classes"
cout << s.find("classes", 17);

//displays 19 - started searching past the first 'a'
cout << s.find('a', 6);
```

It is sometimes more convenient (or efficient) to search backward from the end of the string. You can use the rfind() method in this case. It searches for a particular character sequence, from a specified point, just like find(), except that it searches backward. Here are the declarations for the rfind() functions:

```
size_type rfind(const basic_string& s, size_type i = npos) const;
size_type rfind(const C* p, size_type i, size_type n) const;
size_type rfind(const C* p, size_type i = npos) const;
size_type rfind(C c, size_type i = npos) const;
```

As you can see, not much has changed, other than the method name. The default values for the arguments are a notable exception. For find(), the default value for the start position was 0 (start at the beginning), but for rfind(), it is npos (start at the end). Here are some examples:

```
string s = "The string class sure has a lot of methods.";
string s1 = "of";

//displays 32
cout << s.rfind(s1);

//displays 4294967295 - couldn't find it
cout << s.rfind(s1, 31);

//displays 35 - the position of "meth"
cout << s.rfind("methane", string::npos, 4);
```

You can also search for a particular character from a sequence of characters. The method find_first_of() does this job. It searches forward from a given point, and if it runs across a character also in the character sequence, the function returns the position of that character. The method find_last_of() does the same thing, except that it searches backward (just as rfind() does). Here are the declarations for the find_first_of() functions:

```
size_type find_first_of(const basic_string& s, size_type i = 0) const;
size_type find_first_of(const C* p, size_type i, size_type n) const;
size_type find_first_of(const C* p, size_type i = 0) const;
size_type find_first_of(C c, size_type i = 0) const;
size_type find_last_of(const basic_string& s, size_type i = npos) const;
size_type find_last_of(const C* p, size_type i, size_type n) const;
size_type find_last_of(const C* p, size_type i = npos) const;
size_type find_last_of(C c, size_type i = npos) const;
```

Here are some examples of this group of functions:

```
string s = "We need a bigger gun.";
string s1= "Mercenaries.";

//displays 1 - the position of 'e'
cout << s.find_first_of(s1);

//displays 15 - the position of 'r' in "bigger"
cout << s.find_last_of("tree.", 16);
```

You might want to do the opposite at times. You can search for the first (or last) character in a string that isn't also in a particular sequence of characters. You do so using the find_first_not_of() and find_last_not_of() methods. Here are the declarations:

```
size_type find_first_not_of(const basic_string& s, size_type i = 0) const;
size_type find_first_not_of(const C* p, size_type i, size_type n) const;
size_type find_first_not_of(const C* p, size_type i = 0) const;
size_type find_first_not_of(C c, size_type i = 0) const;
size_type find_last_not_of(const basic_string& s, size_type i = npos) const;
size_type find_last_not_of(const C* p, size_type i, size_type n) const;
size_type find_last_not_of(const C* p, size_type i = npos) const;
size_type find_last_not_of(C c, size_type i = npos) const;
```

Here are examples of using this group of functions:

```
string s = "The sock is on the floor.";
string s1 = "These rocks";

//displays 9 - the position of 'i' in "is"
cout << s.find_first_not_of(s1);

//displays 20 - the position of 'l' in "floor."
cout << s.find_last_not_of("roof.");
```

You can create new strings from parts (substrings) of a string. For example, if you have a string that stores "Hello World", you could create another string from it that stores "World". You use the substr() method to accomplish this task. By indicating a position and a length, you can specify exactly which part of the string you want. Here is the declaration for substr():

```
basic_string substr(size_type i = 0, size_type n = npos) const;
```

Here i is the position to start from, and n is the number of characters to use. Here is an example:

```
string s = "annihilation";
string s1 = s.substr(4,2);

cout << s1.c_str(); //displays "hi"
```

Notice that the default values for the arguments create a copy of the string.

As a counterpart to substr(), the standard library provides a way to put two strings together to form a new one. You use the + operator for this task. Putting two strings together is called concatenation. All the concatenation functions are declared outside basic_string. Here are the concatenation functions for strings:

```
template<class C, class T, class A>
basic_string<C,T,A> operator+ (const basic_string<C,T,A>&,
                                const basic_string<C,T,A>&);

template<class C, class T, class A>
basic_string<C,T,A> operator+ (const C*, const basic_string<C,T,A>&);

template<class C, class T, class A>
basic_string<C,T,A> operator+ (C, const basic_string<C,T,A>&);

template<class C, class T, class A>
basic_string<C,T,A> operator+ (const basic_string<C,T,A>&, const C*);

template<class C, class T, class A>
basic_string<C,T,A> operator+ (const basic_string<C,T,A>&, C);
```

With these functions, you can create a string from two strings, a string and a character array, or a string and a character. Here are some examples:

```
string s = "Hello";
string t = "World";

cout << s + ' ' + t; //displays "Hello World"
cout << s + ' ' + "Everyone!"; Displays "Hello Everyone!"
```

The `basic_string` class also provides some memory functions to handle the memory used for the data and statistics about the string. One such statistic is the `size()` method. It returns the number of characters stored in the string. The `length()` method does the same thing. The `empty()` method returns `true` if the string is empty (otherwise, it returns `false`). The `max_size()` method returns the largest possible size that a string can be. Here are the declarations for these methods:

```
size_type size() const;
size_type length() const {return size();}
bool empty() const { return size == 0;}
size_type max_size() const;
```

Manipulating Strings

The capability of manipulating strings in a number of different ways is essential for a string class. Fortunately, `basic_string` more than fulfills this requirement. You have many options when you need to manipulate a string.

One of the simplest and most useful ways to change a string is to use the assignment operator (=). The basic_string class overloads these operators to make the string seem more like a built-in data type. Here are the declarations for these assignment methods:

```
basic_string& operator= (const basic_string& s);
basic_string& operator= (const C* p);
basic_string& operator= (C c);
```

These functions enable you to assign a string, a character array, or a single character to a string object. Keep in mind that whatever was stored in the string before the function call is destroyed.

For these operations, a normal method called assign() allows more flexibility in arguments. Here are the declarations for the assign() method:

```
//a whole string
basic_string& assign(const basic_string&);

//a partial string, starting at position pos and taking n characters
basic_string& assign(const basic_string& s, size_type pos, size_type n);

//the first n elements from p
basic_string& assign(const C* p, size_type n);

//all of p
basic_string& assign(const C* p);

//n copies of c
basic_string& assign(size_type n, C c);

//everything from first to last
typedef<class I> basic_string& assign(I first, I last);
```

This mimics the versatility of the constructor. It wouldn't make sense to create an object a certain way and not be able to assign that way as well. The basic_string& that is returned is the same as the value that is assigned, but you can ignore it if you don't need it.

Appending (adding characters to the end) is an operation commonly performed on a string. The basic_string class provides either the += operator or the append method to append things to strings. Here are the declarations for the appending functions:

```
basic_string& operator+= (const basic_string& s);
basic_string& operator+= (const C* p);
basic_string& operator+= (C c);

basic_string& append(const basic_string& s);

//append partial string
basic_string& append(const basic_string& s, size_type pos, size_type n);

//append partial character array
basic_string& append(const C* p, size_type n);

//append whole character array
basic_string& append(const C* p);

//append n copies of c
basic_string& append(size_type n, C c);

//append values from iterator
template<class I> basic_string& append(I first, I last);
```

Using the += operator, you can append a string, character array, or character to a string. Using the append method, you can append a string, a partial string, a partial character array, a whole character array, n copies of a character, or the values from an iterator.

If the values that you want to add don't necessarily go at the end of the string, you can use the insert method to put them somewhere in the middle. Here are the declarations for the insert method:

```
//insert string right before character at pos
basic_string& insert(size_type pos, const basic_string& s);

//insert partial string right before character at pos
basic_string& insert(size_type pos, const basic_string& s,
                     size_type pos2, size_type n);

//insert partial array at pos
basic_string& insert(size_type pos, const C* p, size_type n);
```

```
//insert array at pos
basic_string& insert(size_type pos, const C* p);

//insert n copies of c at pos
basic_string& insert(size_type pos, size_type n, C c);

//insert c right before character at pos - return iterator at c
iterator insert(iterator pos, C c);

//insert n copies of c at pos
void insert(iterator pos, size_type n, C c);

//insert sequence at pos
template<class I> void insert(iterator pos, I first, I last);
```

Every version of the insert method inserts the specified characters before the character at pos. Every character after this is moved up to make room.

You can use the replace() method to change part of a string to something else. Here are the declarations:

```
//replace characters from pos to pos+n
basic_string& replace(size_type pos, size_type n, const basic_string& s);

basic_string& replace(size_type pos, size_type n, const basic_string& s,
                            size_type i2, size_type n2);

basic_string& replace(size_type pos, size_type n, const C* p, size_type n2);

basic_string& replace(size_type pos, size_type n, const C* p);

basic_string& replace(size_type pos, size_type n, size_type n2, C c);

//replace characters from pos to pos2
basic_string& replace(iterator pos, iterator pos2, const basic_string& s);

basic_string& replace(iterator pos, iterator pos2, const C* p, size_type n);

basic_string& replace(iterator pos, iterator pos2, const C* p);
```

```
basic_string& replace(iterator pos, iterator pos2, size_type n, C c);

template<class I> basic_string& replace(iterator pos, iterator pos2,
                                                    I first, I last);
```

You can also just get rid of a substring from your string if you desire. To do so, you use the erase() method. Here are the declarations:

```
//erase all characters from position i to i+n
basic_string& erase(size_type i = 0, size_type n = npos);

//erase single character at position i
iterator erase(iterator i);

//erase all characters from first to last
iterator erase(iterator first, iterator last);
```

The first version of this method clears the string by default.

Using Vectors

As your programs get more complex, the need for more advanced data storage arises. Arrays are not bad for storing data, but they are pretty low-level. In other words, you have to deal with many of the inconveniences yourself.

The standard library containers provide an optimal solution to this problem. There are many different containers to suit many different needs. In your programming experience, you will encounter most of them. To get you started, this section presents the most common one: the vector. The vector has properties that make it ideal in some situations and quite inefficient in others. It is up to you to decide which container suits your needs.

Vectors are similar to arrays. They hold a series of values, each of which can be accessed as though it were its own variable (and not part of a data structure). In fact, the data in a vector is stored in a single-dimensional array. Because of this, you can easily access any element in the vector simply by providing the index number. This kind of access to the elements is called random access, because you can access any random element easily.

A vector automatically resizes itself if you add elements to it. It does so by creating a new, larger array and copying each element from the old array to the new one. This procedure is inefficient and is one of the main disadvantages of the vector.

If you insert or remove an element from the middle of the vector, every element must be shifted up or down, respectively, to make sure that no empty spots are in the array. This shifting up or down of all the elements can be costly.

A vector is a class template and is in the header `<vector>`. The declaration looks fairly similar to `basic_string`:

```
template <class T, class A = allocator<T>> class std::vector;
```

IN THE REAL WORLD

Many programmers ignore or don't know about all the utilities provided by the standard library. When I started programming my first computer game, I needed to figure out a way to store units. The number of units in the game is not something a programmer can predict (at least not without great difficulty), so I needed to store the units dynamically, which was a complicated concept for me at the time. As a result, I did a great deal of research to find a way. When I stumbled upon vectors in the standard library, I was pleasantly surprised. Not only had programmers already encountered this problem, but they had also provided a well-thought-out solution. Without a doubt, the standard library can save you immeasurable time and is well worth careful study.

The allocator for `vector` behaves much the same way that it does for `basic_string` (that is, in most cases, you won't need to access it). `T` is the type of data stored in the vector.

Like `basic_string`, `vector` uses `typedef` to define some standard names:

```
//the type of data stored
typedef T value_type;

//the type of memory allocator
typedef A allocator_type;

typedef typename A::size_type size_type;

//a way to iterate through the elements
typedef compiler_dependent iterator;
```

```
//iterates backwards
typedef std::reverse_iterator<iterator> reverse_iterator;

//pointer to an element
typedef typename A::pointer pointer;

//reference to an element
typedef typename A::reference reference;
```

Though these names can come in handy, they are used mostly for internal implementations, so you don't have to worry about them too much (as long as you know what each one refers to).

The constructors for vector provide a variety of ways to create a vector object:

```
vector(const A& = A());

//vector with n copies of val
vector(size_type n, const T& val = T(), const A& a = A());

//vector copied from input sequence
template<class I> vector(I first, I last, const A& a = A());

//vector created from another vector
vector(const vector& a);
```

The first constructor creates a designated number of elements. Each element is initialized with a default constructor (or a constructor of your choosing). The second acts exactly like the basic_string constructor that takes a sequence of characters. It takes a sequence of elements of the same type that the vector stores (obviously). You use the third constructor to create a vector from another vector. Here are some examples of how you might construct a vector:

```
//default constructor - empty vector
vector<float> fv;

//vector of 10 strings
vector<string> sv(10);

//vector of 10 ints, each initialized to 3
vector<int> iv(10,3);
```

```
string s = "Hello World";
vector<string> sv2(s.begin(), s.end());
```

```
vector<int> iv2(iv);
```

The vector class also has a destructor:

```
~vector();
```

Accessing and Manipulating Vectors

Using vectors is similar to using strings. Most of the interface is the same. For example, here are the methods to obtain a vector iterator:

```
//points to first element
iterator begin();
```

```
//points to one past the last element
iterator end();
```

```
//points to last element
reverse_iterator rbegin();
```

```
//points to one before first element
reverse_iterator rend();
```

As you can see, iterators work here exactly the same as they do for strings. Note that these iterators are random access iterators, because strings and vectors have random access to their elements.

To access individual elements in a vector, you can use the subscripting operator or the `at()` method, as with strings. You can also access the first element in the vector with the `front()` method and the last element with the `back()` method. Here are the declarations for these two methods:

```
reference front(); reference back();
```

The vector has two methods of assigning values to it: with the assignment operator or with the `assign()` method. Here are the declarations:

```
//copy a vector
vector& operator=(const vector& x);
```

```
//assign all values from first to last
template<class I> void assign (I first, I last);
```

```
//assign n copies of val
void assign(size_type n, const T& val);
```

The vector's assign() methods are similar to the string versions and, so, are fairly self-explanatory.

Two of the operations that a vector can perform are referred to as stack operations. They are push_back() and pop_back(). push_back() adds a value to the end of a vector, and pop_back() removes the last element from a vector. Here are their declarations:

```
void push_back(const T& x);
void pop_back();
```

Three of a vector's operations are called list operations. They are insert(), erase(), and clear(). insert() includes a set of values at a certain position in the vector, erase() deletes a sequence of elements from a vector, and clear() deletes all the elements from the vector. Here are the declarations:

```
//insert x at pos
iterator insert(iterator pos, const T& x);
```

```
//insert n x's at pos
void insert(iterator pos, size_type n, const T& x);
```

```
//insert a sequence at pos
template <class I> void insert(iterator pos, I first, I last);
```

```
//erase element at pos
iterator erase(iterator pos);
```

```
//erase a sequence of elements
iterator erase(iterator first, iterator last);
```

```
//erase all elements
void clear();
```

The vector class provides the size(), empty(), and max_size() methods. These methods behave the same way they do in the basic_string class.

Finally, the `vector` class provides the comparison operators (`==`, `!=`, `<`, `>`, `<=`, `>=`) just like the `string` class does.

CREATING THE MYSTERIOUS STORE GAME

While stumbling through the vast wilderness known as Vector Valley, you come across a small town. This town is not like other towns you have seen. Everyone in this town appears to have everything they need. No one is short of supplies. While pondering this oddity, you come across a strange little store. The store appears to be the source of everyone's supplies. Looking at your own supplies, you decide that you could use more, so without another thought you enter the store. Compile the following code to see what happens.

```cpp
//8.1 - The Mysterious Store - Mark Lee
#include <iostream>
#include <vector>
#include <string>

using std::string;
using std::vector;

#define MAX(a,b) a<b ? b: a //the common macro

struct Item //used to store a single item from the store.
{
    string name;
    int price;
};

class Store //used to handle everything to do with the store
{
    vector<Item> inventory;
    vector<Item> forSale;
    int money;
public:
    Store(Item* itemList, int n);
    ~Store() {}
    string BuyItem(int item);
    string viewInventory();
    string ListItems();
```

✦

```cpp
        int getMoney() { return MAX(money,0); }
};

Store::Store(Item* itemList, int n)
{
        for(int i = 0; i < n; i++)
                forSale.push_back(itemList[i]);
        money = 20;
}

string Store::BuyItem(int item)
{
        money -= forSale[item-1].price;
        if (money < 0)
                return "\nSorry, you don't have enough money.\n\n";
        inventory.push_back(forSale[item-1]);
        return "You bought a " + forSale[item-1].name + '\n';
}

string Store::ListItems()
{
        string s;
        for(int i = 0; i < forSale.size(); i++)
        {
                s += "[";
                s += i + 49;
                s+="]Buy a ";
                s+= forSale[i].name;
                s+= " ($";
                s+= forSale[i].price + 48;
                s+= ")\n";
        }
        return s;
}

string Store::viewInventory()
{
        string s;
```

```cpp
        for(int i = 0; i < inventory.size(); i++)
            s += inventory[i].name + '\n';
        return s + '\n';
}


int main(void)
{
        using std::cout;
        using std::cin;

        int input;
        Item f[3];
        f[0].name = "Clown";
        f[0].price = 2;
        f[1].name = "Cracker Jack";
        f[1].price = 6;
        f[2].name = "Camel";
        f[2].price = 9;
        Store s = Store(f,3);

        while(true) {
                do {
                        cout << "Welcome to the store.\n"
                                << "You have " << s.getMoney() << " dollars.\n"
                                << "\nWhat would you like to do?\n"
                                << s.ListItems()
                                << "[4]View your inventory\n"
                                << "[5]Leave\n";
                        cin >> input;
                } while(input<1||input>5);
                switch(input) {
                case 4:
                        cout << s.viewInventory();
                        break;
                case 5:
                        goto END;
                default:
                        cout << s.BuyItem(input);
```

```
            }
        }
END:
        cout << "See ya!";
        return 0;
}
```

SUMMARY

In this chapter, we covered many important topics, including templates, strings, and vectors. Consider this chapter your first major introduction to the C++ standard library, a powerful tool that you will probably want to delve into more deeply over time. You don't have to memorize every method of the `basic_string`.

CHALLENGES

1. Create a vector that stores a set of vectors that each store a set of integers.
2. Create a template class called `Store` that stores an array of T (where T is the template parameter).
3. Create an iterator, called `random_iterator` that uses another iterator to iterate through a container in random order.
4. Name three places where you can get quick information about the components of the standard library (not including this book).

Using Streams and Files

Streams and files are two of the most complex subjects in the C++ language. However, in this chapter, we intend to make learning about these topics painless. Although much more can be written about these topics, when you finish this chapter, you definitely will be able to complete tasks using streams.

In this chapter, you learn about the following:

- The vocabulary associated with streams and I/O
- The various kinds of manipulators
- Binary files and text files
- Dividing a data type into smaller bit fields
- The wonders of bit shifting
- Creating an encryption program

Understanding the Vocabulary of I/O

The core of this chapter is I/O (input/output). I/O refers to sending (outputting) and receiving (inputting) data from various hardware devices, such as hard drives, modems, and keyboards.

In order to learn I/O, you need to know the terminology. Here are several of the definitions we use throughout this chapter:

- **Stream object.** Acts as both a source and a destination for bytes. The stream object manipulates an ordered linear sequence of bytes. This series of bytes can represent a screen, a file, or anywhere else the programmer wants bytes to go. You find the classes that handle streams in several of the library files: `<fstream>`, `<iomanip>`, `<ios>`, `<iosfwd>`, `<iostream>`, `<istream>`, `<ostream>`, `<sstream>`, `<streambuf>`, and `<strstream>`.

- **Manipulator.** Manipulates the data of the stream in some way. For example, a manipulator can make all characters uppercase or can convert numbers using decimal notation to hexadecimal notation.

- **Insertion.** Places bytes into the stream. The methods that perform the insertions are called inserters.

- **Extraction.** Takes bytes from the stream. The methods that perform the extractions are called extractors.

UNDERSTANDING THE HEADER FILES

In the preceding section's bullet on stream objects, we listed several header files. Each of these header files encapsulates a section of the overall C++ stream architecture. All these files come together to give the complete I/O support provided by C++. Each of these files completes its specific task to give C++ the most diverse I/O functionality of any programming language. The purpose of each of the headers is as follows:

- `<fstream>`. Contains the definition for several template classes that support the `iostream` header file's operations on sequences stored in external files.

- `<iomanip>`. Contains several single-argument manipulators.

- `<ios>`. Contains a majority of the format manipulators basic to the operation of `iostream` header file's classes.

- `<iosfwd>`. Contains the forward declarations for the `iostream` header file's classes.

- `<iostream>`. Contains the declarations for the standard global stream objects such as `cin` and `cout`.

- `<istream>`. Contains the extractors for inputting data from streams and includes the template class `basic_istream`. In other words, `<istream>` puts the I in I/O.
- `<ostream>`. Contains the inserters for outputting a series of bytes and includes the template class `basic_ostream`. Basically, `<ostream>` puts the O in I/O.
- `<sstream>`. Supports streams defined on `string` objects.
- `<streambuf>`. Defines the `basic_streambuf` template class.
- `<strstream>`. Supports streams defined on arrays.

With the exception of the `ios_base` class, each template class has a specialization class for characters. Figure 9.1 shows the most commonly used template classes and their character specialization classes. However, this is not a complete list because several of the stream classes are beyond the scope of this book.

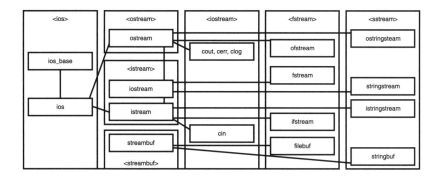

FIGURE 9.1

The class contained within each header file and the classes from which they are derived. Terms in bold represent header files, and terms without bold represent classes. The lines that link the classes indicate from which classes each class is inherited.

THE IOS_BASE CLASS

The `ios_base` class contains the byte storage common to all streams and the methods that are not dependent on template parameters. This byte storage stores the bytes that are being input and output until they reach their final destination.

The several data types contained within the `ios_base` class provide the basis for controlling streams.

The following list outlines the purpose of several data types that can be used to control streams:

- `event`. Use the event information in the data type `event` to store callbacks. Callbacks are pointers to methods that are registered with and called by the operating system when a specified significant event happens.
- `fmtflags`. Use format flags in the data type `fmtflags` to specify information about the format of the stream.
- `iostate`. Use I/O state information in the data type `iostate` to keep track of the current state of I/O operations. Use the `iostate` data type to check for stream corruption.
- `openmode`. Use open mode to specify a stream's type of read/write access.
- `seekdir`. Use seek direction to specify where the stream data should be sought and store it in the type alias `seekdir`.

In addition, you can use several methods provided by the `ios_base` and in its derived classes (all other stream classes). Here they are in alphabetical order:

- `flags()`. Sets or returns format flag information.
- `getloc()`. Returns an internal local object that encapsulates the stream's information.
- `imbue()`. Stores a local object that encapsulates the stream's information and returns its previously stored object.
- `ios_bas()`. This is the constructor.
- `iword()`. Returns a reference to a specified element of the extensible array having elements of type `long`.
- `operator =()` **(overloaded assignment operator)**. Copies everything in the object to a new stream object including formatting information and extensible arrays.
- `precision()`. Determines the number of decimal places in the display's precision.
- `pword()`. Returns a reference to a specific element of the `void*` array.
- `register_callback()`. Stores callback information for stream callback events.
- `setf()`. Sets new flags for the stream and returns the previously set flags.
- `unsetf()`. Clears all flags.
- `width()`. Sets or retrieves the field width of a stream.
- `xalloc()`. Returns a unique static variable to be used in `iword()` or `pword()` as an array index.

Much more could be written about the `ios_base` class. However, to keep this book interesting and within its intended page count, we decided to focus on applying streams to their most common uses. However, if, like us, you are one of those strange individuals who can't learn enough about streams, you can extend your knowledge in the Library section on the MSDN Web site at http://www.MSDN.Microsoft.com.

INTRODUCTION TO FILE STREAMS

To increase the functionality of games, you often need to store millions of pieces of data—for example, map information or data for a player's last saved game. You store this data by using several specialized file I/O classes: `ofstream`, `ifstream`, and `fstream`, contained in the `ofstream`, `ifstream`, and `fstream` header files, respectively.

OPENING FILES

Generally, your first action with a file stream object, such as one derived from the `ofstream`, `ifstream`, and `fstream` classes, is to associate it with the file with which you want to work. You make the association using the `open()` method or the constructor of each of the classes.

The `open()` method's prototype looks like this:

```
void open (const char * filename, openmode mode);
```

`filename` is a string of characters representing the filename, and `mode` is a combination of the flags shown in Table 9.1.

Flags are connected with the bitwise or (|) operator. Say that you want to open `"level1.map"` to output in binary mode. The `open` function might look like this:

```
ofstream file;
file.open ("level1.map", ios::out | ios::binary);
```

Each of the file classes includes the `open()` method; however, each stream has several default flags specifying its use. The default values, however, are applied only if the method is called without flags. The default flags are shown in Table 9.2.

TABLE 9.1 FLAGS FOR OPENING A FILE

Flag	Function
ios::in	Opens file for reading.
ios::out	Opens file for writing.
ios::ate	Initial position is at the end of the file.
ios::app	Appends every output at the end of the file.
ios::trunc	Erases a file, if one already existed.
ios::binary	Access to the file is in binary mode.

TABLE 9.2	DEFAULT FLAGS FOR THE FILE CLASSES
Class	**Flags**
ofstream	ios::out | ios::trunc
ifstream	ios::in
fstream	ios::in | ios::out

You can also open a file by including the filename in the constructor. The class constructors use the same argument as the open() method. For example, if you use the ifstream class, the prototype for the constructor will look like this:

```
ifstream::ifstream(const char * filename, openmode mode);
```

Here filename and mode mean the same thing as in the open() method.

You can check whether a file opened correctly by calling to the method is_open():

```
bool is_open()
```

is_open() returns true if the file is properly open and false if not.

Here are the usual reasons why a file does not open correctly:

- **A bad filename**—for example, a name for a file that doesn't exist.
- **A corrupt file**—for example, one on a bad sector of a hard drive.
- **Another program has exclusive access**—this means that only the program with exclusive access can access the file. The file is therefore unusable by other programs until the program with exclusive access relinquishes its exclusive access privileges.
- **Windows protects the file**—Windows sometimes automatically protects files in particular folders or of certain types. Contact your system administrator if this happens.

CLOSING FILES

In order to make a file accessible to other programs, you must close the file. Also, an object can open only one file at a time. To close a file, you use the close method. For each of the three classes, use the close member to close a file, as follows:

```
void close();
```

If a file stream object is destroyed, its destructor will automatically close the file associated with that object.

WORKING WITH TEXT FILES

Inputting and outputting to files is exactly like inputting and outputting onscreen because the cin and ifstream classes are both derived from the istream class, as shown earlier in Figure 9.1. Likewise, cout and ofstream are both derived from the ostream class. Both use the overloaded insertion operator <<.

The following code exemplifies this point:

```
//9.1 - Outputting Text - Dirk Henkemans
#include <fstream>
using namespace std;
int main(void)
{
    //contains the default flags ios::out | ios::trunc
    ofstream dragons("dragons.txt");
    if(dragons.is_open())
    {
        dragons << "Copper Dragon" << "\n"
                << "Bronze Dragon" << "\n"
                << "Silver Dragon" << "\n"
                << "Gold Dragon" << "\n";
    }
    dragons.close();
    return 0;
}
Output:
Copper Dragon
Bronze Dragon
Silver Dragon
Gold Dragon
```

"dragons.txt" will normally be in the same folder as your project. However, if you don't find it there, go to the Windows taskbar, click Start > Find (or Search) > Files or Folders. A window entitled something like Find: All Files will appear. Type the name of the file and select the drive on which it is stored. Then click Find Now, and Windows will find the file for you. (Note that your program might have slightly different names.)

If you run the program twice, you will notice that the text file always contains the same information. This is because the implied ios::trunc uses the ofstream class if you do not specify mode parameters. Remember that ios::trunc restarts a file if it already exists.

Although you can input from the file with the overloaded shift operator (>>), it becomes impossible to know when you reach the end of your file. The easiest way to input from a text file is to input the data line by line using the istream::getline() method. This is also the most useful method because most data are stored line by line, so you input the line and then dissect the line of data into its respective fields.

You have three options for using the istream::getline() method:

```
istream& getline(char* pch, int nCount, char delim = '\n');
istream& getline(unsigned char* puch, int nCount, char delim = '\n');
istream& getline(signed char* psch, int nCount, char delim = '\n');
```

The parameter placeholders mean the following:

- pch, puch, psch. A pointer to a char array. Remember that the getline method overwrites data stored in the array.

- nCount. The maximum numbers that the getline method should store, including the terminating null.

- delim. The delineating character to which getline() goes.

Last, you probably want to read to the end of a file, except how do you know where the end is? You use the ios::eof() method:

```
int eof();
```

The eof() method returns a non-zero integer when the end of the file is reached.

You can put it all together now and read from the "dragon.txt" file. A sample implementation of this is shown here:

```cpp
//9.2 - Inputting Dragons - Dirk Henkemans
#include <fstream>
#include <iostream>
using namespace std;

int main(void)
{
    //contains the default flags ios::in
    ifstream dragons("dragons.txt");
    char buffer[50];
    if(!dragons.is_open())
    {
```

```
        cout << "Error opening file\n";
        //non 0 exit means there was an error
        exit(1);
    }
    while(!dragons.eof())
    {
        dragons.getline(buffer, 49);
        cout << buffer << "\n";
    }
    dragons.close();
    return 0;
}
```
Output:
```
Copper Dragon
Bronze Dragon
Silver Dragon
Gold Dragon
```

The getline() method deletes the delineators (in this case, the default line breaks), so the program compensates by adding a line break after reading each line.

You now have read your first file!

VERIFYING STREAM

When you send a message asking a stream to perform a task, how do you know that the stream accomplished the task? The interface with stream objects provides several methods that enable you to know whether a stream successfully completes its tasks. Table 9.3 provides several of the stream verification methods.

In order to reset all the preceding stream verification methods, use the ios::clear() method (no parameters).

TABLE 9.3   VERIFICATION METHODS

Method	Description
bad()	Returns true if a severe error occurs when you are trying to read or write from a file. For example, this might occur when you are trying to write to a device with no space left.
eof()	Returns true if the stream reaches the end of the file. This works only when you are inputting from a file.
fail()	Returns true if there is a formatting error. For example, the stream tries to read an integer, but finds an alpha character.
good()	This is a general method that returns false if any one of the preceding methods bad, eof, or fail, returns true.

WORKING WITH BINARY STREAMS

Although working with text is convenient, it is inefficient in many cases. When using a 28.8 modem, you often will send as little data as possible. In a game such as *StarCraft*, by Blizzard, you can specify ahead of time what data types will be sent. This enables you to use more than one data type (such as characters).

The solution is binary streams, which can send multiple data types. The program must know the order and kind of data types being sent in order to read the data. Figure 9.2 shows a text stream and a binary stream.

In order to make correct interpretations, the program must know to which structure the bytes in a binary stream are related. This means that the binary stream must apply a programmed algorithm (such as int, char, or long) to decipher the data, but a text stream can assume that every byte is a character. In Figure 9.2, note that the top data stream is a text file, and each byte means the same thing—one character. The bottom stream is a data stream in which bytes are part of larger structures; your program must know what the structure is to use the byte properly.

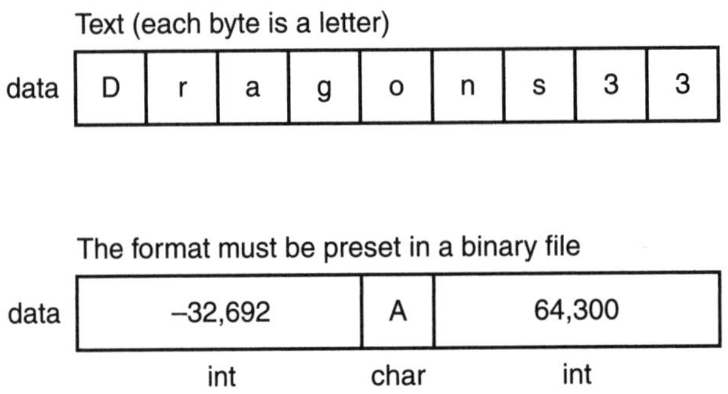

Text (each byte is a letter)

data	D	r	a	g	o	n	s	3	3

The format must be preset in a binary file

data	−32,692	A	64,300
	int	char	int

FIGURE 9.2

A text stream and a binary stream.

THE GET AND PUT STREAM POINTERS

Memory is indexed for our enjoyment, but more importantly, it is indexed to ensure random access. Random access enables you to access portions of files of streams in any order. For example, you can read a file backward almost as easily as you can read it forward. Two pointers, generally referred to as stream pointers, indicate the location where you are reading or writing. These stream pointers are the get pointer and the put pointer. The get pointer indicates where you are reading, and the put pointer indicates where you are writing.

All I/O streams have at least one stream pointer, depending on the stream's method. Here are the ones for the common classes:

- ifstream. Like istream, this class has the get pointer.
- ofstream. Like ostream, this class has the put pointer.
- fstream. Because it is derived from istream and ostream, this class has both pointers.

INTERFACING WITH THE STREAM POINTERS

The two stream pointers gain their functionality when an interface is created to adjust them. The interface consists of the following methods:

- istream::tellg(). Returns the number of bytes the get pointer is from the beginning of the file (not the address to which the get pointer is pointing). The streampos data type is effectively type alias for an integer. The prototype for this method is streampos tellg();.
- ostream::tellp(). Returns the number of bytes the put pointer is from the beginning of the file. The prototype for this method is streampos tellp();.
- istream::seekg(). Sets the position of the get pointer in the stream. The prototype for this method is seekg (pos_type position);.
- ostream::seekp(). Sets the position of the put pointer in the stream. The prototype for this method is seekp (pos_type position);.
- seekg() and seekp(). Sets the direction of the offset of the pointer and the amount of offset. The prototypes for these methods are:
  ```
  seekg ( off_type offset, seekdir direction );
  seekp ( off_type offset, seekdir direction );.
  ```

The offset directions specified in the second parameter, direction, are shown in Table 9.4.

TABLE 9.4	OFFSET DIRECTIONS

Direction	Description
ios::beg	The offset is specified from the beginning of the stream.
ios::cur	The offset is specified forward from the current position of the pointer.
ios::end	The offset is specified from the end of the stream.

The following example uses a number of methods just discussed to determine the size of a file:

```
//9.3 - Binary File Size - Dirk Henkemans
#include <iostream>
#include <fstream>
using namespace std;
int main(void)
{
    int n1, n2;
    ifstream dragons("dragons.txt", ios::in|ios::binary);
    n1 = dragons.tellg();
    dragons.seekg (0, ios::end);
    n2 = dragons.tellg();
    cout << "The size of dragons.txt is " << n2 - n1 << "\n";
    return 0;
}
Output:
The size of dragons.txt is 58
```

WRITING AND READING BINARY STREAMS

File streams introduce two new methods that are designed especially for sequential input and output of data: ostream::write() and istream::read(). The prototypes of both these files are as follows:

```
write (char * buffer, streamsize size );
read( char * buffer, streamsize size );
```

write() places the number of bytes specified by size after the put pointer, thereby writing them to the file.

read() places the number of bytes specified by size taken from the get pointer and places the bytes after the buffer pointer parameter.

To exemplify these two methods, examine the following program, which takes the "dragons.txt" file and copies it to another file named "dragons2.txt".

```
//9.4 - File Copier - Dirk Henkemans
#include <iostream>
#include <fstream>
using namespace std;

int main(void)
{
    char buffer;
    int index = 0;

    //the file names
    const char filename1[] = "dragons.txt";
    const char filename2[] = "dragons2.txt";

    //opening the files
    fstream file1(filename1, ios::in);
    fstream file2(filename2, ios::out);

    //points to the beginning of the files
    file1.seekg(0, ios::beg);
    file2.seekp(0, ios::beg);

    //reads the first char
    file1.read(&buffer, 1);

    //writes the remainder of the chars
    while(file1.good() && file2.good())
    {
        file2.write(&buffer, 1);
        index++;
        file1.seekp(index);
        file2.seekg(index);
        file1.read(&buffer, 1);
    }

    //closes the files
    file1.close();
```

```
    file2.close();

    return 0;
}
```

When you open `"dragons2.txt"`, it should be the same as `"dragons.txt"`.

WORKING WITH COMMON MANIPULATORS

Manipulators are used to manipulate the data in a stream. For example, you can use some manipulators to turn all lowercase alpha characters to uppercase or to adjust the way a number displays. Most manipulators are included in the `ios` header file. In the following section, you use only the common manipulators found in the `ios` header file.

Although we can't list all the manipulators in this book, Table 9.5 lists several of the most common ones and their functions.

TABLE 9.5 COMMON MANIPULATORS IN THE `<IOS>` HEADER

Flag	Function
dec()	Displays in the base-10 number system.
hex()	Displays in the base-16 number system.
oct()	Displays in the base-8 number system.
fixed()	Inserts floating-point values.
scientific()	Inserts floating-point values in scientific format using exponents.
internal()	Pads to a field width as needed by inserting internal whitespace.
left()	Left-justifies characters by padding with whitespace on the right.
right()	Right-justifies characters by padding with whitespace on the left.
boolalpha()	Symbolic representation of true and false.
noboolalpha()	Cancels boolalpha().
showbase()	Shows the base of the number prefixing octal and hex numbers with 0 and 0x, respectively.
noshowbase()	Cancels showbase().
showpoint()	Displays a decimal point even if there is no fractional portion.
noshowpoint()	Cancels showpoint().
showpos()	Inserts a positive (+) sign before non-negative numbers.
noshowpos()	Cancels showpos().
skipws()	Skips whitespace.
noskipws()	Cancels skipws().
unitbuf()	Flushes out after each insertion.
nounitbuf()	Cancels unitbuf().
uppercase()	Inserts uppercase equivalents of lowercase alpha characters.
nouppercase()	Cancels uppercase().

You can use the manipulators in Table 9.5 on any stream by using the `ios::setf()` method and by placing a flag as the parameter. The next program clearly demonstrates this procedure and the results when used on the `cout` object.

```cpp
//9.5 - Manipulators - Dirk Henkemans
#include <iostream>
#include <ios>
using namespace std;

int main(void)
{
    cout << "Default True, False \n" << true << " " << false << "\n";
    cout.setf(ios::boolalpha);
    cout << "\nwith ios::boolalpha:\n" << true << " " << false << "\n";
    cout << "\n140 in hex\n";
    cout.setf(ios::hex, ios::basefield);
    cout.setf(ios::showbase);
    cout << 140 << "\n";
    float f[2] = {1.0f, 775.374f};
    cout << "\nDefault numeric formula\n" << f[0] << "\n" << f[1] << "\n";
    cout.setf(ios::showpos);
    cout<< "\nand with showpos\n" << f[0] << "\n" << f[1] << "\n";

    //indicates that cout should always use 6 digit precision
    cout.setf(ios::fixed);
    cout<< "\nand with a precision of 6\n" << f[0] << "\n" << f[1] << "\n";
    return 0;
}
```

USING BIT FIELDS

Standard data types are built into C++; however, often it is more efficient to divide a standard data type into several fields of bits in order to store multiple smaller values. These subsections of bits are called bit fields. For example, imagine that you want to subdivide an unsigned character into bit fields. An unsigned character is composed of 8 bits. This means that the sum of all the bit fields must contain 8 bits.

You declare a bit field by placing a colon after the declaration and specifying the number of bits that will be in the bit field. You must declare bit fields inside a structure, as shown here:

```
struct shortBits
{
    short member1 : 2;
    short member2 : 7;
    short member3 : 7;
};
```

member1 can store only three values: 1 + 2.

member2 and member3 can store 127 values: 1 + 2 + 4 + 8 + 16 + 32 + 64.

Figure 9.3 visually represents what the shortBits structure might look like in memory.

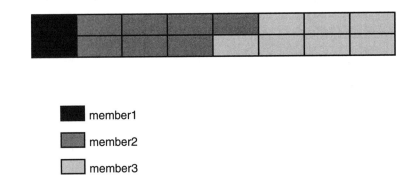

FIGURE 9.3

In this figure, the total memory for the short data type is divided into three individual members.

member1

member2

member3

Fun with Bit Shifting

The << (left shift) and >> (right shift) are the bit shift operators. When you bit shift, you take the bits of a data type and shift them over 1 bit. For example, if you want to bit shift a char to the left by 2 bits, all the bits of the char are shifted to the left 2 bits. The leftmost 2 bits are truncated, and 2 false bits are added to the rightmost position, as illustrated in Figure 9.4.

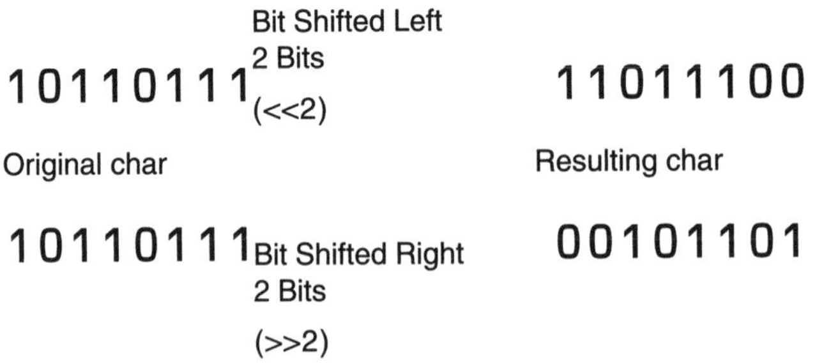

FIGURE 9.4

The original character on the left is shifted over two places to form the resulting character on the right.

Bit Shifted Left 2 Bits (<<2)

10110111   11011100

Original char   Resulting char

Bit Shifted Right 2 Bits (>>2)

10110111   00101101

Bit shifting one place right is the equivalent of multiplying by two, and bit shifting one place left is the equivalent of dividing by two and truncating the remainder.

CREATING AN ENCRYPTION PROGRAM

Your goal, agent, should you accept it, is to develop a high-security encryption program for the British S.A.S. covert operations force. The program must be quick and efficient, allowing S.A.S. agents the ability to work quickly in enemy territory. If you are caught, we, the authors, will deny all knowledge of your existence.

Good luck, agent!

The encryption algorithm used on this assignment is not difficult. Your program will take the first four bits and last four bits of every byte and switch them. You can do this using the bit shift operator and dividing by 128 while truncating the fractional section.

Try to solve the problem by yourself, but if you get stuck, you can check out the solution in the following "Encryption Program."

```cpp
//9.6 - Encryption Program - Dirk Henkemans
//A text data encryption program

#include <iostream>
#include <fstream>

using namespace std;

class Encryption
{
    fstream file1; //source file
    fstream file2; //destination file
public:

    Encryption::Encryption(char* filename1, char* filename2)
    {
        file1.open(filename1, ios::in | ios::out | ios::binary);
        file2.open(filename2, ios::out|ios::binary);
    }

    //encrypts the file
    void Encrypt(void)
```

```cpp
{
    char currentByte;
    bool currentBit;
    int index = 0;

    //sets the pointers to the beginning of the file
    file1.seekg (0, ios::beg);
    file2.seekp (0, ios::beg);

    //reads the first value
    file1.read(&currentByte, 1);
    while(file1.good())
    {
        //loop for four bits
        for(int c = 0; c < 4; c++)
        {
            //finds out if the first bit is a one
            currentBit = (int)((unsigned char)currentByte / 128);
            //shifts the byte over
            currentByte <<= 1;
            //if the first bit was a one then we add it to the end
            if(currentBit)
            {
                currentByte += 1;
            }
        }

        //writes the character
        file2.write(&currentByte, 1);

        //increments the pointer
        file1.seekg (++index);
        file2.seekp (index);

        //reads the next value
        file1.read(&currentByte, 1);
    }
}
```

```
        //closes both of the files
        void close(void)
        {
            file1.close();
            file2.close();
        }
};

int main(void)
{
    cout << "Welcome to the S.A.S encryption program.";

    Encryption delta("dragons.txt", "output1.txt");
    delta.Encrypt();
    delta.close();

    Encryption gamma("output1.txt", "output2.txt");
    gamma.Encrypt();
    delta.close();

    return 0;
}
```

Don't try to use the "Encryption Program" on large or important files. Neither the author nor Course PTR hold any responsibility for loss or alteration of data or for the program's security.

When you first use this program to encrypt a file, if you open the encrypted file in a text editor such as Notepad or DOS Edit, the file will look strange and often be all on one line. For example, it might look like this (no kidding):

@#|#!%$%^&*7gfh@#$#4

When you run the program the second time, the program should decrypt the file, causing it to look the same as the original file.

SUMMARY

You started this chapter by looking at the hierarchy and learning the definitions for streams. Then you used the file streams on some text files in text mode. Later, as you expanded your knowledge, you continued to use file streams to copy files and learned about the get and put pointers. With some common manipulators from the <ios> header library, you manipulated the cout stream and produced several cool outputs. Last, you developed an encryption program.

CHALLENGES

1. Create a program to write the following two lines of text to a file called Question1.txt:

```
Programming is fun.
I love programming.
```

2. What method can you use to test whether a file has reached its end? What method can you use to test whether a file has an error? What method can you use to test whether a file has reached its end and has an error?

3. What is the result when the letter A is bit-shifted to the left three places (<<3)? What is the result when the letter A is bit-shifted to the right two places (>>2)?

4. Explain why the encryption program needs to be run a second time in order to decrypt the file placed into the program.

ERRORS AND EXCEPTION HANDLING

You've learned much about C++ so far, good reader. Now, you are ready to find out how to make your programs secure and safe from crashing. In this chapter, you learn how to ensure that certain conditions remain true. You learn how to safeguard against going out of array bounds. In short, you learn how to make your programs very stable, capable of handling the unexpected. In this chapter, you learn how to:

- Use assertions
- Handle exceptions
- Catch every exception

ASSERTING CONDITIONS

Sometimes, certain operations can be dangerous. They can corrupt memory, freeze your computer, or worse. Normally, you know what must be true in order for the operation to succeed. You know that certain conditions must be true. If these conditions are not true, the results could be disastrous. It is your duty, as a programmer, to test for these conditions before proceeding with the operation. If the condition fails, you must immediately end the program or risk catastrophe.

Okay, that was a little melodramatic. It's true that some operations can cause problems, but it is rare for them to be permanent or disastrous. However, to make your program execute successfully, it is a good idea to test to be sure that conditions are true before performing a major operation (or a potentially risky one). If a condition fails while you are testing your program, you might simply exit the program and have the program display a message saying what happened and on which line.

C++ provides a special macro, called an assertion, for exiting the program and displaying a specified message for a specified condition. Assertions are macros that test a condition and exit the program if the condition fails. A standard version of this macro is defined in `<cassert>`. The prototype for an assertion is as follows:

```
void assert(int expression);
```

Even though `expression` is an integer, it is treated as a boolean expression (for example, 5 <3). Thus, testing a condition might look like this:

```
assert (y > 0);
```

This assertion does nothing if `y` is greater than 0, but if `y` is not greater, the program stops, and an error message is displayed. To see this error message for yourself, try compiling the following program:

```
//10.1 - An Assertion Failure - Mark Lee
#include <cassert>

int main(void)
{
    assert(5>6); //always fails
    return 0;
}
```

This assertion will always fail, no matter what, because 5 is never greater than 6. So, what happens when this assertion fails? First, this message is displayed:

```
Assertion failed: 5>6, file C:\Projects\Temp\Test13\Test13.cpp, line 5
```

On my computer (I'm using Windows Vista Professional and Visual Studio 2008 Express Edition) a window pops up displaying a message saying that the program terminated abnormally, as shown in Figure 10.1.

The `assert` macro ends the program when it fails by calling a function called `abort()`. The `abort()` function is included in `<cstdlib>`. This function takes no arguments and returns no value. It simply ends the program. This is the function that caused the message box in Figure 10.1 to appear. This function also outputs the message, `abnormal program termination`.

If this assertion does not meet your needs or you want your program to keep running after a failed assert, you need to define your own assertion. However, if you are using the assert macro just to debug your programs, you should be fine.

You can use assertions to ensure that you don't walk off the end of an array. You also use them at the beginning of functions to ensure that the user applied the function correctly, and you use them to validate the result of code that you are not sure is correct.

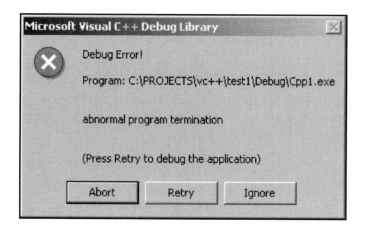

FIGURE 10.1

If you have an assertion failure in your programs, you will see a message box like this one. The filename and directory of the executable file are displayed.

Keep in mind that you use assertions to debug code, so before you release something or give it to other people to use, be sure to remove all the assertions. (The users of your program do not need to know that an assertion failed on line 675 of a code file.) If you want to handle unexpected errors happening in your program when you release it, use exception handling.

HANDLING EXCEPTIONS

When you write code that is not a complete program (such as a class or a set of functions), unexpected errors can happen in your code. You can't always count on the values that you expect, and you can't always assume that users of your code will know what they are doing. A graceful piece of code will prevent a program from crashing when these kinds of things happen. One way to make your code "graceful" is by using exception handling, which enables you to manage non-routine circumstances in a program.

With exception handling, you can actually prevent unpredictable occurrences and exceptional events. Exceptions mean that a part of your code cannot perform a task that it was asked to do. Exception handling enables you to try another method of completing the task or to attempt to fix the problem.

An exception occurs because a section of code throws an exception. One example of an unexpected event, or exception, is a computer running out of hard drive space. However, running out hard drive space does not mean that a program will necessarily crash or completely fail at its task. You can write code that handles such exceptions by specifying that the program catch a certain kind of exception.

In order to catch an exception, you must use a try-block. A try-block is a section of code with the keyword `try` at the beginning. This keyword keeps track of whether an exception is thrown. The syntax for a try-block is as follows:

```
try { someCode }
```

Using a try-block tells the computer that the code inside a try-block might throw an exception, so watch out.

After you establish a try-block, you can use it to catch an exception. You do this by using a `catch` statement. Here is the syntax for the `catch` statement:

```
catch(exceptionName) { whatToDo }
```

Here `exceptionName` is the name of an exception. When the code inside a try-block throws an exception, the computer starts executing the code inside the `catch` statement. In order for a `catch` statement to be connected with a `try` statement, the `catch` statement must occur immediately after the `try` statement. You cannot have any code between them:

```
try
{
      someCode
}
catch (exceptionName)
{
      whatToDo
}
```

You can have as many `catch` statements after `try` statements as you want:

```
try {
      someCode
}
catch (exceptionName1)
{
      whatToDo1
}
```

```
catch (exceptionName2)
{
     whatToDo2
}
```

When an exception is thrown, the appropriate `catch` statement is called.

An exception is thrown using the `throw` statement. Here is the syntax:

```
throw exception;
```

Here `exception` is the exception.

`exceptionName` (from the `catch` statement) is the name of a type—any type at all. It can be `int`, `char*`, or `string`. In fact, it is very similar to a function argument, except that it doesn't need a variable name.

`exception` must be an expression. Using a `throw` statement is like calling a function. Think of all the `catch` statements as an overloaded function. Based on the type of `exception`, the computer can decide which `catch` statement is the most appropriate one to use (if any).

Here is an example:

```
#include<iostream>

using namespace std;

int main (void)
{
     try
     {
          int x = 10;
          if (x == 10)
               throw x;
     }
     catch(int x)
     {
          cerr << "Oh No! x equals " << x << "!!!!";
     }
     catch(float f)
     {
          cerr << "How did I get here?";
```

```
        }
        return 0;
}
```

In the preceding example, the variable x is initialized to 10. Then the program checks to see whether x is 10 and throws an exception if so. This is obviously a useless example, but it illustrates our point.

The exceptionNames for the catch statements are not just type names. There is also a variable declaration, because catch statements work exactly like functions. The value of x (10) is passed to the catch statement so that the catch statement can deal with the error properly (it helps if the catch statement knows what the error is).

Also, even though there are two catch statements, the computer, using the rules for function overloading, figured out which statement is the correct one to call.

Using a built-in data type for an exception is usually not a good idea. When an integer is thrown, you can't tell exactly what the error is. You might assume that the error is related to the value of an integer, but you can't tell for certain.

Fortunately, there is a standard way to pass this information. Normally, you define a new type for every kind of exception. Here is an example:

```
class FileError {};
```

Notice how this class is completely empty? This is because the class doesn't need anything in it. The class is just being used for its name. Here is an example of how you might use this:

```
#include <iostream>
#include <istream>
#include <fstream>

using namespace std;

class FileError {};

int main (void)
{
        try
        {
                char* filename = "hello.txt";
                fstream file;
```

```
                file.open(filename, ios::in);
                if (!file.is_open())
                        throw FileError();
        }
        catch (FileError)
        {
                cerr << "Error with file.";
        }
        return 0;
}
```

If your code throws an exception that is not caught (there is no appropriate catch statement), the computer decides what to do. Unfortunately, a computer is not very forgiving. It thinks the best way to handle an exception is to immediately close the program. To do so, the computer calls the terminate() or unexpected() functions; both are included with <exception>. Also, neither of the two have arguments or a void return type. To see what happens when these functions are called, compile and run the following program:

```
int main (void)
{
        throw 5; //an arbitrary value
        return 0;
}
```

You might have noticed that the error message displayed is exactly the same as for the abort() function. This is because terminate() calls abort(). You can make terminate() call a custom function as well by calling the set_terminate() function. Here is the declaration:

```
typedef void (*terminate_function)();
terminate_function set_terminate(terminate function term_func);
```

This declaration looks really complicated, but you just pass the name of the function as the parameter. Here is an example:

```
#include <exception>
#include <iostream>

using namespace std;

void error_handler()
{
```

```
        cerr << "There was an uncaught error.";
}

int main (void)
{
        set_terminate(error_handler);
        throw 5;
        return 0;
}
Output:
There was an uncaught error.
```

BUILDING AN EXCEPTION HIERARCHY

If you use really specific exceptions for a large program, you can quickly have an unmanageable number of exceptions. Having a ton of catch statements after every try-block is annoying at best. You can easily forget to include one and wind up with quite a problem. Fortunately, as you program, you will discover personal techniques to alleviate this problem.

However, one common way is to use inheritance (refer to Chapter 8, "Introducing Inheritance," for more on that topic). If you make a hierarchy of exceptions, you can deal with only the most general one, rather than be specific. Or you can be very specific for some and very general for others. This technique gives you the flexibility to design your programs so that they adapt to meet any situation.

Here is an example of such a hierarchy:

```
class MathError {};
class DivideByZero : public MathError {};
class Overflow : public MathError {};
```

With this hierarchy, you can choose to handle a specific exception, such as DivideByZero, or deal only with all math errors in one catch statement. Here is an example:

```
#include <iostream>
using namespace std;

int divide(int a, int b);

class MathError {};
class DivideByZero : public MathError {};
```

```
class Overflow : public MathError {};

int divide(int a, int b)
{
      if (b == 0)
      {
            throw DivideByZero();
            return false;
      }
      return a/b;
}

int main (void)
{
      try
      {
            if (!divide(5,0))
                  throw MathError();
      }
      catch(DivideByZero)
      {
            cerr << "Whoops! You tried to divide by zero";
      }
      catch (MathError)
      {
            cerr << "There was an unexplained math error.";
      }
      return 0;
}
Output:
Whoops! You tried to divide by zero
```

Here you see that if you try to divide by zero, a `DivideByZero` exception is thrown, but if there is some other problem, a general `MathError` is thrown.

This example also illustrates another important point. If you call a function within a try-block and that function throws an error, the try-block can catch it.

CATCHING EVERY EXCEPTION

You can catch every possible exception in your programs, making them virtually crash proof. To do so, you use a form of the catch statement that can handle any exception that hasn't already been handled. Rather than an exception type as the argument for the catch statement, you use an ellipsis (...). When the computer searches the catch statements for one that will handle an exception, the computer will use this one as a last resort (if you include it). Here is the syntax:

```
catch(...) { handleTheException }
```

Here is an example of how you might use the default catch statement:

```cpp
#include <iostream>

using namespace std;

int main (void)
{
    try
    {
        throw 6;
    }
    catch(...)
    {
        cerr << "There was an exception, but it was caught!";
    }
    return 0;
}
Output:
There was an exception, but it was caught!
```

If you use this version of the catch statement with other catch statements, it must be at the end of the list. If not, no subsequent catch statements beyond the default catch statement will ever have the possibility of being called. However, if the default catch statement is used at the end of the list of catch statements, the default catch statement will be used only as a last resort.

CREATING THE MINEFIELD GAME

You are part of the elite Soviet team XJ77. You have been sent out to disarm a deadly minefield. The work is extremely dangerous. Only the best and brightest will survive a day in the minefield. Compile this program, and see if you have what it takes.

```
//10.2 - MineField - Mark Lee
#include <iostream>
#include <exception>
#include <string>
#include <vector>
#include <cstdlib>
#include <ctime>

using std::string;
using std::vector;
using std::srand;
using std::time;


class StepOnMine {};
class FailedDisarm {};
class MineField
{
    vector<bool> minefield;

    //stores where the player has been
    vector<bool> beenThere;

    //current location of player
    int location;

    int menu(string choices[], int numChoices)
    {
        using std::cout;
        using std::cin;

        int choice;
        do {
```

```cpp
            for (int i = 0; i < numChoices; i++)
            {
                    cout << i+1 << ") " << choices[i] << "\n";
            }
            cin << choice;
        while (choice < 1 || choice > numChoices);
        return choice;
    }

public:

    MineField() //4X4 minefield
    {
        srand((unsigned int)time(0));
        location = 0;
        for (int c = 0; c <16; c++)
        {
            minefield.push_back(false);
            beenThere.push_back(false);
        }
        for (int i = 0; i <10; i++) //place 10 random mines
            minefield[rand()%15+1] = true;
        beenThere[0] = true;
    }

    bool IsAMine(int location)
    {
        return minefield[location];
    }

    string draw()
    {
        string s;
        for (int i = 0; i <4; i++)
        {
            for (int c=0; c<4; c++)
            {
                if (location == i*4+c)
```

```
                                s+='P';
                        else
                        {
                                if (beenThere[i*4+c])
                                        s+= "X";
                                else
                                        s+= " ";
                        }
                        s+="|";
                }
                s+= '\n';
        }
        return s;
}

bool moreMines()
{
        for (int i=0; i<16; i++)
                if (beenThere[i])
                        return true;
        return false;
}

int Directions()
{
        string options[4];
        options[0] = "North";
        options[1] = "East";
        options[2] = "South";
        options[3] = "West";
        return menu(options, 4);
}

int& place() { return location; }

void goThere(int place) { beenThere[place] = true; }
};
```

```
void Detonate()
{
    using std::cout;
    cout << "You detonated the mine. Ka-boom!!!\n";
}

void disarm()
{
    int temp = rand()%2+1;
    if (temp-1)
        throw FailedDisarm();
}

int main (void)
{
    using std::set_terminate;
    using std::cout;
    using std::cin;
    set_terminate(Detonate);
    MineField m; //create the minefield
    string input;

    cout << "Welcome to the MineField!!\n"
        << "You are part of the elite Soviet mine team "
        << "XJ77,\n sent to clear a deadly minefield full"
        << " of remote heat-sensing claymore mines.\n"
        << "Most of your team will not survive.\n"
        << "Only the best of you will see then end of "
        << " the day.\n Do you have what it takes?\n";
    cin >> input;
    if(input == "no" || input == "No")
        goto TOO_BAD;
    cout << "You are in the NorthWest corner.\n";
PLAY:
    try
    {
        int goTo;
        while(m.moreMines())
```

```
    {
        cout << endl << m.draw();
        cout << "Your position is marked with a P.\n"
            << "Which direction would you like to go?" <<endl;
        bool proper = false;
        do {
            goTo = m.Directions();
            if (goTo == 1 && m.place() >3)
                proper = true;
            if (goTo == 2 && (m.place()-3)%4 != 0)
                proper = true;
            if (goTo == 3 && m.place() <12)
                proper = true;
            if (goTo == 4 && m.place()%4 != 0)
                proper = true;
            if (!proper)
                cout << "\nYou cannot go that way.\n";
        } while (!proper);

        if (goTo == 1)
            m.place() -= 4;
        if (goTo == 2)
            m.place()++;
        if (goTo == 3)
            m.place() += 4;
        if (goTo == 4)
            m.place()--;
        m.goThere(m.place());

        if (m.IsAMine(m.place()))
            throw StepOnMine();
    }
}
catch(StepOnMine)
{
    int input;
    do {
        cout << "\nYou have encountered a mine.\n"
```

```
                       << "What would you like to do?\n"\
                       << "[1]Attempt to Disarm it.\n"
                       << "[2]Run Away.\n";
                cin >> input;
        } while(input <1 && input >2);

        if (input == 1)
        {
                try
                {
                        disarm();
                }
                catch(FailedDisarm)
                {
                        terminate();
                }
                cout << "You have disarmed the mine!!!\n";
                goto PLAY;
        }
        cout << "You have failed the XJ77 team.\n";
        goto TOO_BAD;
    }
    return 0;
TOO_BAD:
    cout << "\nMaybe next year kid.\n";
    return 0;
}
```

SUMMARY

This chapter, although short, is an important one. Even the most advanced programmers too often ignore the concept of this chapter, and it is true that exception handling does not add to the functionality of your program. However, exception handling makes your programs stable, and if you want to advance from being a good programmer to being an excellent one, we strongly suggest that you make a habit of using it.

CHALLENGES

1. What does the keyword `try` do?
2. What is the purpose of an exception hierarchy?
3. How can you design your programs so that they will not crash?
4. What is the definition of an exception?
5. At what point in your program's development should you use assertions?

CHAPTER 11

CREATING THE PIRATE ADVENTURE

L ast chapter! If you started at the beginning of this book, you've traveled far, good reader. This chapter shows you how to apply all the information in the earlier chapters to design a computer game. In this chapter, you find the code for a basic game engine. You will use Dark GDK, a game development kit, which is distributed with Visual Studio Express Edition, and much of the C++ programming covered in the rest of this book. It is up to you, as a new programmer, to develop this code, make it your own, and produce a fully functional game. Good luck!

In this chapter, you learn about the following:

- Declaring the global variables of the game engine
- Creating the Ship class, which is used to represent a ship
- Creating the game chassis
- Moving the ship across the screen
- Drawing the game to the screen
- Visiting towns within the game

Introducing Dark GDK

There are many things one needs to be able to program in order to write a graphical computer game that we have not yet taught. The details of many of these things are beyond the scope of this book, but, fortunately, there is a library available, called Dark GDK, which provides all of the functionality we require. This library is freely available for download at http://www.microsoft.com/express/samples/gamecreators/default.aspx.

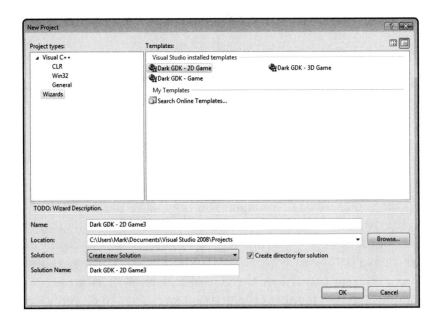

Figure 11.1

Creating a Dark GDK project.

Once you've successfully installed Dark GDK, you'll be able to create Dark GDK projects, as shown in Figure 11.1. The code for a "Dark GDK – 2D Game" project is shown below:

```
// Dark GDK - The Game Creators - www.thegamecreators.com

// the wizard has created a very simple 2D project that uses Dark GDK
// it can be used as a starting point in making your own 2D games

// whenever using Dark GDK you must ensure you include the header file
#include "DarkGDK.h"

// the main entry point for the application is this function
void DarkGDK ( void )
{
```

```
// in this application a backdrop is loaded and then several
// animated sprites are displayed on screen

// when starting a Dark GDK program it is useful to set global
// application properties, we begin by turning the sync rate on,
// this means we control when the screen is updated, we also set
// the maximum rate to 60 which means the maximum frame rate will
// be set at 60 frames per second
dbSyncOn    ( );
dbSyncRate ( 60 );

// a call is made to this function so we can stop the GDK from
// responding to the escape key, we can then add in some code in our
// main loop so we can control what happens when the escape key is pressed
dbDisableEscapeKey ( );

// now we will set the random seed value to the timer, this will
// help us to get more random values each time we run the program
dbRandomize ( dbTimer ( ) );

// we are going to display a backdrop for the scene, to do this
// we load our image and give it an ID number of 1, this particular
// image is of a sky at night with stars
dbLoadImage ( "backdrop.bmp", 1 );

// the next step is to create a sprite that uses this image, this
// is achieved by calling dbSprite and passing in a value of 1 for the
// sprites ID, 0 for the X coordinate, 0 for the Y coordinates and a
// value of 1 for the image
dbSprite ( 1, 0, 0, 1 );

// next we will load in some animated sprites, before doing this
// we need to adjust the image color key, by using this function we
// can make a specific color be transparent, in our case we want this
// to be bright pink
dbSetImageColorKey ( 255, 0, 255 );

// in this loop we're going to create some animated sprites, the image
// we load contains frames of animation for an asteroid
for ( int i = 2; i < 30; i++ )
```

```cpp
{
     // create an animated sprite and give it the ID number from the
     // variable i, next is the filename, now we come to how many frames
     // across and down, in our case this is 4, finally we come to the
        image
     // ID that the sprite will use, again we use i
     dbCreateAnimatedSprite ( i, "sprite.bmp", 4, 4, i );

     // position our sprite at a random location
     dbSprite ( i, dbRnd ( 640 ), -dbRnd ( 1500 ), i );
}

// now we come to our main loop, we call LoopGDK so some internal
// work can be carried out by the GDK
while ( LoopGDK ( ) )
{
     // run a loop through all our sprites
     for ( int i = 2; i < 30; i++ )
     {
          // move the sprite down and play its animation
          // moving from frame 1 to 16 with a delay of 60 ms
          dbMoveSprite ( i, -2 );
          dbPlaySprite ( i, 1, 16, 60 );

          // check the position of the sprite, if it has gone off screen
          // then reposition it back to the top
          if ( dbSpriteY ( i ) > 500 )
               dbSprite ( i, dbRnd ( 640 ), -dbRnd ( 1500 ), i );
     }

     // here we check if the escape key has been pressed, when it has
     // we will break out of the loop
     if ( dbEscapeKey ( ) )
          break;

     // here we make a call to update the contents of the screen
     dbSync ( );
}
```

```
// when the user presses escape the code will break out to this location
// and we can free up any previously allocated resources

// delete all the sprites
for ( int i = 1; i < 30; i++ )
    dbDeleteSprite ( i );

// delete the backdrop image
dbDeleteImage ( 1 );

// and now everything is ready to return back to Windows
return;
}
```

This code, though littered with helpful comments, might be rather overwhelming at first glance. But do not lose hope! By the end of the chapter, this code will seem perfectly natural.

So, studious reader, the first thing you should do is compile and run this code to see exactly what it does. Remember to start by creating a "Dark GDK – 2D Game" project. The running program is shown in Figure 11.2.

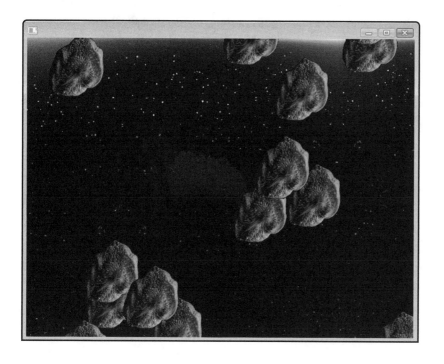

FIGURE 11.2

The asteroids sample Dark GDK program.

Now, let's begin taking this code apart to figure it out. The first thing you'll notice is the complete lack of a `main()` function. When using Dark GDK, instead of `main()`, you must create a `DarkGDK()` function. This function has no arguments and a `void` return value. All the code in this program is contained within this one function, and that code can be split into three parts: initialization, the main loop, and cleanup.

The initialization is the longest of the three sections. It includes everything from the beginning of the `DarkGDK()` function up to these lines:

```
// now we come to our main loop, we call LoopGDK so some internal
// work can be carried out by the GDK
while ( LoopGDK ( ) )
```

The first step in the initialization section is the following two lines:

```
dbSyncOn   ( );
dbSyncRate ( 60 );
```

Every function provided by Dark GDK starts with the prefix "db". This is to make sure that the function names do not conflict with any of your own; similar to how the C++ Standard Library uses the `std` namespace.

These two lines of code set the maximum frame rate. With a graphical computer game, it is important to control the rate at which things happen, because on modern computers things can become way too fast if they simply run as fast as possible. The frame rate here is set to 60. This means that the image on the screen will be updated 60 times every second (at most).

By default, a Dark GDK program will respond to the escape key by immediately quitting. Often you would like to be able to perform some actions before quitting, or you'd like to use the escape key for something else. The call to `dbDisableEscapeKey()` disables Dark GDK's default action.

The C++ Standard Library provides functionality to generate random numbers, but Dark GDK provides its own. Just like you use `srand()` to seed the standard library random generator, you used `dbRandomize()` to seed the Dark GDK random number generator. Using `dbTimer()` as a seed value is just like using `time()`.

Now we get to the exciting part! The call to `dbLoadImage()` reads the background from an image file to get it ready to be displayed. This function takes two arguments: the filename of the image, and an id number that you assign. You must remember this number so that you can refer to the loaded image in later code.

Speaking of which, the loaded image is used in the very next line. In order to display an image on the screen, we must first load it into a "sprite". A sprite in Dark GDK is a two-dimensional image that can be displayed on the screen. When we create a sprite, we give it an id and a position. The position refers to the top-left corner of the image and, since this is a background for the whole screen, is set to the top-left corner of the screen, or (0,0). The image id is used as the fourth parameter to refer to the previously loaded image file.

Using the `dbSetImageColorKey()` function, you can make a certain color be displayed as transparent onscreen. This can be a convenient way to convert a square image file into, say, an asteroid shaped image onscreen.

The last step is to create the 28 asteroid sprites at random locations. These sprites are different from the background in that they are animated. Take a look at Figure 11.3 to see the image file these sprites are created from. As you can see, all the different frames of animation are stored in the same file. Instead of `dbLoadImage()`, we use `dbCreateAnimatedSprite()` to load the images for an animated sprite. You must provide the number of animation frames per row and the number of columns. Even though the sprite is created with this function call, we must still call `dbSprite()` to give this sprite a position. `dbRnd()` is used to create random values for the sprite's position.

FIGURE 11.3

The image file for the asteroid sprite.

Now that everything is initialized, it is time to enter the main loop. This loop has the following structure:

```
while(LoopGDK())
{
    ...
}
```

The call to `LoopGDK()` performs all internal operations needed and only returns 0 when the program is ready to quit. All of the code included in this loop is executed once per frame.

The first thing done in the main loop is to loop through all of the asteroid sprites and move them down. This is accomplished with the `dbMoveSprite()` function. Also, the `dbPlaySprite()` function is used to automatically cycle through all of the animation frames at a rate of 60 frames per second. When a particular asteroid sprite has gone past the bottom of the screen, its position is reset to a new random location.

Every frame, `dbEscapeKey()` is used to check if the escape key has been pressed. If it has, we break out of the main loop, effectively ending the program.

Finally, `dbSync()` is called to update the screen with all the changes performed previously in the main loop.

When the program ends, either by the user pressing the escape key or the window being closed, we enter the cleanup phase. Here, the resources for all of the sprites are freed with a simple call to `dbDeleteSprite()`. Finally, the loaded image file is unloaded with the call to `dbDeleteImage()`.

Table 11.1 summarizes all of the Dark GDK functions that we'll be using in this chapter.

TABLE 11.1 IMPORTANT DARK GDK FUNCTIONS

Function Name	Purpose
DarkGDK()	Replaces the main() function.
dbSyncOn()	Allows the maximum frame rate to be set.
dbSyncRate()	Sets the maximum frame rate.
dbSetDisplayMode()	Sets the number of pixels on the screen.
dbMaximizeWindow()	Maximizes the display.
dbSetWindowOff()	Exits window mode for full-screen display.
dbDisableEscapeKey()	Disables Dark GDK's default handling of the escape key.
dbRandomize()	Seeds the random number generator.
dbTimer()	Returns the current time.
dbSetImageColorKey()	Sets the color that will be treated as transparent.
dbLoadImage()	Loads an image from a file.
dbCreateAnimatedSprite()	Loads a set of animated frames from a file.
dbSprite()	Creates a sprite, or gives it a new position.
dbSetSpritePriority()	Used to control which sprites are in front onscreen.
dbHideSprite()	Disables the visibility of the sprite.
dbShowSprite()	Enables the visibility of the sprite.
dbRnd()	Returns a random number.
LoopGDK()	Used to implement the main loop.
dbMoveSprite()	Moves the specified sprite a certain amount up or down.
dbPlaySprite()	Automatically cycles through the animation frames.
dbSetSpriteFrame()	Changes the sprite to a specified animation frame.
dbEscapeKey()	Returns true if the escape key has been pressed.
dbReturnKey()	Returns true if the return key has been pressed.
dbLeftKey()	Returns true if the left arrow key has been pressed.
dbRightKey()	Returns true if the right arrow key has been pressed.
dbUpKey()	Returns true if the up arrow key has been pressed.
dbDownKey()	Returns true if the down arrow key has been pressed.
dbSync()	Updates the display. Should be called once per frame.
dbDeleteSprite()	Destroys the specified sprite.
dbDeleteImage()	Destroys the specified image.

GETTING AN OVERVIEW OF THE GAME

When you are designing a game, we suggest creating the graphics first because the graphics help give the game shape. After all, what's more exciting, six hours of programming looking at a screen with only the words Insert Title Screen Here running across it or the artful title screen you labored to create? After you have several graphics in place, you can use them to test whether your code works.

You will use 11 screens for the "Pirate Adventure" game: the title screen (which is displayed before the game starts), a screen to display a city when the player enters it, and 9 screens for the game maps.

The basic idea of this game engine is that you follow a map to sail around the Caribbean. The map will be divided into 9 pieces (9 squares forming a 3 x 3 grid). Each piece will be the size of a computer screen (800 x 600). Each of the 9 pieces will be divided into a separate bitmap (.bmp) file, with names ranging from map1.bmp to map9.bmp, shown respectively in Figures 11.4 through 11.12.

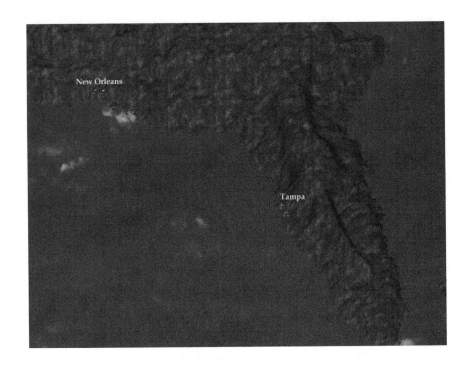

FIGURE 11.4

The northwest corner of the map shows the bottom of the United States, including Florida.

FIGURE 11.5

The large sea area with New Providence near the bottom is the upper-center section of the map.

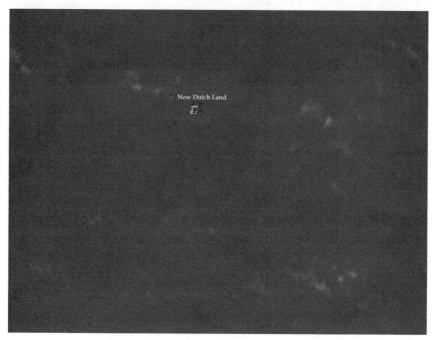

FIGURE 11.6

New Dutchland (a fictional city) is isolated in the middle of the upper-right section of the map.

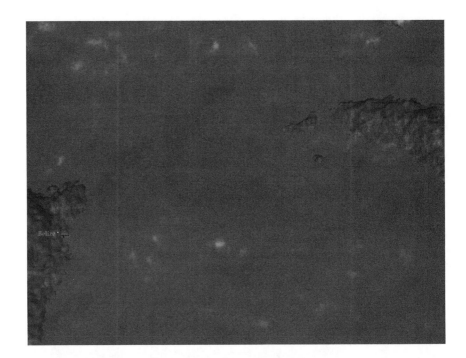

FIGURE 11.7

Right below map 1 comes the center-left section of the map, showing Belize.

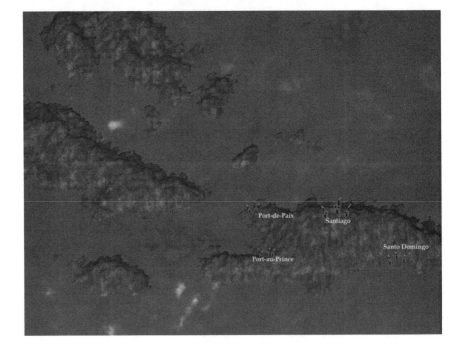

FIGURE 11.8

The exact center of the map shows a thriving area, with many cities.

FIGURE 11.9

Immediately below map 3 and beside map 5 is the center-right portion of the map.

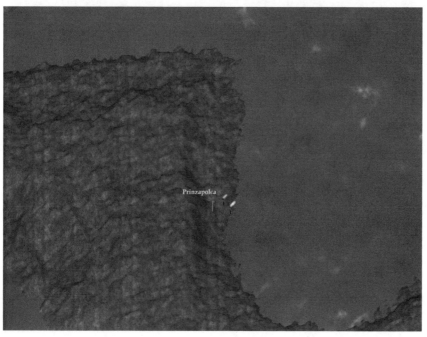

Prinzapolca

FIGURE 11.10

A lot of land, but few cities, are on the lower-left corner of the map.

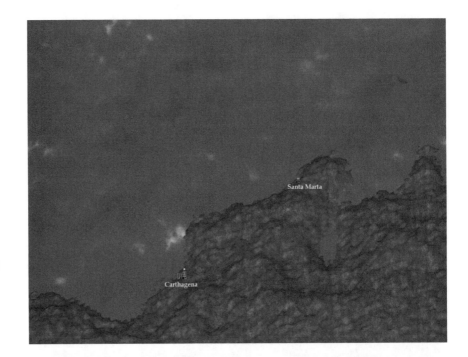

On the lower-center section of the map you see Santa Maria and Carthagena.

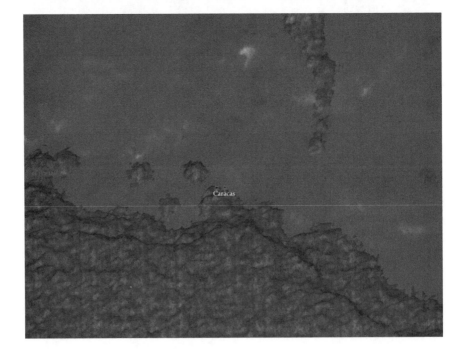

On the lower-right corner of the map you see Caracas all by itself.

In order to appear like a professional game, the "Pirate Adventure" needs a title screen. A title screen generally displays the title of the game (on most games, the title screen will also be where you can choose to start a new game). The title screen (Figure 11.13 shows the title screen for the "Pirate Adventure") displays until the enter key is pressed, and then the "Pirate Adventure" begins.

Finally, the city screen (see Figure 11.14) displays whenever the player enters a city. This gives some variation to the game. The player isn't always on the same screen for the entire game.

Now that you have the background on the screen images, you can turn your attention to the graphics for the ship. In this game engine, there is only one ship (the player), but you could easily reuse the graphics for the first ship and create a second one on the screen. Because the ship travels in only four directions, you need only four graphics for the ship, one image for each direction. Fortunately, all these images are small enough to fit into one image. When you need one, you just copy that part of the image.

Each picture of the ship is called an animation frame. See Figure 11.15 for the ship image file. Because the ship must sit seamlessly on the map screen, its background needs to be transparent.

FIGURE 11.13

Here is the "Pirate Adventure" title screen in all of its glory.

FIGURE 11.14

This is what the city screen looks like.

FIGURE 11.17

You use the ship sprites to give the ship a sense of direction.

PROGRAMMING THE GAME ENGINE

Now that you have the graphics all sorted out, it is time to start programming. The first thing to do is create a new "Dark GDK – 2D Game" project, called "Pirate Adventure". You will need to copy all of the images into the project folder, alongside your code.

Because Dark GDK does not play along well with the C++ Standard Library, there is one additional change we must make. Right-click on the project name in the Solution Explorer and select Properties. See Figure 11.18.

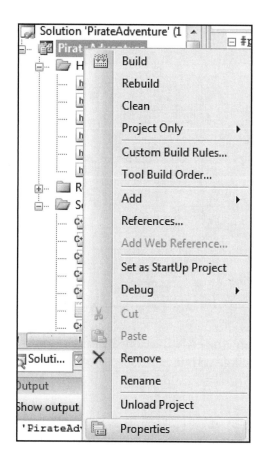

FIGURE 11.18

Editing the project properties.

Next, under Configuration Properties and then C/C++, select Code Generation. The setting you want to change is Runtime Library. You want to change it from Multi-threaded Debug (/MTd) to Multi-threaded (/MT). See Figure 11.19.

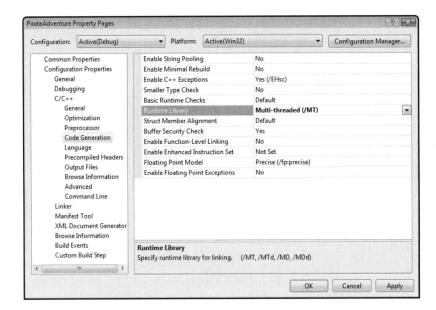

FIGURE 11.19

Making Dark GDK get along with the C++ Standard Library.

Then you can proceed to add the following code files, one by one. You can find a listing of the complete game engine in the following sections.

Storing Locations

Throughout this game engine, we are going to need a way to store locations. Since the location of things either onscreen or on the map has both a horizontal (x) and vertical (y) component, a simple integer will not be sufficient. We will create a new class to store locations, called `Point`. The declaration of the `Point` class is stored in Point.h and the implementation in Point.cpp.

```
//Point.h
#pragma once

#include <istream>

using std::istream;

class Point
{
    int m_x, m_y;
public:
    Point(int x, int y) : m_x(x), m_y(y) {}
```

```
        Point(istream& input);
        int x() { return m_x; }
        int y() { return m_y; }
        Point operator+(const Point& p);

};


// Point.cpp
#include "Point.h"


Point::Point(istream& input)
{
        input >> m_x >> m_y;
}


Point Point::operator+(const Point& p)
{
        return Point(m_x + p.m_x, m_y + p.m_y);
}
```

There are two constructors for the Point class. One simply sets the x and y components of the Point directly, and the other reads them in from an input stream. There are two accessor methods used to obtain the x and y components of the point, named x() and y() respectively. Finally, the addition operator is overloaded to allow for adding two Point objects together. Predicatively, this function simply creates a new Point object by adding the respective x and y components together.

Creating a Ship Class

The first file is Ship.h. This is the declaration file for the Ship class. The actual implementation of this class is in Ship.cpp.

```
//Ship.h
#pragma once

#include "DarkGDK.h"

#include "Point.h"
```

```
class Ship
{
      static char* m_spriteFileName;
      static const int m_numFramesAcross = 4;
      static const int m_numFramesDown = 1;
      static const int m_spriteID = 1;
      static const int m_imageID = 1;

public:
      Ship();
      void show(Point theLoc);
      void hide();
      void moveLeft();
      void moveRight();
      void moveUp();
      void moveDown();
      ~Ship();
};

// Ship.cpp
#include "Ship.h"

char* Ship::m_spriteFileName = "sprites.png";

Ship::Ship()
{
      dbCreateAnimatedSprite(m_spriteID, m_spriteFileName, m_numFramesAcross,
m_numFramesDown, m_imageID);

      dbSprite(m_spriteID,0,0,m_imageID);
      dbSetSpritePriority(m_spriteID, 1);
      this->hide();
}

void Ship::show(Point theLoc)
{
      dbSprite(m_spriteID, theLoc.x(), theLoc.y(), m_imageID);
      dbShowSprite(m_spriteID);
```

```
}

void Ship::hide()
{
        dbHideSprite(m_spriteID);
}

void Ship::moveLeft()
{
        dbSetSpriteFrame(m_spriteID,3);
}

void Ship::moveRight()
{
        dbSetSpriteFrame(m_spriteID,1);
}

void Ship::moveUp()
{
        dbSetSpriteFrame(m_spriteID,4);
}

void Ship::moveDown()
{
        dbSetSpriteFrame(m_spriteID,2);
}

Ship::~Ship()
{
        dbDeleteSprite(m_spriteID);
}
```

The constructor for this class loads the ship sprites with the dbCreateAnimatedSprite() function, gives the ship a random position, and hides the ship for the title screen. The dbSetSpritePriority() function is used to ensure that the ship is always drawn in front.

The show() member function moves the ship to the specified location with dbSprite() and shows the ship onscreen with dbShowSprite(). The hide() member function simply calls dbHideSprite() to ensure the ship is not shown. This is used for the title screen and the city screen.

The moveLeft(), moveRight(), moveUp(), and moveDown() member functions call dbSetSpriteFrame() to change the direction that the ship is facing.

Finally, the destructor simply calls dbDeleteSprite() to destroy the sprite for the ship.

Creating a City Class

There are a total of 13 cities in this game engine, each with its own name, bounding box, and ending location for the ship. The bounding box defines the area in which the ship must enter to visit the city. The ending location is the position the ship is set to once it exits the city. The City class is declared in City.h and implemented in City.cpp.

```cpp
// City.h
#pragma once

#include <string>

#include "Point.h"

using std::string;

class City
{
        string m_name;
        Point m_topLeft;
        Point m_bottomRight;
        Point m_endLoc;

public:
        City(string name, Point topLeft, Point bottomRight, Point endLoc);
        bool isInside(Point thePoint);
        Point endCoordinates();
        string name();
        ~City();
};

//City.cpp
#include "City.h"
```

```
City::City(string name, Point topLeft, Point bottomRight, Point endLoc) :
        m_name(name), m_topLeft(topLeft), m_bottomRight(bottomRight),
m_endLoc(endLoc)
{
}


bool City::isInside(Point thePoint)
{
        if (thePoint.x() < m_bottomRight.x() && thePoint.x() > m_topLeft.x() &&
                    thePoint.y() < m_bottomRight.y() && thePoint.y() >
m_topLeft.y())
                return true;
        return false;
}


string City::name()
{
        return m_name;
}


Point City::endCoordinates()
{
        return m_endLoc;
}


City::~City()
{
}
```

This class is very simple. Really the only function with any complication is the isInside() member function, which tests if a specified location counts as being in the city or not. If the provided location is inside the City object's bounding box, the function returns true, otherwise it returns false.

Implementing the Map Screens

The entire map is divided into 9 screens, each with its own image file, sprite, location, and set of cities. The Screen class encapsulates all of the functionality of each of these screens. It is declared in Screen.h and implemented in Screen.cpp.

```cpp
// Screen.h
#pragma once

#include "DarkGDK.h"

#include <vector>
#include <string>
#include <fstream>

#include "City.h"

using std::vector;
using std::string;
using std::ifstream;

class Screen
{
    int m_spriteID;
    int m_imageID;
    string m_fileName;
    Point m_topLeft;
    vector<City*> m_cities;
    ifstream m_mapFile;

public:
    Screen(int spriteID, int imageID, string fileName, Point topLeft);
    void addCity(string cityName, Point topLeft, Point bottomRight, Point
endLoc);
    Point topLeft() { return m_topLeft; }
    void hide();
    void show();
    bool isLandCollision(Point thePoint);
    City* isEnteringCity(Point thePoint);
    ~Screen();
private:
    Screen(const Screen& rhs);
    Screen& operator=(const Screen& rhs);
};
```

```
// Screen.cpp
#include "Screen.h"

Screen::Screen(int spriteID, int imageID, string fileName, Point topLeft) :
     m_spriteID(spriteID), m_imageID(imageID), m_fileName(fileName),
m_topLeft(topLeft)
{
     char fileNameBuffer[500];
     strcpy(fileNameBuffer,m_fileName.c_str());
     dbLoadImage( fileNameBuffer, m_imageID );
     dbSprite( m_spriteID, 0, 0, m_imageID );
     this->hide();

     m_mapFile.open(m_fileName.c_str());
}

void Screen::addCity(string cityName, Point topLeft, Point bottomRight, Point
endLoc)
{
     m_cities.push_back(new City(cityName, topLeft, bottomRight, endLoc));
}

void Screen::hide()
{
     dbHideSprite( m_spriteID );
}

void Screen::show()
{
     dbShowSprite( m_spriteID );
}

bool Screen::isLandCollision(Point thePoint)
{
     int green;
     int blue;

     m_mapFile.seekg(3 * (599 - thePoint.y()) * 800 + 3 * thePoint.x() + 54);
```

```
        blue = m_mapFile.get();
        green = m_mapFile.get();

        if (green < blue)
                return false;
        return true;
}


City* Screen::isEnteringCity(Point thePoint)
{
        for (int i = 0; i < m_cities.size(); i++)
        {
                if (m_cities[i]->isInside(thePoint))
                        return m_cities[i];
        }
        return 0;
}


Screen::~Screen()
{
        for (int i = 0; i < m_cities.size(); i++)
        {
                delete m_cities[i];
                m_cities[i] = 0;
        }

        // delete the backdrop sprite
        dbDeleteSprite ( m_spriteID );

        // delete the backdrop image
        dbDeleteImage ( m_imageID );

        m_mapFile.close();
}
```

The constructor for the Screen class simply calls dbLoadImage() to load the image file of the map and then dbSprite() to create a sprite from it. This is the same procedure we saw for the backdrop in the asteroids program. Take a look at the following lines of code:

```
char fileNameBuffer[500];
strcpy(fileNameBuffer,m_fileName.c_str());
dbLoadImage( fileNameBuffer, m_imageID );
```

You may wonder why we don't just pass m_fileName directly to dbLoadImage(). First, dbLoadImage() takes a char* and m_fileName is a string. Also, the c_str() member function returns a const char* instead of a regular char*, so we must copy it into a new string in order to pass it to dbLoadImage().

The member m_mapFile is a file stream of the bitmap image of the map. We use this member in the isLandCollision() member function to ensure the ship does not travel on land.

The addCity() member function passes its arguments on to the City constructor, which is called to create a new City object on the heap. The pointer to this new City object is stored in the m_cities vector.

The hide() and show() member functions simply call dbShowSprite() and dbHideSprite() to show or hide this particular portion of the map depending on whether or not the ship is currently on this screen.

The isLandCollision() member function takes a Point object and returns true if the map has land instead of water at that location. First, the file stream is positioned to read that exact location from the file. The formula for computing this location has much to do with the internal storage of bitmaps, but, basically, there are 54 bytes at the beginning that are irrelevant and then there are 3 bytes per pixel, a red, a green, and a blue value. We read the green and blue values and test if the green is less than the blue. If so, this is water. Otherwise, it must be land.

The isEnteringCity() member function takes a Point object and returns a pointer to a City object if that Point is inside a city. Otherwise, it returns 0. The function simply iterates through all of the cities and calls the isInside() member function.

The destructor iterates through all of the cities and frees them, destroys the sprite and image, and closes the file stream.

The Game Class

The Game class ties everything together, storing all of the Screen objects and keeping track of the game state. It is declared in Game.h and implemented in Game.cpp.

```
// Game.h
#pragma once
```

```cpp
#include <sstream>
#include <fstream>
#include <istream>

#include "Screen.h"
#include "Ship.h"
#include "Point.h"

using std::stringstream;
using std::ifstream;
using std::getline;
using std::istream;

class Game
{
        int m_gameState;
        Ship m_theShip;
        vector<Screen*> m_theScreens;
        Screen* m_currentScreen;
        Point m_shipPos;
        int m_shipPos_x;
        int m_shipPos_y;
        City* m_currentCity;

        Point toLocal(Point global);
        Screen* toScreen(Point global);
        Point toGlobal(Screen* theScreen, Point local);
        void readCity(istream& input);

public:
        Game();
        void doIntroScreen();
        void doMapScreen();
        void doCityScreen();
        void update();
        ~Game();
};
```

```cpp
// Game.cpp
#include "Game.h"

Screen* Game::toScreen(Point global)
{
      int currentScreen_x = global.x()/800;
      int currentScreen_y = global.y()/600;
      return m_theScreens[(currentScreen_y*3)+currentScreen_x];
}


Point Game::toLocal(Point global)
{
      return Point(global.x() % 800, global.y() % 600);
}


Point Game::toGlobal(Screen* theScreen, Point local)
{
      Point screenTopLeft = theScreen->topLeft();
      return Point(local.x() + screenTopLeft.x(), local.y() +
screenTopLeft.y());
}


void Game::readCity(istream& input)
{
      string cityName;

      Screen* theScreen;

      getline(input,cityName);
      Point topLeft(input);
      Point bottomRight(input);
      Point endLoc(input);
      input.ignore();
      input.ignore();
      theScreen = toScreen(topLeft);
      topLeft = toLocal(topLeft);
      bottomRight = toLocal(bottomRight);
      endLoc = toLocal(endLoc);
```

```
        theScreen->addCity(cityName,topLeft,bottomRight,endLoc);
}


Game::Game() : m_shipPos(0,0)
{
        dbLoadImage ( "openingScreen.bmp", 11);
        dbSprite(11,0,0,11);
        dbHideSprite(11);
        dbLoadImage ( "city.bmp", 12);
        dbSprite(12,0,0,12);
        dbHideSprite(12);

        for (int i = 0; i < 9; i++)
        {
                stringstream fileName;
                fileName << "map" << i+1 << ".bmp";
                m_theScreens.push_back(new
Screen(i+2,i+2,fileName.str(),Point(i%3*800,i/3*600)));
        }

        m_currentScreen = m_theScreens[0];

        do {
                m_shipPos = Point(dbRnd(800), dbRnd(600));
        } while (m_currentScreen->isLandCollision(m_shipPos));
        m_gameState = 1;


        ifstream citiesFile("cities.txt");
        for (int i = 0; i < 13; i++)
        {
                readCity(citiesFile);
        }
        m_currentCity = 0;
}


void Game::doIntroScreen()
{
```

```
        m_theShip.hide();
        dbShowSprite(11);

        if (dbReturnKey())
        {
                dbHideSprite(11);
                m_gameState = 2;
        }
}

void Game::doMapScreen()
{
        int move_x=0, move_y=0;

        m_currentScreen->hide();

        if (dbLeftKey())
        {
                move_x = -6;
                m_theShip.moveLeft();
        }
        if (dbRightKey())
        {
                move_x = 6;
                m_theShip.moveRight();
        }
        if (dbUpKey())
        {
                move_y = -6;
                m_theShip.moveUp();

        }
        if (dbDownKey())
        {
                move_y = 6;
                m_theShip.moveDown();

        }
```

```cpp
        Point newPos = m_shipPos + Point(move_x,move_y);
        Point localPos = toLocal(newPos);
        Screen* newScreen = toScreen(newPos);

        if (m_currentCity = newScreen->isEnteringCity(localPos))
            m_gameState = 3;

        if (!newScreen->isLandCollision(localPos))
        {
            m_shipPos = newPos;
        }

        m_currentScreen = toScreen(m_shipPos);

        m_currentScreen->show();
        m_theShip.show(toLocal(m_shipPos));

}

void Game::doCityScreen()
{
        m_theShip.hide();
        m_currentScreen->hide();
        dbShowSprite(12);

        if (dbReturnKey())
        {
            dbHideSprite(12);
            m_shipPos = toGlobal(m_currentScreen, m_currentCity-
>endCoordinates());
            m_gameState = 2;
        }
}

void Game::update()
{
        switch(m_gameState)
        {
```

```
    case 1:
        doIntroScreen();
        break;
    case 2:
        doMapScreen();
        break;
    case 3:
        doCityScreen();
        break;
    }
}

Game::~Game()
{
    for (int i = 0; i < 9; i++)
    {
        delete m_theScreens[i];
        m_theScreens[i] = 0;
    }
}
```

There are four private utility member functions used within the Game class. Three of these, toScreen(), toLocal(), and toGlobal(), are used to convert between global (over the entire 9-screen map) locations and local (just the position on the current screen) locations.

The toScreen() member function takes a Point object that stores a global location and returns a pointer to the Screen object within which that Point object is located. The toLocal() member function takes a Point object that stores a global location and returns the corresponding local location. The toGlobal() member function takes a Screen object pointer and a Point object that stores a local location and returns the corresponding global location.

The readCity() member function is used to read one city from the cities file, create a corresponding City object, and add it to the appropriate Screen object. The contents of the cities file is shown below:

```
New Orleans
90 100 190 150
140 160

Tampa
```

```
460 310 530 365
440 330

New Providence
840 460 945 500
960 440

New Dutch Land
1950 150 2020 200
1930 175

Belize
20 980 90 1010
120 1000

Port-de-Paix
1220 945 1320 990
1270 920

Port-au-Prince
1235 1030 1320 1070
1180 930

Santiago
1360 940 1435 1000
1380 900

Santo Domingo
1485 1030 1580 1090
1420 1110

Prinzapolca
335 1530 460 1595
480 1550

Santa Marta
1250 1460 1370 1525
1230 1440
```

```
Carthagena
1030 1630 1130 1705
1010 1610

Caracas
1960 1510 2010 1545
1980 1490
```

All the locations in the cities file are in global coordinates, so they must first be converted to local locations.

The Game constructor creates sprites for the introduction screen and the city screen, creates a Screen object for each of the 9 map screens, gives the ship a random non-land position on the first map screen, and reads all of the cities from the cities file.

The game state can be one of three values: 1 for the introduction screen, 2 for the main game play, and 3 for the city screen. The update() member function checks the current state and calls the corresponding member function to handle it.

The doIntroScreen() member function simply hides the ship, shows the introduction screen, and waits for the return key to be pressed. Once it has been pressed, the introduction screen is hidden and the game state is set to 2.

The doMapScreen() member function handles most of the work of the game engine. First, the current screen is hidden and each of the four arrow keys is checked to see which way the ship should move. The ship is pointed in the appropriate direction with a call to the moveLeft(), moveRight(), moveUp(), or moveDown() member function, and the movement direction is stored. The ship's new position is calculated and is checked to see if it is inside a city or on land. If the new location is inside a city, the game state is changed to 3. If the new position is on land, the ship does not move. Finally, the ship's location is updated and is drawn at its new position.

The doCityScreen() member function is almost exactly the same as the doIntroScreen() member function, except that when the return key is pressed the ship's location is set to the value read from the cities file. This value needs to be converted back to global coordinates before it can be used.

Creating the Game Chassis

The next file is main.cpp. This is the main file, from which all other files are included (see Chapter 5 for more on creating a chassis for your classes). In this file, you find Dark GDK's version of the main method: DarkGDK().

```
// Main.cpp

// Dark GDK - The Game Creators - www.thegamecreators.com

// the wizard has created a very simple 2D project that uses Dark GDK
// it can be used as a starting point in making your own 2D games

// whenever using Dark GDK you must ensure you include the header file

#include "Game.h"


// the main entry point for the application is this function
void DarkGDK ( void )
{
      // set the display to 800 x 600 with 32bit depth
      dbSetDisplayMode ( 800 , 600 , 32 );

      // when starting a Dark GDK program it is useful to set global
      // application properties, we begin by turning the sync rate on,
      // this means we control when the screen is updated, we also set
      // the maximum rate to 60 which means the maximum frame rate will
      // be set at 60 frames per second
      dbSyncOn   ( );
      dbSyncRate ( 60 );
      dbMaximizeWindow();
      dbSetWindowOff();

      // a call is made to this function so we can stop the GDK from
      // responding to the escape key, we can then add in some code in our
      // main loop so we can control what happens when the escape key is pressed
      dbDisableEscapeKey ( );

      // now we will set the random seed value to the timer, this will
      // help us to get more random values each time we run the program
      dbRandomize ( dbTimer ( ) );

      Game g;
```

```
// now we come to our main loop, we call LoopGDK so some internal
// work can be carried out by the GDK
while ( LoopGDK ( ) )
{
      g.update();

      if ( dbEscapeKey ( ) )
            break;
      dbSync();
}

}
```

Since the Game class handles most everything, there is not much to do here. In the initialization section, the display is set up to be full-screen, the escape key default behavior is disabled, the random number generator is seeded, and a Game object is created. In the main loop, almost everything is handled by a call to the update() member function of the Game object. The Game destructor handles all cleanups.

CONGRATULATIONS, READER!

You've made it. Only the best of the best make it this far. You can genuinely call yourself a programmer now. We suggest you take the code for this game engine and play with it. Make it your own. Research the Dark GDK and see if you can add sound. Maybe add enemy ships. You could have battles complete with explosions! Maybe in the cities you could buy ship upgrades, or commodities to sell at other cities. The options are limitless! Go forth, young reader, and code!

ANSWERS TO CHAPTER CHALLENGES

This appendix provides the answers to the challenges from the end of each chapter. As we say throughout the book, we highly recommend that you try to solve the challenges before looking at the following answers. (Note that in some cases, the answers we provide are only suggested ways to answer the questions.)

If you get stuck on a challenge, review the appropriate chapter for help.

CHAPTER 1

1. Create a program that displays a picture of a house that looks like the ASCII house in Figure 1.7.

ANSWER:

```
//displays a house
#include <iostream>

int main( void )
{
    using std::cout;
    cout << "    / \\ " << "\n";
    cout << "   /   \\ " << "\n";
    cout << "  /     \\ " << "\n";
    cout << " |       | " << "\n";
    cout << " |[] []| " << "\n";
    cout << " |       | " << "\n";
    cout << " ------- " << "\n";
    return 0;
}
```

2. What is the output of the following program?

```
#include <iostream>
#include <string>

int main( void )
{
    using std::cout;
    using std::string;
    int x = 25;
    string str2 = "This is a test\n";
    cout << "Test" << 1 << 2 << "3";
    cout << 25 %7 << "\n" << str2.c_str();
    return 0;
}
```

ANSWER:

```
Test1234
This is a test
```

Remember that the `cout` statement does not automatically skip a line at the end of a line of code.

3. Write a program that asks users for their names, greets them, asks them for two numbers, and then provides the sum.

ANSWER:

```cpp
#include <iostream>
#include <string>

int main( void )
{
    using std::cout;
    using std::cin;
    using std::string;

    string name = "";
    int number1;
    int number2;

    //asks the user for their name
    cout << "What is your name? ";

    //the user inputs their name and
    //it's stored in the name variable
    cin >> name;

    //The program says hello and skips a line
    cout << "Hello " << name << "\n";

    //the user inputs the first number
    cout << "Enter the first number to add together: ";
    cin >> number1;

    //the user inputs the second number
```

```
        cout << "Enter the second number: ";
        cin >> number2;

        // displays the sum of the two numbers
        cout << "the sum is " << (number1 + number2) << "\n";

        return 0;
}
```

4. What happens when you store 10.3 as an integer? What about 0.6? Can you store −101.8 as an integer?

ANSWER:

C++ will truncate (remove) the decimal, making the numbers 10, 0, and −101.

5. Write code that will multiply some number by 2 if the number is between 1 and 100 (including 1 or 100) and if it is evenly divisible by 3; otherwise, multiply by 3 if it is between 1 and 100 but not divisible by 3; finally, if it isn't between 1 and 100, multiply the number by the number modulus 100. (Hint: Use the nested if statement.)

ANSWER:

```
#include <iostream>

int main( void )
{
        using std::cout;
        using std::cin;
        int number;
        cout << "Enter a number" ;
        cin >> number;
        if (number >= 1 && number <= 100 && (number % 3 == 0))
        {
                number = number * 2;
        }
        else if (number >= 1 && number <= 100 && !(number % 3 == 0))
        {
                number = number * 3;
        }
        else if (!(number >= 1 && number <= 100))
```

```
    {
            number = number * number % 3;
    }
    cout << "The final result is " << number << "\n";
    return 0;
}
```

CHAPTER 2

1. What is the correct variable type for storing the following data:

- The number of books in a bookshelf
- The cost of this book
- The number of people in the world
- The word Hello

ANSWER:

- The best approach is probably to store the number of books on a bookshelf in an unsigned integer or unsigned short because you cannot have a negative number or partial number of books on a bookshelf.
- Store the cost of this book as a floating-point data type because a float will enable you to store both dollars and cents.
- Store the number of people in the world as a float because the float stores numbers in scientific notation, thereby allowing very large numbers.
- Store the word Hello either as a string or as an array of characters.

2. Provide meaningful variable names for the variables in the first challenge.

ANSWER:

Your variable identifiers can differ, but each expresses the variable's purpose. This allows other programmers, and you, to understand your code. Sample variable identifiers for Challenge 1 are `numOfBooks`, `bookCost`, `numOfPeople`, and `helloString` for each section, respectively.

3. Name two reasons to use constants rather than literals.

ANSWER:

You have to change only one value, where the constant is declared, to change the value in the whole program. Also, using constants makes your code more readable.

4. Write a program that calculates and displays the sizes of all the fundamental types.

ANSWER:

```
//displays the size of fundamental variable types
#include <iostream>

int main( void )
{
```

```
    using std::cout;
    cout << "Here is the size of the fundamental variable types:";
    cout << "\nint - " << sizeof(int);
    cout << "\nshort - " << sizeof(short);
    cout << "\nfloat - " << sizeof(float);
    cout << "\ndouble - " << sizeof(double);
    cout << "\nbool - " << sizeof(bool);
    cout << "\nchar - " << sizeof(char);
    cout << "\n And that concludes the experiment :)";
    return 0;
}
```

5. Test what happens if you declare a character as unsigned. Do you get the results you expected? Formulate a reason why or why not.

ANSWER:

The results for the ASCII characters are the same whether the character is signed or unsigned. However, when you attempt to use negative values with the signed character or values above 127, the ASCII table becomes erratic because it is not standardized.

CHAPTER 3

1. Write a conditional statement (an `if` statement) that will assign x/y to x if y doesn't equal 0.

ANSWER:

```
if(y != 0)
{
      x = x/y;
}
```

2. Write a `while` loop that calculates the summative of positive integers from 1 to some number n (if you want to check this, the formula is n (n + 1) / 2).

ANSWER:

```
int i = 0;
int sum = 0;
while(i < n)
{
      i++;
      sum += i;
}
```

3. Write a conditional statement that assigns x * y if x is even; otherwise, if x is odd and y doesn't equal 0, assign x to x / y; if neither of the preceding cases is `true`, output to the screen that y is equal to 0.

ANSWER:

```
if(x % 2 == 0)
{
      x = x * y;
}
else if((x % 2) == 1 && y != 0)
{
      x = x / y;
}
else
{
      cout << "y = 0" << endl;
}
```

CHAPTER 4

1. Write a function, called `multiply`, that multiplies two numbers and returns the result.

ANSWER:

```
long multiply(int x, int y)
{
    return (x * y) ;
}
```

2. Change the function you wrote in Challenge 1 so that it remembers how many times you called it.

ANSWER:

```
int multiply(int x, int y)
{
    static int staticMember;
    staticMember++;
    return (x * y) ;
}
```

3. What is the difference between a global variable and a static variable? Which is better in which situation and why?

ANSWER:

Both the global and static variables exist for the entire program. The difference arises when you look at the two kinds of variable scopes. You can access the global variable from anywhere in the program, whereas you can access the static variable only in the method in which the variable is created. So, a static variable is better when you access the variable only from within the function. You, therefore, use a global variable if you must access the variable in more than one function.

4. Try rewriting "The Cave Adventure Game" so that it does not use functions (an exercise to convince you how useful functions are).

ANSWER:

You can do this; however, trying to conglomerate all your code into one function (called spaghetti coding) makes the code confusing. Trust me, the functions are useful!

5. If you actually made it through the last question, buy yourself a Slurpee.

ANSWER:

The five steps to getting a Slurpee are:

1. Earn $1.50.
2. Run to the nearest convenience store.
3. Remember, programmers never walk; drive to the convenience store.
4. Pay for the Slurpee.
5. Enjoy the Slurpee.

CHAPTER 5

1. Create a class that can be used to represent a character in a role-playing game. Store the character's name, class, and race.

ANSWER:

```
class Player
{
        string name;
        string charClass;
        string race;
        Player(string lname, string lclass, string lrace);
};

//a constructor that uses an intializer list
Player::Player(string lname, string lclass, string lrace)
        : name(lname), charClass(lclass), race(lrace);
{
}
```

2. Explain the three main principles of OOP.

ANSWER:

The three main principles are:

- **Data abstraction.** Hides and protects the data inside the object. The data must then be extracted by using a method.
- **Encapsulation.** Each task is encapsulated into a single object.
- **Polymorphism.** Each object can accomplish its task in any program it's used in. This allows for portability and reusability of code.

3. What is the difference between a class and an object?

ANSWER:

A class is like a template in that a class tells the computer how to create something. Declaring a class essentially is saying to the compiler, "Here is a new data type, and here is what it is capable of doing." A class is similar to a function that hasn't been called. An object is an instance of a class; basically, you are taking the class and creating something from it. An object consumes space in memory, but a class does not.

4. If you have a choice between declaring something public, private, global, or local without loss of functionality, which scope should you pick?

ANSWER:

Select local because it protects the data in a smaller scope more than any of the other scopes do. This follows the OOP principle of Data Abstraction.

5. What attributes present in constructors and destructors are not present in other functions?

ANSWER:

- Neither the constructor nor the destructor can return values.
- The destructor cannot have parameters.
- The destructor is the only function to start with a tilde.
- Both the constructor and destructor have the same name as the object.

CHAPTER 6

1. What is the size of the string "Hello World"? What is the length of the array named s?

```
char s[] = "Hello World";
```

ANSWER:

The size of the string "Hello World" is 12 bytes. This is because each of the alpha characters requires 1 byte, plus one space and the terminating character at the end of the string, resulting in an array length of 12. Remember, though, that the array indexes extend only from 0 to 11.

2. List five reasons to use pointers.

ANSWER:

Possible uses include

- Pointers give you access to specific indexes in an array.
- Pointers can enable you to pass a reference to a data value, instead of passing the data itself.
- Pointers are the basis for using dynamic memory.
- Pointers are the basis for binary file access.
- Pointers are the basis for iterators.
- Pointers are fun!

3. What are the problems with the "Tic Tac Toe" game at the end of the chapter? How can you improve the game?

ANSWER:

The interface is rather awkward. Entering a row and column number (0–2) requires knowing that the numbering starts at 0. You can improve it by labeling the rows and columns.

Also, you can add a computer opponent. The computer opponent AI (artificial intelligence) will have to check first to see whether it can get three Xs or Os in a row, then check to see whether the opponent can receive three in a row, and finally try to set itself up for three in a row.

4. List three reasons to use dynamic memory.

ANSWER:

- You can create an array of arbitrary length.
- Dynamic memory is more plentiful than system memory. The system memory is assigned to the program by the operating system, whereas the program "borrows" dynamic memory from big blocks of free memory.
- The program can decide when to gain or release the memory.

CHAPTER 7

1. Create a weapon hierarchy with at least four weapons derived from a single parent class. What kind of data members should each contain? What about methods?

ANSWER:

A possible weapon hierarchy can use a weapon class as its base class and have specific weapons classes derive from this class. Examples include a sword, a dagger, and a bow. Each class should then have several class-specific methods that highlight the weapon's capabilities.

2. Design and fully implement an abstract Shape class. What should be included? What should be left to the derived classes?

ANSWER:

Leave everything but the interface to the derived classes. The abstract class should have only an object interface. Here is an example of how a Shape class might look:

```
class Shape
{
     //draws the shape onto the screen.
     virtual void Draw() = 0;
};
```

CHAPTER 8

1. Create a vector that stores a set of vectors that each store a set of integers.

ANSWER:

```
typedef vector<int> Vi;
vector<Vi> vvi;
```

2. Create a template class called Store **that stores an array of** T **(where** T **is the template parameter).**

ANSWER:

```
template<class T> Store
{
    T array[5];
};
```

3. Create an iterator, called random_iterator, **which uses another iterator to iterate through a container in random order.**

ANSWER:

```
template<class Iter> class random_iterator :
    public iterator<iterator_traits<Iter>::iterator_category,
                    iterator_traits<Iter>::value_type,
                    iterator_traits<Iter>::difference_type,
                    iterator_traits<Iter>::pointer,
                    iterator_traits<Iter>::reference>
{
protected:
    //used to internally iterate randomly
    //with a normal iterator
    Iter current;
    int size;
public:
    //give the iterator type a standard name
    typedef Iter iterator_type;

    //default constructor
    random_iterator() : current() {srand(time(0));}
    //constructor from a normal iterator
```

```
    random_iterator(Iter x, int y) : current(x), size(y) {}
    //construct from another random_iterator
    template<class U> random_iterator (const random_iterator<U>& x)
            : current(x.base()) {}

    //return the normal iterator that this class uses
    Iter base() const {return current;}

    reference operator* () const
    {
        Iter tmp = current;
        return *-tmp;
    }

    //dereferencing
    pointer operator-> () const;

    //access member operator
    reference operator[] (difference_type n) const;

    // increment and decrement return random positions
    random_iterator& operator++ () {return current[rand()%(size + 1)] }
    random_iterator& operator- () { return current[rand()%(size + 1)];}

    random_iterator operator+ (difference_type n) const;
    random_iterator operator+= (difference_type n);
    random_iterator operator- (difference_type n) const;
    random_iterator operator -= (difference_type n);
};
```

4. Name three places where you can get quick information about the components of the standard library (not including this book).

ANSWER:

- The source files
- http://www.cplusplus.com
- Your compiler's help files

CHAPTER 9

1. Create a program to write the following two lines of text to a file called Question1.txt:

```
Programming is fun.
I love programming.
```

ANSWER:

```cpp
#include <fstream>

int main ()
{
        using std::ofstream;

        //opens the file
        ofstream file("Question1.txt");

        //makes sure the file is open
        if (file.is_open())
        {
                //writes two lines to the file
                file << "Programming is fun.\n";
                file << "I love programming.\n";

                //closes the file
                file.close();
        }
        return 0;
}
```

2. What method can you use to test whether a file has reached its end? What method can you use to test whether a file has an error? What method can you use to test whether a file has reached its end and has an error?

ANSWER:

- `eof()` is used to test whether a stream has reached the end of a file.
- `fail()` and `bad()` can be used to test whether a file stream has an error.
- `good()` can be used to test both.

3. What is the result when the letter A is bit-shifted to the left three places (<<3)? What is the result when the letter A is bit-shifted to the right two places (>>2)?

ANSWER:

Without any bit shifting, A is 01000001 (or 65). When shifted left three places, A becomes 00001000, and when shifted right two places, A becomes 00010000.

4. Explain why the encryption program needs to be run a second time in order to decrypt the file placed into the program.

ANSWER:

When the program is originally encrypted, the program is simply switching the first and last 4 bits in every byte. When they are switched again, you end up with every byte returning to normal, producing the original file.

Chapter 10

1. What does the keyword `try` do?

ANSWER:

Use `try` to tell the computer that a section of code might throw an exception. If you use a `try` statement, you can catch the exception.

2. What is the purpose of an exception hierarchy?

ANSWER:

Having numerous different exceptions can make exception handling unmanageable, but having a few generalized ones is not always optimal. With an exception hierarchy, you can choose exactly how detailed you need to make your exception catches.

3. How can you design your programs so that they will not crash?

ANSWER:

You will never be able to create programs that will never crash. However, designing your program carefully, using exception handling, and doing a good job with debugging will definitely help in this regard.

4. What is the definition of an exception?

ANSWER:

An exception is a non-routine circumstance that a section of code can't handle.

5. At what point in your program's development should you use assertions?

ANSWER:

You should use assertions throughout your program's development, but you should remove them when the program is released to the public.

Using the Octal, Hexadecimal, Binary, and Decimal Systems

To most people, the standard number system is the decimal system (also called base-10). All numbers in the decimal number system are based on exponents of 10. Each digit holds 10 possibilities (1, 2, 3, 4, 5, 6, 7, 8, 9, or 0). Based on theories of permutations, if you have two digits in the decimal system, you can have 100 different values (1 to 99 and 0). This principle is behind all numeric systems.

In the binary number system (also called base-2), if you have two binary digits, you have four possibilities, as follows (equivalent values appear in parentheses): 00 (0), 01 (1), 10 (2), and 11 (3).

The hexadecimal number system (also called hex and base-16) is useful in computers (and, so, to programmers). Each digit has 16 possibilities (0–9 and A–F). The decimal number system has only 10 unique digits, so to represent 16 unique digits, the first five letters of the alphabet are used. A represents 10, B represents 11, C represents 12, D represents 13, E represents 14, and F represents 15. Hex numbers are written with 0x prefixing the number; for example, 0x3E1 is a hexadecimal number.

Octal is a base-8 number system, which is also useful in computers. Each digit has eight possibilities (0–7). Octal is represented with an "x" prefixing the number—for example, x95.

CONVERTING TO DECIMAL

Don't be intimidated by number systems other than the decimal system. All your old, familiar numbers are still there; other systems just represent them differently. So, how exactly do you convert a number in other systems to a number in the decimal system? It's easy. Take the first digit (the one on the far right) and multiply it by n (the base of the system) raised to digit number −1. That is, the value of the first digit is multiplied by n^0, the second by n^1, the third by n^2, and so on. Then you add all the resulting numbers.

As an example, convert the hexadecimal number 0x3E1. Remember that the 0x is just telling you that the numeric representation is in hexadecimal and does not actually contribute to the number. Also, remember that E is the same thing as 14 in the hexadecimal system.

```
1 x 16^0 = 1
E x 16^1 = 224
+3 x 16^2 = 768
```

Then you add them all together to get the resulting decimal number, 993.

CONVERTING FROM DECIMAL

The process for converting from the decimal system to a base-n system is slightly harder. First, take a number and divide it by the base raised to the digit number. That is, the first column is 1, and the second is 2, and so on. Then subtract the remainder from the original number. To find the value of the digit in the column, divide the remainder by the base raised to the power of 1 less the digit number. Although this concept might seem confusing, it is not too difficult. For example, convert 993 back to hexadecimal:

Column number 1:

    993 / 16^1 = 62 Remainder: 1

    Hexadecimal digit = 1 / 16^0 = 1

    Hexadecimal number so far: 1

    993 − 1 = 992

Column number 2:

    992 / 16^2 = 3 Remainder: 224

    Hexadecimal digit = 224/16^1 = 14 (E)

    Hexadecimal number so far: E1

    992 − 224 = 768

Column number 3:

768 / 16^3 = 0 Remainder: 768

Hexadecimal number so far: 3E1

768 − 768 = 0

Hexadecimal digit = 768/16^2 = 3

You're finished! 0x3E1 is the hexadecimal number.

WORKING ON MAC AND LINUX PLATFORMS

indows is a very popular platform, but, increasingly, Mac and Linux are becoming notable alternatives. Programming on these two platforms, while slightly different, is a breeze after a short introduction.

PROGRAMMING ON MAC OS X

So you've got your spiffy new MacBook or iMac and you're all ready to learn how to program. But, where to begin? Well, luckily, OS X comes with an integrated development environment called Xcode.

To create a new C++ project, with Xcode running, follow these steps (note that the names of menus, dialog boxes, and other options might be different if you have a different version of Xcode):

1. From the File menu, select New Project.... See Figure C.1.

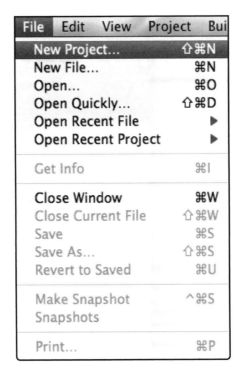

2. Scroll down to the section titled Command Line Utility and under that select C++ Tool. Click Next. See Figure C.2.

3. Type **HelloWorld** in the Project Name field. You will see that the Project Directory also gets filled in as you type. Click Finish. See Figure C.3.

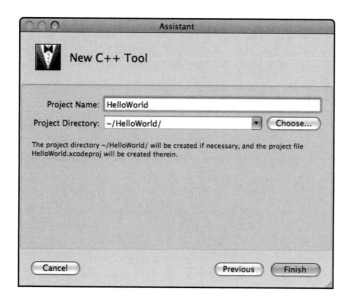

FIGURE C.3

Naming the new project.

4. The project window appears. From here you modify every aspect of your project. For now we are only interested in the file listed called main.cpp. See Figure C.4.

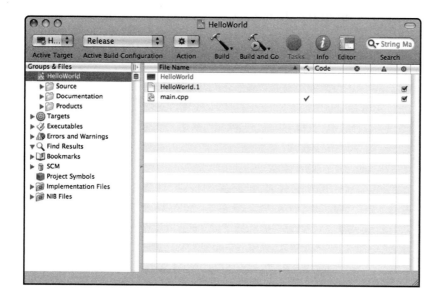

FIGURE C.4

The project window.

5. Double-click on main.cpp to open it for editing. The editor window appears with some automatically generated source code. Fortunately, this code already displays Hello, World! to the screen, so there is no need to edit it. See Figure C.5.

FIGURE C.5

The editor window.

6. To compile and run the program, first select Console from the Run menu. See Figure C.6.

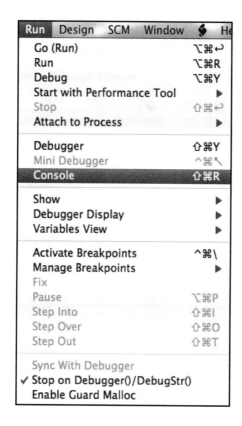

FIGURE C.6

Displaying the console.

7. Click on the Build and Go button on the console window's toolbar. You will see the output of the HelloWorld program displayed. See Figure C.7.

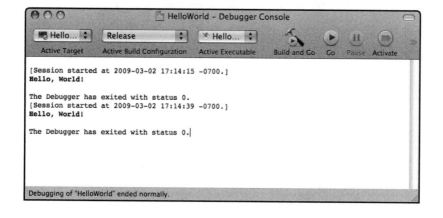

FIGURE C.7

Running your project.

You now know the basic steps to working with Xcode. You should head to http://developer.apple.com/documentation/DeveloperTools/Xcode-date.html to read up on further details.

PROGRAMMING ON LINUX

Linux is an extremely versatile operating system, offering many different choices from the windowing environment to the text editor. As such, there are many different ways to program in Linux, but in this section we will only touch on the most universal. You may want to check out some of the Integrated Development Environments (IDEs) for Linux, such as KDevelop or Code Crusader, but the installation and usage of these software packages is beyond the scope of this book.

The first thing you'll want to do is start a terminal, from which we can issue commands. You'll want to search your window manager's list of programs for a terminal emulator. Often it is located in the Utilities menu and called something like color-xterm, regular-xterm, gnome-terminal, konsole, or terminal. Once you have started a terminal window, follow these steps to create, compile, and run a new C++ project.

1. Create a new directory called HelloWorld by typing `mkdir HelloWorld` and pressing enter. Change into this directory by typing `cd HelloWorld` and pressing Enter. See Figure C.8.

FIGURE C.8

Creating a
directory.

2. Open an editor to start writing the code for our project. There are many editors to choose from such as vim, pico, nano, gedit, emacs, nedit, and kate. Feel free to use your favorite if you are already accustomed to one. We will use emacs. You can start emacs by typing `emacs HelloWorld.cpp`. See Figure C.9.

FIGURE C.9

Starting emacs.

3. When emacs first opens you will see a primarily blank screen with a status bar at the bottom. See Figure C.10.

```
-uuu:---F1  HelloWorld.cpp    All L1    (C++/l Abbrev)-------------------
Loading cc-mode...done
```

FIGURE C.10

The emacs text editor.

4. Type in the Hello World program from Chapter 1. See Figure C.11.

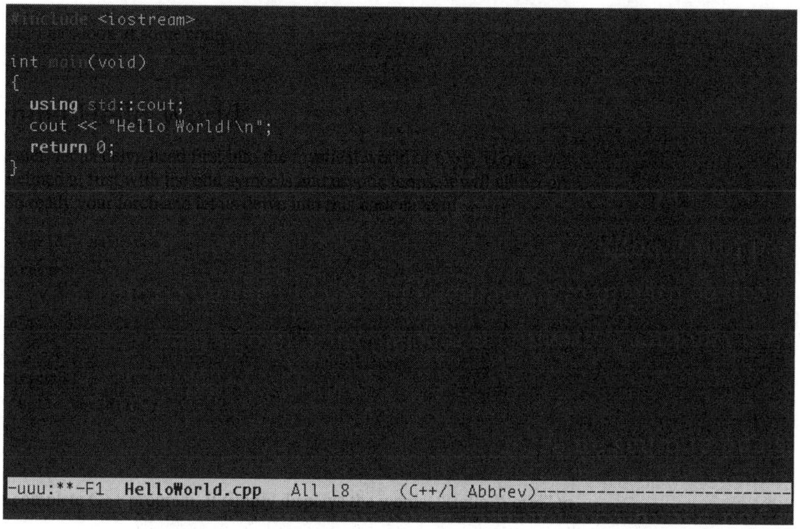

```
#include <iostream>

int main(void)
{
  using std::cout;
  cout << "Hello World!\n";
  return 0;
}
```

```
-uuu:**-F1  HelloWorld.cpp    All L8    (C++/l Abbrev)-------------------
```

FIGURE C.11

Typing in the Hello World program.

5. Press Ctrl-X and then Ctrl-S to save your code. You will see an update indicating it was saved successfully in the status bar. See Figure C.12. Now press Ctrl-X and then Ctrl-C to exit emacs.

FIGURE C.12

Saving your code.

```
-uuu:---F1  HelloWorld.cpp    All L8    (C++/l Abbrev)------------------------
Wrote /Users/marklee/Documents/Projects/c++/HelloWorld/HelloWorld.cpp
```

6. To compile the program, type in g++ -o HelloWorld HelloWorld.cpp. g++ is the name of the C++ compiler in Linux, HelloWorld.cpp is the name of our source file, and HelloWorld is the name of the executable we are creating. See Figure C.13.

FIGURE C.13

Compiling
HelloWorld.

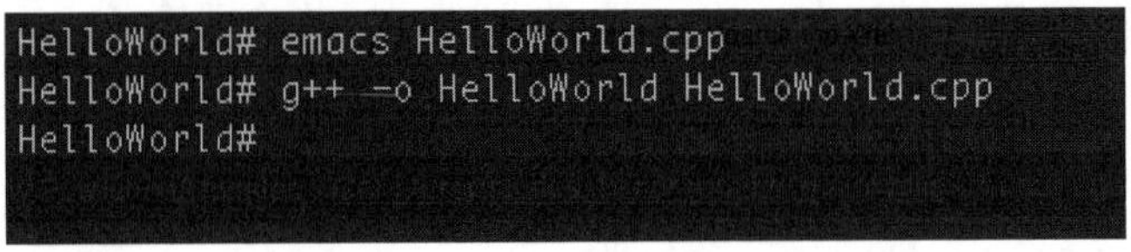

```
HelloWorld# emacs HelloWorld.cpp
HelloWorld# g++ -o HelloWorld HelloWorld.cpp
HelloWorld#
```

7. Type in ./HelloWorld to run your project. You will see Hello World! displayed on the screen. See Figure C.14.

FIGURE C.14

Running your
project.

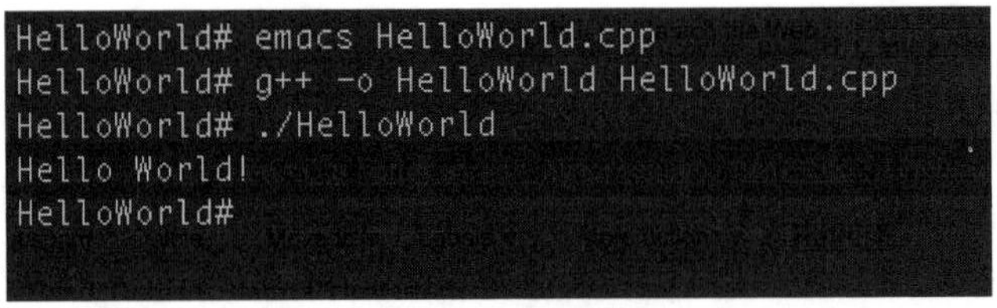

```
HelloWorld# emacs HelloWorld.cpp
HelloWorld# g++ -o HelloWorld HelloWorld.cpp
HelloWorld# ./HelloWorld
Hello World!
HelloWorld#
```

Congratulations, you have now compiled your very first program in Linux! A very good place to start learning more about working in Linux is the Linux Documentation Project, located at http://www.tldp.org.

WHERE TO GO FROM HERE

U se this appendix as a reference for books you might find helpful if you choose to further your programming skills. The books are sorted by topic.

THE C++ LANGUAGE

- *C++ Coding Standards: 101 Rules and Guidelines*, Herb Sutter, Andrei Alexandrescu
- *C++ FAQs*, Marshall Cline, Greg Lomow, Mike Girou
- *The C++ Programming Language*, Bjarne Stroustrup
- *The C++ Standard Library*, Nicolai M. Josuttis
- *C++ Templates*, David Vandevoorde, Nicolai M. Josuttis
- *The Elements of C++ Style*, Trevor Misfeldt, Gregory Bumgardner, Andrew Gray
- *Thinking in C++*, Brue Eckel

SOFTWARE DESIGN

- *Code Complete (2nd edition)*, Steve McConnell
- *Design Patterns: Elements of Reusable Object-Oriented Software*, Richard Helm, Ralph Johnson, John Vlissides

GAME PROGRAMMING

- *Beginning DirectX 10 Game Programming*, Wendy Jones
- *C++ for Game Programmers*, Mike Dickheiser
- *Data Structures and Algorithms for Game Developers*, Allen Sherrod
- *Windows via C/C++*, Jeffrey M. Richter, Christophe Nasarre

GLOSSARY

abstract class A class with a pure virtual function. You cannot create an object from an abstract class.

access specifiers Specify the scope of members of a class.

address A unique number that represents a memory location.

algorithm The logic that accomplishes a specific task.

allocate memory To declare and reserve a certain portion of memory.

ANSI (American National Standards Institute) An organization that develops standards for the computer industry.

argument Data sent to a called function by a calling function.

array A list that holds data with each data element referenced by its subscript.

array, multidimensional An array of arrays.

ASCII code (American Symbolic Code for Information Interchange code) A code that determines a unique bit pattern for 256 characters represented by computers.

assertion A statement (typically a macro) that ensures a certain condition holds true.

automatic memory Memory where all local variables are stored by default.

base class (also called super class and parent class) A class from which another class is derived.

binary A numbering system that uses the digits 1 and 0.

binary file A file, unlike text files, in which data is stored in a compressed format.

bit The smallest unit of memory; typically represented by 1 or 0.

block A section of C++ code offset by braces.

Boolean A fundamental data type that represents two possible values, true or false.

boolean logic The study of the relationship between boolean data types.

bug A computer error.

byte A unit of memory represented by 8 bits; can store any one of 256 values.

calling The act of initiating a function from another part of the program.

calling procedure A function that calls another function.

character A variable that can store one of 256 different characters from the ASCII character set.

child class See derived class.

class A structure that defines the characteristics of an object, including the object's data and function members.

class hierarchy A tree-like structure that shows the inheritance relationship between classes.

class template A class that is not specific to a certain kind of data; uses templates in order to accomplish this feat.

code fragment A section of a program.

command A programming language instruction.

comment Informational code placed in the source code for the convenience of the programmer or someone trying to understand the code. The compiler ignores comments.

compiler Converts source code to an executable format.

compiling The act of sending your source code through a compiler to be converted to an executable format.

complexity The measurement of an algorithm's efficiency.

concatenation Merging of two or more strings.

conditional statement See control statement.

console application An application that uses a DOS-based text window rather than the Windows libraries.

control statement A statement that alters the flow of a program based on a condition.

constructor A function with the same name as its class. The constructor is executed every time an object derived from that class is created. Used to declare memory and assign initial properties to an object.

C-style strings An array of characters terminated by 0.

debugging The process of removing errors from a program.

declare To inform the computer about the name and attributes of a variable, function, or class.

decremental operators The -- operators used to decrease the value of a variable by one.

derive To create a class from another class.

derived class (also called a sub class or child class) A class formed from a base class that inherits all the base class's characteristics.

derives-from Another name for a type-of relationship.

destructor A member function that is automatically executed when an object is deleted. The destructor has the same name as the class, preceded by a ~.

development cycle The general steps taken when creating and debugging a program.

disk memory The memory—made up of hard drives, CD-ROMs, floppy drives, zip drives, and so on—that stores data on a semi-permanent basis.

dynamic memory (also called the free store and heap) A section of memory that programmers can access for new data. Allocated and deallocated with the new and delete operators.

element One piece of data from an array.

encapsulation A principle of OOP in which objects do one, and only one, specific task.

escape characters A special set of characters used to represent other characters that cannot easily be in literal form (for example, a line break).

exception handling Handling of non-routine circumstances in a program.

extractions Removal of bytes from a stream.

extractors The functions that perform extractions.

free store See dynamic memory.

freeing memory The process of telling the computer that you are finished with a particular section of memory.

function A section of code that performs a specific task when called.

function declaration Introduces a function to a program and defines the function's return type, name, and arguments. Also called a prototype.

function definition The implementation of code inside a function.

function template A function that is not specific to any one data type. It uses a template to accomplish this.

fundamental types The data types built into the C++ language.

Global A variable that can be accessed anywhere within a source file.

heap See dynamic memory.

header files The files you include in C++ programs that often represent the C++ standard library files.

hexadecimal A base-16 numbering system that uses the numbers 0–9 and the letters A–F to create 16 unique digits.

identifiers Names given to variables so that programmers can conveniently refer to the variables later in the program.

implementation The definition of a function.

incremental operators The ++ operator that increments a variable by one.

index (also called a subscript) A number used to access a particular element of an array.

inheritance The derivation of one class from another.

inheritance chain The inheritance line of a class.

initializer list for arrays A list of values separated by commas; used to initialize an array.

initializer list for objects A list of values after the constructor that initializes the variables of an object.

input/output (I/O) A term used to describe the way in which a computer communicates with the outside world. Input devices include the mouse, keyboards, joysticks, and so on. Output devices include monitors, printers, speakers, and so on.

inserters The functions that perform stream insertions.

insertions Place bytes into an I/O stream.

integer A variable type that stores only whole numbers (can be positive, negative, and zero).

integer wrapping When an integer reaches one more than its maximum value, it "wraps," thereby setting the integer to its minimum value.

Integrated Development Environment (IDE) A graphical interface that incorporates your compiler, file browser, settings, and source code editor.

iterative control statements Control statements that allow the repetition of code based on a condition.

jump statements Keywords used to jump the flow of a program from one part to another bypassing everything in between.

kilobyte A unit of memory made up of 1024 bytes. One of the primary units of memory measurement.

libraries Sets of compiled code that you can use in your programs.

line break A meta-character that represents a new line.

linking The process of checking to see whether the code works with all the files that you include in a program, not only your files, but also external libraries such as DirectX.

literals A representation of actual data values in a program. Numbers are literally represented by the Arabic number system (1, 2, 3, and so on); strings are represented by letters and numbers enclosed within quotation marks.

local A variable that is declared within a function. It can be accessed only within that function.

lvalues Expressions that can be assigned to or located on the left side of an equal sign in an assignment statement.

machine language The compiled, executable version of a program.

main function The first function to execute when a program begins. The most common prototype is `int main(void)`.

manipulators Manipulate the data of the stream in some way. For example, a manipulator might make all characters uppercase or convert decimal numbers to hexadecimal.

mathematical operator An operator that performs mathematical functions such as addition and subtraction.

memory The part of the computer where data is stored and retrieved. The most common sources are hard drives, disks, and random access memory (RAM).

meta-character A character that doesn't display onscreen but that is used by the computer for special formatting or to represent other characters. These characters include tabs, line breaks, and so on.

modulus operator (%) The remainder of x divided by y (x % y).

namespace A C++ keyword used to divide a single scope into multiple subscopes.

nesting Placing if statements (and other control statements) inside other control statements.

null pointer (also called undeclared pointer) A pointer that stores the value of 0 and that is assumed not to be pointing to data.

null zero The terminating character of a string; represented by the escape character, \0.

object A specific instance of a class.

object-oriented programming (OOP) A technique of programming that activates data by creating objects that have both characteristics and code.

operands Values that operators manipulate.

operation A phrase containing both an operator and its operands.

operator Any symbol or double symbols such as <=—and, in some cases, even words such as sizeof()—that cause the compiler to take an action.

operator over'oading Creating new uses for existing operators.

order The growth pattern of an algorithm.

order of operation The precedence that some operators have over others. For example, the + operator has a lower precedence than the * operator. Therefore, it is executed after the * operator unless overridden by a higher operator such as parentheses.

order of precedence See order of operation.

overloading To create more than one version of a function with the same name. The computer uses the arguments to determine which version to call.

overriding When a derived class declares a method with the same name as one from its base class. The derived version is preferred when using a derived class object.

parameter See argument.

parent class See base class.

pointer A variable that stores a memory address of another data value.

point of instantiation When a class template or function template is generated from a particular set of template parameters.

polymorphism A principle of OOP in which each object can be used in more than one program.

program A sequence of instructions that is executed by a computer. Also, the process of entering source code into the computer to be compiled and run.

prototype (also called a function prototype) A function's representation; used so that the compiler can set up the function. The prototype contains the return type, function name, and type of variables that should be passed.

pure virtual function A virtual function that is not implemented but that is used only to create abstract classes.

quadratic Any equation that can be expressed in the following form: $ax^{2} + bx + c$.

quotient The result from the division of two numbers.

Random-Access Memory (RAM) The memory that temporarily stores data while the computer is turned on.

random numbers Numbers that appear in seemingly random order; generated from complex mathematical formulas.

recursion A method of programming where a function calls itself.

return value Data that is sent back from a function to the calling function; often used for returning numerical results from a function's calculations.

scalar variables Variables that can hold only one piece of data as opposed to array data.

scope A variable's range defined by how much of the surrounding source code can use the variable.

scientific notation A succinct way to represent numbers of extreme magnitude.

shadow A local variable that is declared with the same name as a global variable; the local variable takes precedence when the variable's name is used.

single inheritance A derived class that has one and only one base class.

source code The text representation of a program, written in a programming language such as C++.

static memory The part of memory where the compiler stores static and global variables.

static variables Variables that retain their values throughout the whole program but do not necessarily have global scope.

stream object Acts as both a source and a destination for the input and output (I/O) of data. The stream object manipulates an ordered linear sequence of bytes.

string An object type that stores a sequence of characters in a character array, terminated by a null zero.

subclass See derived class.

subscript A number that represents a single data element from an array.

substring A string formed from part or all of another string.

super class See base class.

switch statement A statement that utilizes the switch keyword to execute specific code based on selected cases.

template A way of generalizing a class or function so that it doesn't use any particular data type.

template parameter A parameter, such as a function parameter, that stores a type of data.

test chassis A function that is used to test the capabilities of an object.

text file A file whose data is represented by characters.

try-block A section of code that attempts to catch any exceptions that are thrown.

type-of A relationship between two elements where one is a category and the other is an object from that category.

type A representation of data, such as an integer and a floating-point.

type alias Another name for a type; often specified with the typedef keyword.

undeclared pointer See null pointer.

unsigned variable An integer type variable that can store only positive values.

variable A named memory location where data is stored within a program.

variable lifetime The amount of time that the memory used for a variable is reserved.

variable scope The range of a program where a particular variable can be accessed.

vector A complex data structure that is part of the standard library. It is in the `<vector>` library.

virtual functions Polymorphic functions that ensure the correct class is referenced when pointing to a virtual function.

wrapper class A class that extends the basic functionality of a primitive data type or object.

Index

the fun way
to learn programming

Let's face it. C++, Java, and Perl can be a little intimidating. But now they don't have to be. The *for the absolute beginner*™ series gives you a fun, non-intimidating introduction to the world of programming. Each book in this series teaches a specific programming language using simple game programming as a teaching aid. All titles include source code on the companion CD-ROM or Web site.

**DarkBASIC Programming
for the Absolute Beginner**
By Jerry Lee Ford, Jr.
1-59863-385-6 | $29.99 | 432 pages

**Microsoft WSH and VBScript
Programming for the
Absolute Beginner, Third Edition**
By Jerry Lee Ford, Jr.
1-59863-803-3 | $34.99 | 480 pages

**C Programming for the
Absolute Beginner, Second Edition**
By Michael Vine
1-59863-480-1 | $29.99 | 336 pages

**Microsoft Excel VBA Programming for
the Absolute Beginner, Third Edition**
By Duane Birnbaum and Michael Vine
1-59863-394-5 | $29.99 | 544 pages

**Microsoft Access VBA Programming for
the Absolute Beginner, Third Edition**
By Michael Vine
1-59863-393-7 | $29.99 | 384 pages

**Microsoft Windows PowerShell
Programming for the Absolute Beginner**
By Jerry Lee Ford, Jr.
1-59863-354-6 | $29.99 | 376 pages

**Microsoft Visual Basic 2008 Express
Programming for the Absolute Beginner**
By Jerry Lee Ford, Jr.
1-59863-900-5 | $29.99 | 432 pages

**Ajax Programming
for the Absolute Beginner**
By Jerry Lee Ford, Jr.
1-59863-564-6 | $29.99 | 320 pages

**Java Programming for the
Absolute Beginner, Second Edition**
By John Flynt
1-59863-275-2 | $29.99 | 480 pages

COURSE TECHNOLOGY
CENGAGE Learning
Professional • Technical • Reference

**Call 1.800.648.7450 to order
Order online at www.courseptr.com**